TRANSFORMATIONS
ON THE GROUND

TRANSFORMATIONS ON THE GROUND

Space and the Power of Land in Botswana

Anne M. O. Griffiths

INDIANA UNIVERSITY PRESS

This book is a publication of

Indiana University Press
Office of Scholarly Publishing
Herman B Wells Library 350
1320 East 10th Street
Bloomington, Indiana 47405 USA

iupress.indiana.edu

Cataloging information is available from the Library of Congress.

Library of Congress Cataloging-in-Publication Data

Names: Griffiths, Anne M. O., author.
Title: Transformations on the ground : space and the power of land in
  Botswana / Anne M. O. Griffiths.
Description: Bloomington : Indiana University Press, 2019. | Series: Framing
  the global book series | Includes bibliographical references and index.
Identifiers: LCCN 2019013601 (print) | LCCN 2019017133 (ebook) | ISBN
  9780253043580 (ebook) | ISBN 9780253043566 (hardback : alk. paper) | ISBN
  9780253043573 (pbk. : alk. paper)
Subjects: LCSH: Land use—Government policy—Botswana. | Land tenure—Law and
  legislation—Botswana. | Globalization—Economic aspects—Botswana.
Classification: LCC HD996.Z63 (ebook) | LCC HD996.Z63 .G75 2019 (print) | DDC
  333.3096883—dc23
LC record available at https://lccn.loc.gov/2019013601

ISBN 978-0-253-04356-6 (hdbk.)
ISBN 978-0-253-04357-3 (pbk.)
ISBN 978-0-253-04358-0 (web PDF)

1 2 3 4 5   24 23 22 21 20 19

For Ed

CONTENTS

PREFACE

I FIRST CAME TO BOTSWANA IN 1980 TO help set up the Law Department at what was then the University of Botswana, Lesotho and Swaziland (UBLS), now the University of Botswana. The Edinburgh University Law Faculty was providing two years of legal training in Edinburgh to students from these countries as part of a five-year program. As part of that effort, I was brought on board to prepare course materials for teaching family law by my colleague Sandy McCall Smith, who was heading the team to establish the department. This assignment was my introduction to legal scholarship in Botswana in which I have maintained an interest for over thirty years. I remain indebted to the late S. G. Masimega who was my mentor, guide, and interpreter during the earlier years of my research that culminated in the publication of my book *In the Shadow of Marriage: Gender and Justice in an African Community*, published in 1997. As we worked together over the years, people in Molepolole village would comment, "There goes the old man again with his shadow."

I have carried out field research in the country at various periods of time, intensively in the 1980s, with a gap into the 1990s. Building on this earlier research, my study on which this book is based was carried out mainly in 2009–2010, with shorter periods of further research in 2011, 2012, 2013, 2014, 2015, and more extensively in 2016.

My findings are thus the product of work from different periods in time, and I have tried to flag these variations in the text as frequent changes to legislation precluded updating all the elements of my research. So, for example, a new Tribal Land Bill was introduced in 2017, but this book does not deal with its provisions, except to indicate in places where changes are proposed. The same is true for government ministries whose designations changed in 2016. I refer to the ministries and departments as they were when I carried out the bulk of my research in 2009–2010 and 2012. As a result, what is presented is a patchwork of findings woven into a narrative that has been put together over time and space.

One of my major goals has been to highlight the degree to which people in Botswana actively participate in debates about land and land reform at all levels of society. While one participant at a workshop commented that I quoted too extensively from my interviews in a paper I presented, I have consciously adopted this strategy in my book in order to forefront the voices, perceptions, and experiences of people's relationships with land across a wide range of domains and at a number of levels. I believe these firsthand accounts are important because all too often the people who lie at the heart of the research process remain silent.

Over the years, many people and institutions have generously assisted me in my research and with the drafting of this manuscript. Without their ongoing support and encouragement, I would not have been able to write this book. These include my research assistants, Phidelia Dintwe, Kawina Power, Boineelo Borakile, and Phenyo Churchill Thebe, to whom I remain indebted for their hard work and support. I would also like to thank the administrative staff and land board members for Kweneng Land Board (KLB), who made me welcome and showed great patience in dealing with my questions and in making materials available to me. They include David Botlhoko, Frank Nkomo Tshiamo, Oduetse Lekoko, Rra Khuduego, Mma Bantle, Flora Moageng, Rra Mahatshwa, Mma Benjamin, Neo Tshaakane, Henry Matashwa, Asego Ditshilwana, Rra Mabine, Victor Baboloki, Rra Bafitlhile, Rra Dintwe, Ikopoleng Shabance, Itsheakeng Tsheboagae, Thato Pako Chale, Boinyana Keforilwe, Samuel Leero, Simon Marone, Tower Segwale, Punah Sekgetle, Badina Moalatshwang, David Mtebang, Henry Deeds, Major Olebeng Seitiketso, Ata Sakaio, Nr Ntebang, Mma Phakedi, Borra Matshidiso, Sebako, Selioka, Rra V. B. Job, Mma Annah Ramotsisi, Borra Lombhala, Maabang, Letlole, Bomma Botita, Monkutwatsi, Sherbana, Male, and Rra Speerk. I am also grateful to the administration and members of Tlokweng Land Board, who have discussed their development of land policy over the years and provided a contrast to the workings of KLB.

Thanks are also due to Bakwena Tribal Administration and the staff and members of the Customary Court of Appeal, who were so generous in making me at home while listening to disputes and making records available and who participated so willingly in interviews. They include Norman Bakwena, Rra Mhaladi, Patricia Sechele, and especially K. K. Sebele, who remembered working with me in the 1980s and encouraged his staff to support my research project. As part of this process, I would like to give special thanks to the headmen and members of Dikoloing, Lekgwapheng, Mokgalo, Mokgopeetsane, and Ntoloolengwae wards. The families and descendants of brothers Makokwe and Radipati are also owed a debt of thanks. They are too numerous to list here but they are named in the main body of the text.

I am also grateful for all the support and assistance provided by the administrative staff and members of the Land Tribunal. They include Borra Baruti, Nare, Mologelwa, Mma Moremong, Ms. Chuma (now Mrs. Kaisara), Kebalepile Rutherford, Simon Rapinyana, Borra Tobedza, Mareng, Marengi, and Mma Mabua. I am especially indebted to Kabelo Manase who has unfailingly provided me with tribunal transcripts and kept me up to date on the working of the Tribunal.

In addition, my thanks are due to all government personal and members of various ministries and departments who spent time with me over the years in discussing their work and land policies. These include the Department of Land; Department of Housing, Deeds Registry; Department of Surveys and Mapping; Department of Town and Regional Planning; Department of Technical Services; Department of Corporate Services at the Ministry of Lands and Housing; Attorney General's Chambers; Ministry for Defence, Justice, and Security; Department of Housing; Ministry of Labour and Home Affairs; Department of Women's Affairs; Central Statistics Office; and Poverty Eradication Programme within the Office of the President. The individuals concerned are too numerous to be named here but they are acknowledged in the text.

Nongovernmental organizations have also been very supportive of my research, and I would like to thank the Botswana Association of Tribal Authorities (BATLA); Women's Finance House; Ditshwanelo (Center for Human Rights), Gaborone and Kasane branches; Emang Basadi (Stand Up Women); Gender Links; Botswana Institute for Development Policy (BIDPA); Skillshare International; the Botswana Society; and the Citizen Entrepreneurial Development Agency (CEDA).

I am enormously grateful to my colleagues at the University of Botswana who have discussed my research with me over the years. They have been drawn from the Law Department, the departments of Architecture and Town Planning, Political and Administrative Studies, History, the Faculty of Education, and the Department of Civil Engineering. I am especially indebted to Faustin Kalabamu, Clement Ng'ong'ola, and Boipuso Nkgwae, who have supported and debated my research at length with me over many years.

I would also like to thank the following individuals who allowed me to interview them about their experiences of acquiring land or of appealing from decisions made by KLB or the Land Tribunal. These include Bokang Sebobe, Clera Maigas, Doreen Galetshoge, Eva Aaron and Joseph Molale, Judy Tsnope, Kgosi Motlhabane, Louis M. Fisher, Lorato Bolokang, Mmamosinki Kgang, Compton and Punika Taleyana, Mr. Malan, Mr. Moirpula, Morobi Rasina, Mr. Phoi, Richard White, and Sheila Mokabi. I would also like to thank Doreen Khama, Kagalelo Monthe, and Unity Dow, who have given so generously of their time to discuss their perspectives as legal practitioners on land and who have provided me with the transcripts of unreported cases. Any mistakes are mine alone and If I have failed to mention anyone here, please accept my sincere apologies.

Back in Europe, I would like to thank my colleagues at the University of Edinburgh, especially the law librarians, who have made great efforts to help me track down sources for my research. Special thanks are also due to my colleagues at Re:Work, the International Research Centre on Work and the Human Lifecycle in Global History at Humboldt University in Berlin, who supported my work as a senior research fellow in 2010–2011; they have continued to do so ever since, most recently as a research affiliate in 2016, enabling me to draft the text of this manuscript.

In the United States, I would like to thank all my colleagues on the Framing the Global project at Indiana University's Center for the Study of Global Change, who have been so engaging over the years and who have helped me struggle to get to grips with what the *global* is all about. I am indebted to the other fellows for their critical insights, including Tim Bartley, Manuela Ciotti, Deborah Cohen, Stephanie de Boer, Lesley-Jo Fraser, Zsuzsa Gille, Rachel Harvey, Prakash Kumar, Michael Mascarenhas, Deidre McKay, Sean Metzger, Faranak Miraftab, Alex Perullo, and Katerina Teaiwa. I especially want to thank Hilary Kahn and Deborah Piston-Hatlen and the editors of my manuscript at Indiana University Press, including the late Rebecca Tolen, Jennika Baines, Stephanie Smith, and Cindi Dunford, who worked on an earlier version of the manuscript. I also want to thank Pauline Peters, Beverly Stoeltje, and Andreas Eckert, who read and commented extensively on the manuscript, and the anonymous reviewers who commented on the manuscript for the University of Indiana Press.

I am also very grateful to the following institutions for providing the financial assistance that made it possible to undertake the research and to complete this manuscript: the University of Edinburgh, the Leverhulme Trust, the International Research Centre on Work and the Human Lifecycle in Global History, Indiana University Center for the Study of Global

Change, Indiana University Press, the Mellon Foundation, and the British Academy.

Last but not least, I owe a great debt of gratitude to my husband, Ed Wilmsen, without whose love, support, and forbearance this book would not have been possible.

A. G., January 18, 2018,
Edinburgh

TRANSFORMATIONS
ON THE GROUND

INTRODUCTION

Iₙ INTERNATIONAL CIRCLES, THE PUBLIC IMAGE OF THE African nation of Botswana is one of an upwardly mobile state. Among the poorest non-oil producing countries at independence in 1966, it has now acquired the highly desirable status of a middle-income country (MIC) because of its mineral (mainly diamonds) resources.[1] Yet this image of a prosperous country, based on calculations of gross domestic product (GDP) distribution per capita by international institutions such as the African Development Bank (AfDB), belies the reality that faces many of Botswana's citizens on the ground. Indeed, AfDB's 2009–2013 report itself acknowledges poverty and unemployment: "Botswana faces challenges in translating its impressive success in macroeconomic and governance performance into poverty and inequality reduction. The level of poverty, with about a third of the population living below the poverty line, and unemployment rate of nearly 20 percent contradict the MIC status" (5). What lies behind this widely held image of Botswana as one of the highest-ranking African countries in terms of development is reference to an indexed model of development based on comparative figures among states across the globe in relation to per capita distribution of GDP. Botswana, however, presents a dual face of prosperity and poverty when looking inward toward its local spaces.

These differential embodiments of prosperity and poverty are linked to a broader conception of governance that forms part of *global space*, a term used by M. Patrick Cottrell and David M. Trubek (2012, 362) to refer to "an evolving regulatory environment created by globalization and the increasing role international norms play in domestic settings." This space acknowledges the importance of transnational legal and business norms (F. Benda-Beckmann, K. Benda-Beckmann, and Griffiths 2009a, 2009b; Hellum et al. 2011); it blurs the general divide between internal and external state sovereignty, with states increasingly pooling capacity in international organizations at the expense of their mutually exclusive and often divided internal sovereignty (Walker 2014, 13). In light of these transnational forces, is it really appropriate to capture legal and economic processes under the terms of the *global* or *globalization*, and what are the consequences of doing so?[2] These terms feature extensively in popular discourse and scholarly works, yet their meaning remains divided because of the range of activities they encompass. Such activities include the integration of the world economy (Gilpin 2001, 364); power struggles between priorities of time and space (Harvey 1990, 240); deterritorialization and the growth of supraterritorial relations between people (Scholte 2000, 46); the development of security agendas in connection with the global governance complex (Duffield 2001); and hegemonic and counterhegemonic discourses (Santos 2006). These disparate approaches to globalization are associated with an "intensification and increasing density in the flows and patterns of interconnectedness between states and society that constitute the modern world community" (F. Benda-Beckmann, K. Benda-Beckmann, and Griffiths 2005, 1). Such diverse perspectives make it clear that there is no one singular perception about what constitutes the global or globalization. Nor can the relationship between the global and the local be reduced to a simple dichotomy representing sameness and diversity set up in opposition to one another (Tsing 2000, 352). These terms rather reflect sets of relations that connect and reconnect in a variety of ways in a number of different places, which makes for a reenvisaging of both local and global phenomena.[3]

Part of the difficulty in grasping what the global is, lies in the fact that, as Didier Fassin (2012) acknowledges, it is an ambiguous term. It has two potential meanings: one making reference to being worldwide, and the other to being universal. The former denotes a geographic perspective that is planetary in scope, whereas the latter has an ideological dimension "that implies a form of claimed hegemony" denoting a form of superiority (Fassin 2012, 105). Both meanings are at work in processes of globalization and may simultaneously lay claim to territoriality in terms of "spatial expansion," as well as "the affirmation of a moral superiority" on which normative assertions about the world are based (106).

An example of these dual meanings is provided by the promotion of a neoliberal agenda centered on economic and sustainable development associated with international institutions such as the United Nations (UN) and the World Bank that lay claim to a global or universal remit. This ambiguity gives rise to what Marjorie Ferguson (1992) has termed the mythology of globalization insofar as it purports to represent a large-scale phenomenon promoting culturally homogenizing forces over all others. In other words, it elevates what in fact represents a partial, incomplete set of connections into a more encompassing global phenomenon that is accorded universal status of planetary scope.

The dangers of this construction of globalization have been highlighted by scholars such as Frederick Cooper (2001) and James Ferguson (2006), who in an African context point to the deeply misleading projection of normative authority that terms such as *global* and *globalization* come to embody. For Cooper, the concepts of global and globalization have come to represent "a single system of connection—notably through capital and commodities markets, information flows, and imagined landscapes—[that] has penetrated the entire globe" (2001, 189). He argues that in adopting this perspective "crucial questions do not get asked: about the limits of interconnections, about the cases where capital cannot go, and about the specificity of the structure necessary to make connections work" (189). From another perspective, Ferguson argues that what constitutes the global in relation to burgeoning markets and economic development across the globe is not really global at all when it comes to the African continent. He maintains that what is really at work in Africa is a convergence of capital that hops across the continent, connecting at various nodes. The result is that large numbers of the African population are bypassed (in the sense that they do not participate in its operations or share in its benefits, although these deployments of capital do affect their lives). In other words, there is a need for a more informed understanding of what the global and its relationship with local domains entails. For as Ferguson observes, while subventions of capital may indeed be viewed as global "in that they rely on the transnational organization of funding, institutions and moral concerns," nonetheless "their very mode of operation reveals the selectively disordered and starkly divided landscape that . . . is a fundamental feature of Africa's contemporary mode of integration into global society" (J. Ferguson 2006, 48).

These critiques about what constitutes the global and globalization are not incorporated into the discourse or implementation of international agencies' approaches to economic and sustainable development, despite their focus on human rights. Following the end of the Second World War, the Universal Declaration of Human Rights, drafted by representatives from all regions of the world with different legal and cultural backgrounds, was proclaimed by the UN General Assembly in Paris on December 10, 1948 (General Assembly resolution 217A). Its aim was to promote international peace and security and respect for human rights worldwide. To this end, the UN has, since then, promoted the International Covenant on Civil and Political

Rights (ICCPR) and the International Covenant on Economic, Social and Cultural Rights (IESCR), both of which were adopted by the General Assembly of the United Nations on December 16, 1966, and both of which form part of the International Bill of Human Rights. Thus "the UN framework possesses and exercises a depth and scope of normative authority unprecedented in any self-styled planetary legal regime" (Walker 2014, 60). This framework can be seen as integral to the UN and international agencies' promotion of the Millennium Development Goals (MDGs), now Sustainable Development Goals (SDGs), officially known as Transforming Our World: The 2030 Agenda for Sustainable Development (or 2030 Agenda).[4] These goals form part of an agenda that acknowledges the existence of poverty on a global scale and has poverty reduction as its first sustainable development goal (SDG1) along with gender (SDG5) and social equality (SDG19). Such recognition of poverty is not new, and international aid agencies have long been grappling with how to tackle it. A 2008 report by the Commission on the Legal Empowerment of the Poor and the UN Development Program identified property (which includes land) as one of four pillars of legal empowerment, along with access to justice and the rule of law, labor, and business rights.[5] The report marked a recognition of the need to adopt a more holistic approach to development and poverty, including attention to human rights as more broadly construed to include social and economic rights (such as rights to food, housing, water, and health), along with concepts of good governance, accountability, transparency, and attention to informal justice. This broadening of perspective, which has expanded to include policies of social inclusion and participation, has received a mixed response from scholars and development practitioners (O'Meally 2014). Although some are highly critical of the basis on which participation is constructed, others view it as representing a welcome shift from organizations' previous orthodoxy of a political economy to best fit development approaches (World Bank 2012) even if it still has a long way to go. The critical divide occurs over the extent to which the sustainable development agenda is viewed as being underpinned by neoliberal economic policies and deployment of capital that represent a singular, exclusionary approach to development.

Land at the Heart of Global Perspectives

Land features at the heart of these competing global discourses of sustainable development and macrolevel economic empowerment. Land is a recurring topic of discussion in the media, on international agencies' agendas for change, in nongovernmental organizations' (NGOs') plans of action for their constituents, and in scholarly research and publications. For this reason, it is the entry point and focus for my book, which is part of a larger interdisciplinary project, Framing the Global, initiated by the University of Indiana Center for the Study of Global Change and Indiana University Press with funding by the Andrew W. Mellon Foundation. An unprecedented interest in land has been generated by its recognition as a global resource that has come under pressure to meet the often competing demands of macroeconomic development of world population growth (Cotula 2015a, 2015b) and redistribution; the need to generate food security (Stephens 2011; Murphy 2013) and energy security (Borras and Franco 2010); and the longer term goal of securing environmental sustainability (Cotula 2016), including successfully responding to climate change (Habitat III 2016).

The pressure on access to and control over land and the uses to which it is put not only transcends nation-states, forming a core component of macroperspectives centered on competing national, international, and transnational approaches to commerce and sustainability but also forms a critical component at the microlevel. At this level, land engages with individual families and households' provisions for shelter, livelihood, and capital accumulation. The two differing scales of interests may conflict with one another; for example, when large-scale investments in foreign land representing extraterritorial commercial land transactions (colloquially referred to as "land grabs") have the effect of displacing local populations from their homes and livelihoods, thereby exacerbating poverty through dispossession.[6] Although such processes may appear to give rise to a greater degree of interconnectedness (Giddens 1990, 21; McGrew 2010), in reality they result in highly diverse, uneven, and unequal sets of relationships.

Law plays an important role in these processes in regulating relationships, especially with regard to land. Its role is evident from its wide-ranging remit in managing plural legal systems, in regulating security of tenure; in dealing with the distribution of, access to, and control over land, particularly in the light of population density; as well as handling the growing market in land and its commoditization, including informal land transactions and their effects, and land-tenure relations in general.

How then are global and local relations to be perceived? For they relate to one another in ways that undermine any notion of separate, clearly demarcated spheres of action standing in opposition to one another.

As Roland Robertson (1995, 26) observes "much of what is local . . . is constructed on a trans or supra local basis, while Saskia Sassen (2014) asserts that the global "simultaneously transcends the framing of the nation-state and partly inhabits national territory and institutions."[7] Thus a situation is created where, as Sally Engle Merry notes, "the global itself is constituted by various locals" (Merry 2000, 129).[8]

What is key to understanding what global and local relations entail is the standpoint from which they are being addressed. For the range of factors that come into play in the analysis, as my book will demonstrate, depend on where the focus is located and the different dimensions that come into play when it shifts. In my case, this analysis involves exploring the differential and yet overlapping dimensions that are at work in governments', institutions', communities', or individual households' relationships with land because they involve questions of scale and projection and the horizons they embody, ranging along a continuum from more micromanaged and circumscribed parameters to a more macro and wide-ranging set of considerations. As a result, the importance of certain elements will have a differential impact depending on the lens through which they are viewed, as in Boaventura de Sousa Santos's (1987) analogy of the relations between maps and spatial reality, where distortions of scale and projection that are essential to representation vary according to the map's intended function.

So, while the global and the local may share common and overlapping concerns in relation to land, such as its role, for example, in alleviating poverty, the constellation of interests that underpin the way in which these concepts are viewed may differ considerably when addressed from a variety of standpoints. Thus the processes or frameworks that bring the global and the local into communication with one another may be viewed "as a multi-faceted, dialectical process involving complex interconnections between socioeconomic groups, individuals, and institutions worldwide; the ultimate effects of which vary both within and between nations" (Mensah 2008, 37). This process includes the day-to-day workings of globalization as well as the broader discourses that circulate about it.

Spatial and Temporal Dimensions of Land

Thus we return to Cottrell and Trubek's understanding of global space as the increasing interplay between international and domestic domains. However, space in relation to land not only embraces a physical and territorial place but also represents a more intangible domain—one that embraces a more metaphorical state of being that embodies social relationships that coalesce around land. For as Doreen Massey (2013) has observed, a site in space "isn't so much about physical locality so much as relations between human beings." As Max Gluckman (1971, 45–46) noted at an earlier date: "Property law in tribal societies defines not so much rights of persons over things, as obligations owed between persons with respect of things. . . . The crucial rights of such persons are demands on other persons in virtue of control over land and chattels." Thus, whatever its nature, a site in space cannot be divorced from ideology or politics (Lefebvre 1991) because it cannot be viewed as "a natural medium that stands outside of the way it is conceived" (Crang and Thrift 2000, 3).

Adopting this perspective on space allows for diverse interpretations of how relations to land are constituted that may vary, complement, overlap, or even come into conflict with one another and with the broader competing global perspectives in operation at any moment in time. Time and space are intertwined to differing effect: on the one hand, adopting a linear approach to time with the goal of annihilating certain types of space (Harvey 1990); and on the other, by making time subservient to space in the recognition of social states of being. Thus the temporal dimensions of space are important for "space without time is as impossible as time without space" (Crang and Thrift 2000, 3) for temporality forms an integral part of space (Khan 2009). This relationship exists because human behavior, including the realm of law, "is located in and constructed in space" (Low and Lawrence-Zuniga 2003, 1) that is linked through time to human experience. As such, it involves a plurality of spheres that, as Johannes Fabian (1983) demonstrates, give rise to a number of different interpretations of time at different moments in history.

My book explores these diverse interpretations through a social-scientific and anthropological approach that explores power by examining where it is located, how it is constituted, and what forms it takes. This exploration is important because, as Fassin has noted, "globalization is more than anything else a contemporary expression of power: the power to act on people and things as well as on ideologies and subjectivities" (2012, 106). In exploring these dimensions, my book draws on a variety of sources derived from a range of methods in data collection that inform its findings. These include archival research; examination of formal laws in court and land board records; fieldwork on unwritten oral customary law and participant observation of disputes; and interviews with government personnel, members of NGOs, and local citizens. Extended oral life histories of families from Molepolole village are updated from earlier research in the 1980s to cover five generations within two family groups. Combining sources and methods in this way acknowledges the multiple dimensions from which relationships to land may be ascertained. This approach includes recognition of the differing scales that come into play, ranging from the broad-brush sweep of abstract international policies to more nationally constituted perspectives concerning the acquisition and use of land. Both filter into micro-units of family and household experiences of land administration in daily life, highlighting their diverse impact on individuals' well-being and livelihoods.

An Overview of the Book: Disciplinary Perspectives

Using the approaches just described, I move beyond the study of conventional legal sources such as legislation, court records, and court proceedings to more open-ended discussions with social actors on relations to land that highlight what is taking place as an everyday part of their life course. This more socially oriented approach reveals how transmissions of land may proceed as "trouble-less" cases, without resort to disputes (Llewellyn and Hoebel 1941; Holleman 1973). This insight provides an important perspective on the role land plays in everyday life and people's experiences of this role, making visible the context in which ordinary negotiations among individuals over property can lead to voluntary agreements being reached that may differ from those accorded by globalized legal norms and projected legal standards.

To mark the shifts in focus from which relationships to land are addressed, my book is divided into three parts, with the introductory and closing chapters providing situational context and reflection.

Part 1. Historical Dimensions of Land in Botswana: Contemporary Entanglements

The first part comprises chapters 1, 2, and 3, which explore the historical dimensions of land at the international, national, and regional levels. This part adopts a long-term lens covering precolonial, colonial, and postcolonial trajectories. It does so, however, in a way that does not treat these dimensions as time-bound domains that are delineated and separated out from one another in a linear fashion because the treatment of history is informed by archival material and oral life histories stretching across generations and traversing traditional historical periods. Such a perspective challenges conventional historical narratives predicated "on the principle of historicism: the idea that the past is separated from the present" (Hirsch and Stewart 2005, 261). Instead, the book's approach to time acknowledges "that the past, present and future are mutually implicated" (261).[9]

Chapter 1 reveals how international forces have had an impact on the system of land tenure that has developed within Botswana. This history is long, beginning with Botswana's struggles in the region, particularly with regard to its neighbors. It is also indelibly marked by its experience of colonialism while under British indirect rule as the Bechuanaland Protectorate (1885–1966). These encounters have given rise to a spatialization of land in terms of the social organization of *merafe* (tribes)[10] and a nexus involving regular rotation between the village, the lands (where agriculture was and is carried out), and the cattlepost (where livestock were and are kept) that has characterized the life of Batswana[11] into the postindependence period. It also provided a system of access to and control over land that has strengthened the class structure inherent in Tswana social structure that exists today, albeit subject to transformations.

In addition to a historical overview of the development of land tenure in Botswana, chapter 1 documents how the current legal regulation of land that incorporates unwritten, customary law operates alongside statutory and case law derived from European and Cape Colonial law, resulting in three different systems of land tenure that were established during the colonial era and that continue to operate in the country today. As with other African countries, law represented what Martin Chanock observed was "the cutting edge of colonialism" that promoted a particular vision of social order and property rights in its attempts to control and govern its colonial subjects (1985, 4). This superimposition reflected an ideological quest for power through the inscription of law on territory, for as Franz von Benda-Beckmann, Kebeet von Benda-Beckmann, and Melanie Wiber observe, property regimes "cannot be captured in one-dimensional political, economic or legal models" (2006, 2). Nonetheless, the colonial model of law sought to make them so by creating separate legal regimes that distinguished between, and were applicable to, the colonizers and the colonized. This approach that embodied separate and parallel systems of law (Hooker 1975) was one in which one land regime applied to the colonizers while another applied to the colonized assigned to "tribal areas" by their colonial overlords. As a result, colonialism "created and maintained boundaries through dualistic or pluralistic legal structures, boundaries in physical space defined and managed by laws and regulations" (Home 2012, 9).[12] This chapter explores the resulting complex relations to land through spaces embodying territorial, political, economic, and social relations within which land is currently constituted in Botswana. It outlines the contemporary dilemmas that transformations over time have brought about with regard to pursuing policies on land and legal reform.

Chapter 2 situates the context in which a current national policy on land is being developed by the government of Botswana. The focus is on the state as an actor in international and national affairs and as a participant in transnational relations across state borders. For example, Botswana's Vision 2016 represents the ideological framework guiding all national policies and programs seeking to promote development in the country in line with the United Nations Millennium Declaration to which Botswana was a signatory in 2000 (now replaced by the 2030 Global Agenda for Sustainable Development). From a national or state perspective, land administration involves questions of economic development linked to bi- and multilateral treaties negotiated with other national states and transnational organizations like the European Union (EU) or development agencies such as the World Bank. It involves forming an overview of what is in the best interests of the country *as a whole*, in order to facilitate "an educated and informed nation" (Botswana 2009b). This overview requires taking account of all citizens in Botswana as well as the varying sectors that make up the state representing a patchwork of different institutions and interests.

Chapter 3 focuses at a regional level on the Kweneng Land Board (KLB), which was the focus of my 2009–2010 ethnographic case study. A key institution in the administration and management of land, the board oversees the entire spectrum of land allocation in Kweneng District, from rural cattleposts to peri-urban and urban residential and industrial areas, of which a portion falls within the catchment area of the capital city, Gaborone, where around one-third of the population of Botswana lives.[13] The board was also selected because it has been the subject of extensive litigation in the courts and is located in Molepolole, the central village for Bakwena[14] that is also a regional administrative center. Operating at a regional, or district level, KLB administers, allocates, transfers, and resolves disputes over land within its designated territorial and tribal domain. This encompasses both physically grounded space as well as the sociopolitical-administrative structure of the Kwena polity. Thus the district, as a place, embodies a constellation of differing configurations of interest that intersect and come up against one another. Within this setting, KLB must implement policies it considers appropriate for the district in which it operates with regard to the specific needs of its population, while paying heed to national policy on land. These considerations, involving national and district perspectives, raise different questions of scale and projection that make for a delicate balance between land board autonomy and the more global-facing national government intervention in land administration.

Part 2. The Bottom-Up Impact of Land on Diverging Family Lifeworlds and Gender Relations

Part 2, which includes chapters 4 and 5, addresses the impact of land as space on tangible and social relations perceived through the lens of families' and households' social practices and experiences over time. These chapters stress the impact of land management on households as opposed to individuals. The term *individual* carries with it the Western connotation of a single person, whose needs and desires are reflected on largely in isolation, in terms of their autonomous being. In contrast, for Botswana (including Bakwena) the connotation of an individual is much broader, encompassing the extended family. This involves not only situating individuals within networks but also taking account of gender and the lifecycle. It is not enough to refer to *women* and *men* alone, but it is also necessary to mark age and status (e.g., married, unmarried, widowed, childless). These life histories are important because they highlight the ways in which individuals, who form part of a community in terms of genealogical and spatial relationships grounded in place, find their life courses shaped by wider geographic processes that have an impact on their everyday lives. As Massey observes, place "is given its specificity by the fact that it is constructed out of social relations meeting or weaving together at a particular locus" (1994, 154). What it embodies in terms of history is "a product of layer upon layer of different sets of linkages, both local and to the wider world" (156).

Chapter 4 addresses the impact of globalization on structures of inequality concerning class relations and empowerment (or disempowerment) through the study of two family groups descended from two brothers: Makokwe and Radipati. Although related and from the same place, these brothers' descendants have come to experience very different lifeworlds because of the ways in which they have become positioned within social networks. This positioning has affected their access to resources, including land. In the case of Makokwe's family members, relations to land are structured around the need for shelter, subsistence agriculture, and livestock that has provided the basis for their livelihoods. Over time, this spatialized relationship to land has led to intermittent and insecure forms of employment that are not sufficiently remunerative to allow them to expand their agrarian base or to insert themselves into an urban economy in ways that would provide them with greater opportunities for acquiring land. On the other hand, Radipati's descendants, by acquiring a higher degree of education, have been able to diversify their livelihoods so that they no longer engage in subsistence activities. Belonging to a group with stable and secure employment, they have been able to take advantage of government land policy, enabling them to purchase and develop land in a number of areas that can be subsequently rented out or put to commercial use. Thus they are in a position to engage in the entrepreneurial vision of land development that the government envisages for Botswana, one that forms part of agendas promoted by international and transnational agencies. These differing lifeworlds reveal the transformational processes that give rise to the uneven ways in which distribution of resources, such as land, are apportioned through social networks that reflect diverging patterns of human, social, and economic capital. These patterns have implications for the ways in which society in Botswana remains socially stratified, promoting upward mobility for some, while constraining others in ways that perpetuate social inequality.

Chapter 5 explores the question of gender and its impact on women's access to and control over land through a case study of customary land certificates and leases awarded by KLB over a ten-year period (1999–2009). These empirical data make clear that women are featuring in far greater numbers in land transactions than was earlier the case, including an increase in the number of women appointed to manage deceased person's estates and women's inheritance of land. Factors affecting this societal shift are explored, including women's enhanced education and employment opportunities, attitudinal shifts toward women's roles in society, and legal reform. Social differentiation is also addressed, including the inherent tensions and conflicts that arise due to unequal access to resources that make it more difficult for women to acquire land under a consensually based decision-making process. Thus the chapter highlights the importance of understanding the dynamics of social change and their effects, a dimension too often over-looked by international donors who, having taken gender to heart, tend to focus on reforming laws and institutions without having a clear grasp of how these interact with the social aspects of their environment.

Part 3. Law and Space: Negotiating Legal Plurality in Botswana

The last part addresses the legal pluralism found in Botswana today and its impact on global and local issues surrounding land. Within Africa, this form of legal pluralism was a product of colonialism. Colonial powers attempted to impose their legal traditions on local landholding systems by interpreting African land-tenure systems and codifying them in terms of their own understandings of law derived from European perspectives on land that were prevalent at the end of the nineteenth century.[15] They did so in order to bring traditional local power structures within the remit of colonial administration. What emerged from this process was a formulation of land tenure that was reduced to an emphasis on individual and private property rights, on the one hand, and to communal and communitarian forms of land ownership that were taken to represent customary land tenure, on the other. The two became juxtaposed against one another in debates that continue to this day over the supposed failings of customary land-tenure systems to provide for the kind of clearly identifiable, secure, and enforceable rights that underpin the requirements for development under neoliberal capitalism and free markets.

This focus on legal pluralism is important because law is a source of constituting and legitimating power that is highly sought after in local, national, and transnational arenas (F. Benda-Beckmann, K. Benda-Beckmann, and Griffiths 2009a, 1). It is central to creating, producing, and enforcing concepts such as justice, authority, rights, and instantiating notions of legality, and it has a direct bearing "on the way power is deployed and social life structured" (Blomley 1994, xiii). Few negotiations, however, extend beyond daily life into disputes that require handling in a formal legal arena, such as a court. For this reason, some legal scholarship has moved toward studying law as part of the everyday, through the use of individual narratives that may be juxtaposed against those of the official legal system.[16] Such an ethnographic approach, however, is one that is absent from most lawyers' analyses of law. Thus including this perspective of legal pluralism is important because it reveals how transformations can take place at a local level that might otherwise go unnoticed. Alternatively, where conflict does arise, such an approach highlights the competing normative orders brought to bear in both informal and formal dispute forums that have a mutually constitutive bearing on how land is distributed. Such data, which bring differing spatiotemporal logics to the fore, can be used to challenge the more linear construction imposed by conventional legal theory. Such theory renders invisible the economic, social, political, and ideological factors underpinning the construction of legal discourse. As a result, conventional legal theory ignores these considerations, thereby enabling it to uphold abstract legal notions of equality and neutrality.

Chapter 6 presents the workings of the Land Tribunal, which employs a more open-ended approach to law. The Land Tribunal is configured differently from the High Court and Court of Appeal, and its claimants can draw on a plurality of sources in the presentation of their claims in ways that would not be permitted in those courts. Indeed, the tribunal's processes have much in common with customary forums, where less emphasis is placed on findings of fact and their impact on decision making and more on allowing parties to articulate their claims with a view to getting them to reach consensus (Griffiths 1990–1991, 223; 1996). It embodies an approach to oral argument and disputation that is deeply embedded in Tswana culture. Thus it is less geared to promoting adversarial relations, where one legal argument wins over another, and more to establishing what the parameters of the dispute encompass and how they may be dealt with to the satisfaction of all disputing parties. Where this approach is not possible, adjudication takes place, but it is not the primary aim of the process by which disputes are dealt with under the customary system. The move toward this mediatory approach to law in Western jurisdictions that has become prevalent in recent years may be seen to reflect an adoption of local practices and culture applied on a more global scale.

Chapter 7 presents the application of law in the High Court and Court of Appeal and its relationship to spatiotemporal dimensions. The daily workings of these courts represent a form of "time-space" or "space-time" (May and Thrift 2001) that encompasses the routines that structure everyday life. In this case, the organizational and operational dynamics of the courts reflect the way in which "human practices and space-time routines both mirror and mould structures" (Hubbard et al. 2002, 160) with all the consequences that follow from this. Unlike land boards, these courts are highly circumscribed in terms of their organizational framework, where what counts as law is restricted to a set of technical legal questions. These courts reflect a temporal dimension founded on a linear construction of time—one that embodies a singular perception of development to the exclusion of other temporalities through its representation of law as being timeless or representing "all-times" (Greenhouse 1998). This mythic representation makes it possible for law to put itself above social relations, thus privileging a particular narrative of law above all others. This representation also makes it possible for law to reformulate the logic of the past to meet the interests of the present and the future by allowing for the possibility of change without displacing law's ideological claim to timelessness and thus universality.

Final Reflections

My book concludes with final reflections that draw together critical insights concerning how particular dimensions of the research have contributed to refining the concept of what is global. The research highlights different dimensions of scale and content that are at work in the dialectical relationship between local and global domains when viewed from a variety of standpoints. These include international agencies such as the UN and the World Bank, national institutions such as the Ministry of Lands and Housing, district administration in the form of Kweneng Land Board and Bakwena Tribal Administration, and finally families and households located in Molepolole village. The chapter also reflects on how, although these domains vary in range and scope in their relationships with land, they nonetheless have connective threads operating through the numerous forms of access, control, and management of land that embody the nexus of relations taking shape between families, communities, the state, and the world.

Writing this book has been an exploration into the meaning of global as defined through my study of land in Botswana. I invite you to share in this journey as I turn now to the historical context that has framed Botswana's current position with regard to land and the challenges this position represents for its future place within the global community.

Notes

1. This assessment was based on a rise in terms of gross domestic product (GDP) per capita from USD 70 in 1996 to USD 6,270 in 2006–2007. See African Development Bank (2009–2013, 2).

2. See, for example, William Twining's (2000, 2009) distrust of catchall labels such as *global* and *globalization* when analyzing legal processes. As Neil Walker points out, Twining warns against "the overuse of what remains a radically ambiguous and open-ended label,"

along with the dangers of its invocation that "may have a misleadingly reductive effect . . . implying a fake unity, coherence or settlement" (2014, 2).

3. For an example, see Stewart (2011).

4. The 2030 Agenda can be found at the United Nations website, accessed September 14, 2016, http://www.un.org/sustainabledevelopment/development-agenda.

5. Commission on the Legal Empowerment of the Poor and the UN Development Program (2008).

6. Peters (2013) warns against focusing this debate simply on the role of foreign agents. She stresses the need to examine the role of national governments as well as the accelerating process of appropriation by national governments. In the case of Botswana, see *In the Matter between Roy Sesana, Keiwa Setlhobogwa and Others and the Attorney General* (Misca. No. 52 of 2002) BWHC 129 (December 13, 2006), where the applicants sought (1) an order that the government of Botswana had unlawfully removed them from their settlements in the Central Kalahari Game Reserve, and (2) their restoration to these settlements and the provision of basic and essential services to them.

7. Thus Roland Robertson (1995, 26) argues "the contemporary assertion of ethnicity and/or nationality is made within the global terms of identity and particularity." See also Sally Engle Merry (2000, 127), who argues that indigenous groups often define themselves in terms being developed by the global movement of indigenous peoples' human rights.

8. Merry (2000, 129) argues that "global legal language is an amalgam of local law." She observes that in a global meeting, the Beijing Conference Plus Five, held in New York in 2000, the document that the participants sought to develop of the Fourth World Conference on Women in 1995 was one that emerged from participants own local understandings of law in the creation of consensus.

9. For an example of this approach, see Fabian (1996).

10. The term *tribe* or *tribes* was applied by British colonial powers to refer to the indigenous people under their rule. The preferred classification today is the term *polity* (or *morafe*) or *polities* (or *merafe*). However, it is important to note that the word *tribe* is a legal term of art in relation to the legal and administrative regulation in Botswana today.

11. In Setswana, one of the two official languages in Botswana (the other being English), the prefixes *Ba* and *Mo* are the plural and singular modifiers of nouns designating persons. Accordingly, Batswana refers to Tswana people, while the word Motswana refers to a Tswana person.

12. This demarcation of legal systems into separate spheres was advanced by the colonizer. However, these systems did not stand in isolation to one another but did interact. For a discussion on this topic, see Griffiths (1997).

13. Note that the land mass and territorial jurisdiction of KLB covers an area of 38,122 square kilometers, of which 5,000 square kilometers falls within the Gaborone catchment area. Botswana as a whole covers an area of 585,371 square kilometers.

14. *Bakwena* refers to Kwena people as a group, and *Mokwena* refers to an individual Kwena person.

15. For an account of how European perspectives shaped understandings of customary law into the postcolonial period, see John L. Comaroff and Simon A. Roberts (1981).

16. Some examples of this scholarship include Carole Greenhouse, Barbara Yngvesson, and David M. Engel (1994); Alice Lynd and Staughton Lynd (1996); and David M. Engel (1995).

PART I

HISTORICAL DIMENSIONS OF LAND IN BOTSWANA: CONTEMPORARY ENTANGLEMENTS

1

THE INTERNATIONAL LANDSCAPE
AND ITS INFLUENCE ON LAND
IN BOTSWANA

HOW LAND IS SITUATED IN BOTSWANA TODAY IS a product of historical engagement with regional forces such as the Union of South Africa (now the Republic of South Africa), colonialism in the form of British indirect rule under the Bechuanaland Protectorate (1885–1966), and more recent international influences, especially international market forces. The impact of these historical engagements informs current dilemmas around land that Botswana, like other countries across the globe, faces in terms of its growing population, urban migration, and need for land as a market commodity in order to satisfy wider international agendas promoted by the UN, the World Bank, and other transnational institutions. One of these agendas, whose mission is embodied in the UN's Transforming Our World: The 2030 Agenda for Sustainable Development (United Nations 2015a, 2015b), includes goals such as ending poverty in all its forms (SDG 1); achieving food security (SDG 2); achieving gender equality (SDG 5); and promoting sustained, inclusive, and sustainable economic growth (SDG 8). Transforming Our World was agreed to by 193 world leaders in 2015 who sought to create an international, overarching framework within which transnational organizations such as the UN and World Bank can promote global development. This global focus (embracing both spatial expansion and normative application) is one that the 2030 Agenda repeatedly stresses as required in order to meet the needs of "developing countries—including African countries, least developed countries, landlocked developing countries, small island developing States, and middle-income countries" (United Nations 2015b, 25).

How this agenda is being realized with regard to land, however, is open to debate. Although the agreed-on agenda seeks to balance economic and humanistic needs, the functional vehicle within which these needs are being met is based on a strategy that focuses on a particular paradigm of governance based on the legal protection of a Western conception of property rights. This strategy provides for a systematic identification of land, often through a cadastral survey, that confers ownership on an individual through registration of title in a public institution such as the Registry of Deeds. In adopting this approach to property rights, it is argued that greater certainty in land rights will be created, which will empower the poor to unlock their capital in land through obtaining access to credit that can be used to generate greater economic productivity and wealth. The assumption on which this argument is based derives from a view that the main cause of poverty for the poor is their lack of access to formal property rights resulting in their inability to use their land productively to engage with market forces. This view has been and continues to be adopted by the World Bank,[1] a view heavily influenced by the work of Hernando de Soto (2000), who has championed the adoption of formal property law in the developing world in order to facilitate economic development for the poor.[2] Economic development, he maintains, would be achieved through the legalization of assets (currently considered dead capital because it is held on an informal basis) that would enable the poor to benefit from the functions of formal capital to maximize their assets.

The concept of universal legal protection also informs the report of the Commission for the Legal Empowerment of the Poor (2008), which posits that universal legal protection is necessary in order to promote access to justice and effective property rights that are currently lacking because poor people do not have access to a well-functioning justice system that ensures their property and businesses are legally recognized. This Western approach to property rights forms part of a broader, neoliberal approach to a global agenda geared toward the opening up of borders and markets through the free flow of capital supported by access to financial services, including credit.[3]

This approach has been subject to much criticism because it makes particular assumptions about causal connections between formal property, economic development, and poverty (Benda-Beckmann 2003).[4] It has also been subject to criticism because it "pays little attention to locally owned definitions of human being and well-being" that are crucial factors in creating globally sustainable and equitable human progress (Centre for

International Governance Innovation [hereinafter CIGI] 2012, 3). Critics cite its narrow focus on a particular form of land tenure, which is presented as part of an inevitable historical process based on an evolutionary and linear theory of rights. As a result, the underlying basis on which the governance framework is based is never questioned,[5] but rather where there are failures in the achievement of sustainable development goals they are simply "attributed to the people, systems, and governments of the Global South," or sub-Saharan Africa (ibid.). This attitude is inferred in observations such as the following: "Sub-Saharan Africa is not on track to achieve any of the Millennium Development Goals and extreme poverty persists on every continent" (Commission on Legal Empowerment of the Poor 2008, 1). This assumption is founded on a Western construct grounded in aggregation and averages that fails to address the needs of the very poorest. Indeed, as Robert Home has noted, neoliberal aid and policies that include land titling "as a precondition of World Bank structural adjustment from the 1980s" hardly address "the basic inequalities in ownership and access to land" (2012, 11).[6] The failure to take adequate notice of existing inequalities subsisting in the South often leads to misguided assertions, such as Mozambique "is way 'off track' despite strong improvements" (CIGI 2012, 3). Kogo Sebastian Amanor and Sam Moyo (2008) argue that what is required is an analysis of structural interests, access, and equity in addressing questions of sustainable development rather than focusing on the technical management of land and resources.

How then does Botswana, a country in the global South, find itself situated with regard to how land is administered and managed within its borders? To answer this question, one must look to the particular characteristics of the land that constitutes Botswana and how it has come into being (see maps 1.1 and 1.2).

Land in Botswana

Botswana today is a landlocked country about the size of Texas, Kenya, or France that stretches over a land mass of 582,000 square kilometers (224,700 square miles) and that shares a border with Zimbabwe, Namibia, South Africa, and Zambia. It has a semiarid climate with low rainfall and is susceptible to drought that adversely affects agricultural production and the rural economy. Within its borders, which mirror those established during the colonial era, the capital city, Gaborone, and its catchment area are in the southeast of the country where a third of its estimated population

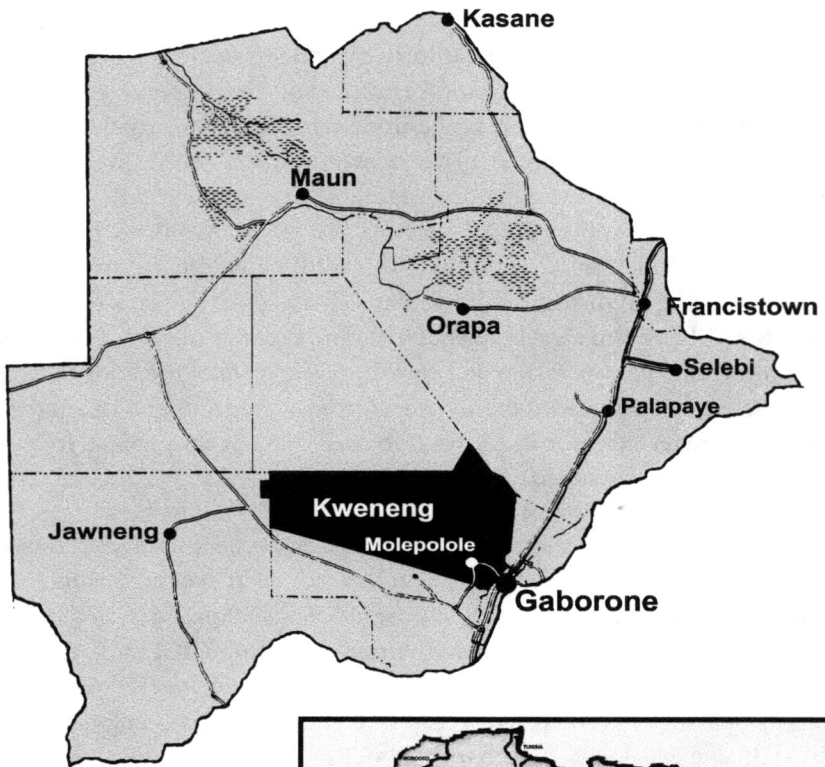

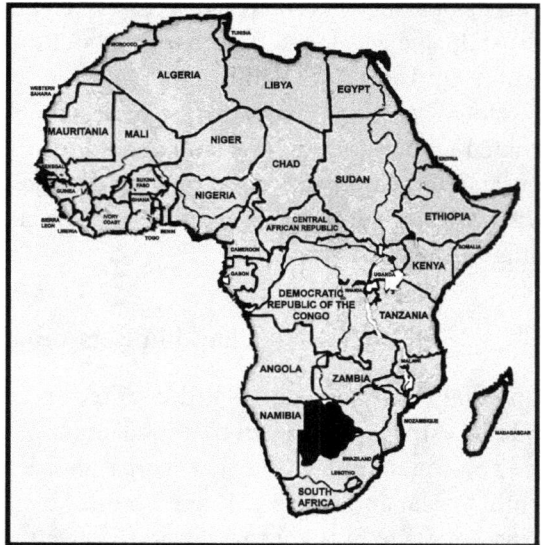

Map 1.1. Map showing Botswana in relation to Africa and locating major places mentioned in the text.

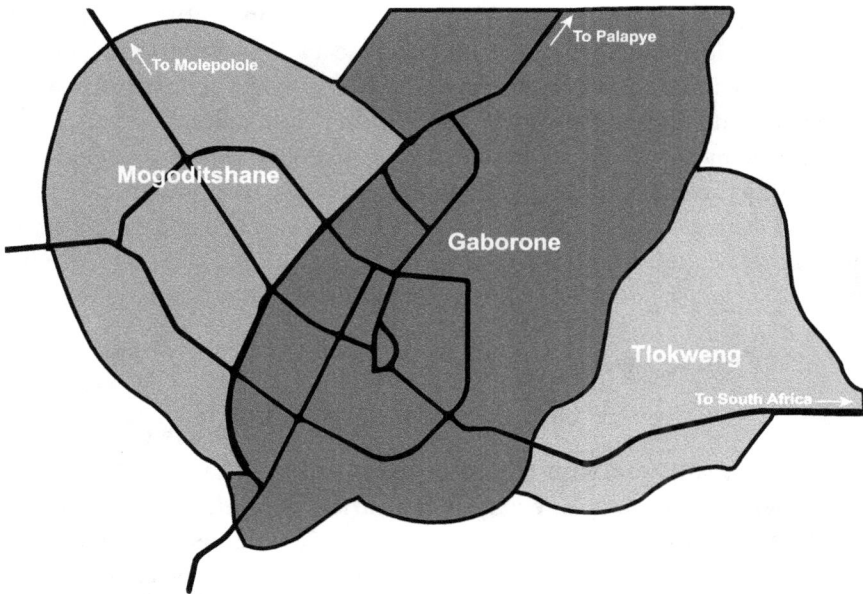

Map 1.2. Map showing the spatial position of Gaborone in relation to the peri-urban areas of Mogoditshane and Tlokweng.

of 2,021,144 lives.[7] It also has large central villages in which the major polities are located,[8] together with commercial ranches, outlying cattleposts, and arable fields that provide subsistence agriculture for many Batswana, as well as large farms for business entrepreneurs. In addition to urban and agricultural uses, land is used for mining activities in which diamonds feature most prominently (centered round the towns of Jwaneng and Orapa), but which also include copper nickel (Selebi-Pikwe and Kgwebe), soda ash (Sowa Spit), and a little gold (Tati and Francistown). A large part of Botswana is taken up with the Central Kalahari Desert, situated in the central and southwest part of the country where the Central Kalahari Game Reserve (CKGR) is located. The CKGR is one of several game reserves in the country that support the growing tourist industry. In contrast to the arid features of the CKGR, the Okavango Delta, the world's largest inland delta, and the Chobe-Linyanti Swamp are situated in the north of the country.

Thus, land in Botswana encompasses a number of topographical, socioeconomic, and cultural features that create the contexts within which it is governed by policy. As Stephanie Lawson notes, "policy making processes occur in spirals of time connecting past, present, and future" (2011, 337). This perception of policy is important because it acknowledges the tensions between the international influence that drives toward a certain future with regard to land and the "institutional structures and cultural expectations established by past policies" (Perche 2011, 403). Policy makers must balance addressing present needs and guiding the nation toward an internationally-minded future with honoring previous local approaches to policy (Perche 2011, 403). To understand how the legal interpretation of land fits into international goals, however, we must first understand the history of the land itself.

Precolonial Dimensions of Land

The current situation with regard to land in Botswana is rooted in the long interaction of peoples engaged in a variety of herding, horticultural, and hunting economies, particularly after Batswana came into the country in the early fourteenth century. Developments that took place beginning in the mid-eighteenth century, stimulated by European-introduced trade on the distance coasts, led to larger settlements characterized by central villages (Okihiro 1976; Parsons 1977; Ramsay 1991; Tlou 1985). By mid-nineteenth century, Sechele I (c. 1833–1892) had consolidated the disunited Bakwena into a single regional power embracing a large central settlement with outlying domains (Griffiths 1997, 64). As part of this consolidation, Sechele I used the land to create a settlement pattern based on agro-pastoral activities that required families and households to move between three locations: the village, where they pursued their social and political life; the agricultural lands, where they pursued farming; and the cattle-posts, where they herded their livestock.

This spatial organization of land, carried out by *dikgosi* (chiefs)[9] and their headmen, created a set of social relations that bound members of the polity together. This form of social organization provided the predominant precolonial context within which people managed their lives. Dependent on labor for their agro-pastoral activities, Bakwena, as in other Tswana *merafe* (polities), moved according to seasonal requirements between village, agricultural land, and cattlepost.

Underpinning this spatial dimension and use of land was a policy where, through kinship and a system loosely resembling share-farming called *mafisa* (Nangati 1982), individuals could acquire rights to control land through reciprocal exchanges of labor such as working the land and building up a herd of livestock. Through this system, the class ranking inherent in Tswana social structure was strengthened by giving local elites direct economic and administrative control over the lower classes in their spheres of assigned responsibility (Wilmsen 1989, 99). Under this system, the power to allocate and distribute land was vested initially in the kgosi, who assigned the land to his male followers, who as ward heads and family elders supervised the process of distribution within the community of their extended kin groups.

Thus, the precolonial community revolved around a local polity built around *dikgotla* (assembly centers). A *kgotla* is an assembly center (both the physical location and socially structured body of members) of a group of households presided over by a male headman or ward head. In the past (but no longer) all household heads were related through the male line. A kgotla forms part of the organization of Tswana society that revolves around the construction of a *morafe* (polity), and each is presided over by a headman. Dikgotla are structured through a tightly organized hierarchy of progressively more inclusive administrative groupings, beginning with households that make up a kgotla and extending through to wards, which are the major units of political and legal organization of the morafe as a whole. In the early 1980s, there were seventy-three dikgotla and six main wards, at the apex of which was Kgosing, where the Chief's Court is situated.

Through this structure, headmen and ward heads allocated lands to kgotla members, and fathers as household heads provided their sons with land when they wished to establish their own households, usually upon marriage. Women acquired rights to work and use arable land, but these were mediated through their fathers or husbands who had control over the land. What emerged under this system was a hierarchical set of social relations with the kgosi at the top, his immediate kin regarded as royals, other members of the morafe as commoners, and serfs at the bottom of the social totem pole.[10]

This social stratification was somewhat flexible, though, and it was possible for individuals to move up and down the social scale through manipulation of kinship genealogies and through the patronage of the kgosi, who possessed the ability to manipulate and balance the varying sectional interests within the polity. As with any group in power, however, the interests of the Sons of Kgabo (Sechele I's ancestors) lay "in promoting and preserving the role of genealogy in defining access to power" (Ramsay 1991, 127). This interest continues to operate among dikgosi in Botswana today. In this environment, the need for labor and the ability to exploit resources extended beyond the boundaries of individual families and households to incorporate the whole society, which was bound together in a system of mutual if somewhat unequal series of exchange relationships that were governed by *mekgwa le melao ya Setswana* (Tswana law and custom), or customary law.

Women's positions regarding land in the precolonial community were subordinate to those of men for a number of reasons having to do with material and psychological inequality (Alverson 1978; Kinsman 1983) that revolved around the gendered position they occupied within familial and social networks.[11] Generally excluded from participating in political life structured around dikgotla and wards, they also found themselves at a disadvantage in accumulating the kinds of resources that would enhance their status and power over time, as the rules governing inheritance favored men over women as custodians of a family's land, property, and interests. Women also found themselves constrained by the types of activities they could undertake compared with those of men. For example, women could not work at a cattlepost because of taboos surrounding women's relationships with cattle. In addition, women's labor was not valued in the same way as that of men. For example, through hunting and herding cattle, men produced meat and hides that not only played an important role in subsistence production but figured prominently in local trade networks. While women did retain control over food they produced in their fields, this food was usually consumed immediately and, in any event, was perishable, so that it could not be accumulated in the same way as the products of men's labor. Although women's agricultural labor might be exchanged for livestock, their chances of building up stock were limited compared to the range of options that made this growth possible for men.

Engaging with Colonial Overrule: The Bechuanaland Protectorate (1885–1966)

The Bechuanaland Protectorate was established in 1885, the result of activity in the region in the 1880s, especially South African Boer incursions into Bechuanaland (now Botswana) that led dikgosi to seek protection from the British. The British were at first reluctant to colonize the territory because it seemed to lack resources, but they acquiesced because they wished to protect their interests from the expansionist tendencies of the Boers in the south, the Germans in the west, and the Portuguese in the east. In safe-guarding their interests, the British opted for a policy of indirect rather than direct rule. Under this arrangement, dikgosi were left in peace to rule their communities except where this interfered with British aspirations and gains in the region. Until 1916, dikgosi were able to consolidate their authority with British support. However, over time, the British began to dismantle this authority because it was seen as being detrimental to British interests. They carried out this divestment, in part, through a series of proclamations.

Under the Native[12] Administration Proclamation (No. 74 of 1934), the British replaced the autocratic leadership of dikgosi with Native Authorities composed of councilors nominated by the Resident Commissioner. Most of the councilors were chiefs' confidants, but they also included educated individuals from the polity (at a time when most members were uneducated) who were not relatives of the chiefs. Each kgosi chaired the Native Authority for his tribe but was obliged to consult the councilors in exercising his functions (Colclough and McCarthy 1980, 25). Thus, the proclamation formalized the rule of dikgosi and of their obligation to consult other people. The same proclamation curtailed automatic accession to chieftainship by requiring the approval of the Resident Commissioner and also gave the High Commissioner power to dismiss any chief, subchief, or headman on the grounds of inefficiency, abuse of power, or unsatisfactory performance of duties.

Dikgosi's powers were further undermined by the Native Courts Proclamation (No. 13 of 1941 as amended by No. 33 of 1943). This proclamation vested judicial powers in native courts composed of chiefs and other members approved by the Resident Commissioner. It also required inclusion of educated individuals in native courts and the recording, in writing, of all court proceedings, judgments, and sentences. Under this proclamation, "natives" were permitted to contest and appeal against decisions and sentences passed by chiefs and their native courts to higher courts, including the High Court. Thus, for the first time, the rule and decisions made by a kgosi and his subordinates could be challenged. This continues to be the case under the legal system in force in Botswana today.

At a fiscal level, under the Native Treasuries Proclamation (1938) and the Native Tax Proclamation (1943, amended), dikgosi were deprived of power to levy taxes at will. They could no longer impose tribal levies without written approval from the Resident Commissioner and without the agreement of the tribe in the kgotla. They were also obliged to carry out all lawful orders issued to them by the Resident Commissioner (Colclough and McCarthy 1980, 25). Some dikgosi challenged these provisions in the High Court but lost when the judge ruled that the High Commissioner had to respect, but was not bound by, native law and custom.

To closely monitor the activities and operations of chiefs and native authorities, the British colonial administration introduced a District Commissioner for each tribal reserve. The District Commissioner was "the most important representative of central government in the district with considerable local executive authority" (Colclough and McCarthy 1980, 39; Picard 1987). The office of the District Commissioner "served as a watch-dog over tribal chiefs and headmen to make sure they ruled their subjects according to what in the view of the colonial administrator, was reasonable governance" (Botswana 2001, 106). The District Commissioner served as a link between local communities and the Resident Commissioner. This system employing a Resident Commissioner, District Commissioners, and officers was one that was replicated across the British Empire where the policy was one of engaging in indirect rule. After independence, the post of District Commissioner as the central government representative was retained, thus maintaining administrative continuity in the postindependent state. This continuity was also to be found in the civil service that continued to be serviced by British expatriates as very few Africans were appointed to its senior ranks at independence (Fawcus and Tilbury 2000).[13]

Local taxes levied through the proclamations, combined with the levying of taxes by the Bechuanaland Protectorate, obliged many men to seek paid employment, especially in South Africa, in effect giving the Protectorate the status of a labor reserve, as local opportunities for wage labor to meet the needs of the local population were insufficient at that time. Thus, the Protectorate became drawn into migrant labor in South Africa. This tax burden had an impact on settlement patterns around land, as many adult men had to leave their lands to spend most of their working lives as migrants, forcing those at home to acquire new forms of labor to maintain their homesteads. While some women also worked as migrants, most women remained at home to look after household needs. This pattern created an environment that had a dramatic impact on family life, such as marriage occurring much later in the life cycle (Schapera 1947, 173; Timaeus and Graham 1989, 392) than in other parts of Africa (Bledsoe 1990), if at all. The phenomenon of unmarried women with children that emerged as a result of these colonial policies continues today (Molokomme 1991; Griffiths

1997, 243) and has given the government of Botswana much cause for concern because unmarried women with children feature among the poorest in the population.

This modification of the traditional land-tenure system during the colonial period through transformations in political, administrative, and social structures exacerbated economic disparities already existing between taxpayers (i.e., ordinary members of the polity) and tax collectors (i.e., dikgosi and headmen). As the rich elite accumulated more and more cattle, they began to benefit from services that were initially offered only to European farmers. The services included disease control and perennial water supplies from boreholes, water sources that were traditionally held under common ownership. With time and "promoted by market forces, [these] boreholes began to be recognized as personal property in the 1930s, and moves towards the private ownership of adjacent grazing lands, a direct and logical extension, soon followed" (Good 1992, 72). Owners of boreholes did not permit cattle belonging to other people to graze close to their boreholes lest they drink water from these private facilities.

As Pauline Peters (1984) observed, it was chiefly the elite dikgosi and headmen with large herds of cattle who benefited unduly from these trends.[14] These quasi-private land rights gave rise to dual-grazing land rights. While other members of the tribe could access or graze within the vicinity of these water sources only with explicit permission of their owners, the elite members could graze their cattle in the communal land at will. In a similar manner, improved crop-farming methods led to people fencing their communal fields, thus having year-round exclusivity and denying other tribe members their traditional rights of grazing on fields after harvesting of crops (Mathuba 1982). Finally, with the decline in the importance of subsistence hunting and gathering, money paid to dikgosi by concession hunters and other Europeans solidified the commoditization and recognition of a market in land.

Postcolonial Developments: From Independence (1966)

The laws concerning land that evolved during the colonial era continue to play an important role today. The land-tenure system in Botswana now contains aspects of unwritten, customary law based on *mekgwa le melao ya Setswana*, as well as written, statutory law derived from European and Cape Colonial case law.[15] As noted earlier, use, control, and allocation of land depends on its legal classification. Three types of land tenure exist, and all mark a continuity with the colonial past. The first is tribal land, with its communal forms of tenure that are the basis of Tswana conceptions of relations to land and the sociopolitical administrative structure in which chieftainship plays a key role. The second type of land is state land, including British Crown land administered by the colonial government, which was converted to state land under the State Land Act (Cap. 32.01). The colonial state asserted rights over this land on the basis of public interest; that is, surplus land was either unoccupied (which involved invoking the concept of *terra nullius* that is now discredited) or was not obviously being used beneficially. The advantage was that once claimed, the state could then transfer the land through grant, sale, or lease to settlers or public bodies that might include central government itself or regional or local authorities. Most of this type of land today is found in urban areas. The third type is freehold land, created for settlers during the colonial era. This type of tenure recognizes individual ownership with a right to free and undisturbed possession, largely with regard to agricultural land. Although this tenure was never widespread and has decreased significantly since independence, it has had a profound influence on the way in which rights to land are perceived because it promotes the primacy of private property rights "through the Lockean philosophy of possessive individualism" (Home 2012, 10). To prevent continuing transfers of freehold land from noncitizens to noncitizens, it was brought under the jurisdiction of the Land Control Act (Cap. 32.11) introduced in 1975.

Among these systems, a major distinction is drawn between tribal land (70 percent of the land in Botswana) and state and freehold land. The former derives its status from oral, unwritten customary law as compared to the Western-derived statutory laws that apply to state and freehold land. The result is a plurality of laws within a formal legal structure that influences how Botswana can respond to global agendas with regard to land.

Although this pluralistic legal structure stems from multiple land Acts, my book focuses on the Tribal Land Act, passed in 1968, which represents the major form of land tenure in Botswana under customary law.[16] This Act forms the basis for the powers given to land boards and was passed barely two years after Botswana acquired its independence in 1966 in order to more readily accommodate "more modern practices of land use, such as more exclusive allocation and utilization of tribal grazing ranges" (Morolong and Ng'ong'ola 2007, 146). Its passage was viewed as a necessary prerequisite for a young country that had acquired statehood and was pursuing a parliamentary democracy to provide for a land administration system that could assure all Batswana access to land. In Botswana, as elsewhere in British colonial Africa, the newly elected rulers were aware that "he who controls the land is in a good position to influence government" (Ghai and McAuslan [1970, 25], quoted in Morolong and Ng'ong'ola [2007, 146]), given the importance of land not only as an economic asset but as a resource that can be used to gain leverage over people.[17]

The Tribal Land Act was the first piece of legislation to propose substantial changes to the Tswana tribal system of land tenure that had been left intact after the proclamation of the tribal reserves during the colonial era (Ng'ong'ola 1997, 14). The Act established land boards for specified tribal areas that corresponded with the nine native reserves proclaimed within the colonial era. However, the Act handed to land boards power previously vested in dikgosi under customary law in relation to allocation, use, and cancellation of land rights (under Section 13). Thus traditional authorities, including dikgosi, "lost the leverage that they [had] over the spatial organization of their subjects" (Ijagbemi 2006, 223), although they continued to play an important role in land matters, especially with regard to inheritance. In 1976, the original nine land boards were expanded to twelve when land "excised from State land was redesignated as Tribal Territories in Chobe, Ghanzi and Kgalagadi districts" (Ng'ong'ola 1997, 15).

The postcolonial introduction of land boards represented a major innovation with regard to the allocation and distribution of land.[18] The devolution of dikgosi's powers to land boards brought land within a different spatial governance structure, one that has promoted conflict over what those powers entail. It is a structure that provides for a decentralized system of land administration where land boards act autonomously, although how autonomous they are in practice has been questioned by Faustin Kalabamu and Siamsang Morolong (2004, 48–49). Botswana did not opt for introducing radical changes to land reform as was pursued in some other African countries, such as Tanzania (D. James 1971), Ethiopia, Kenya, Mozambique, Malawi (Ijagbemi 2006, 319), or postapartheid South Africa (Claassens and Cousins 2008; R. W. James 2007). The Botswana People's Party (BPP), founded in 1960 and based on the structure of the African National Congress (ANC), made an attempt to pursue more radical policies. It stood in opposition to the more traditional Botswana Democratic Party (BDP) led by Seretse Khama, who became the first President of an independent

Botswana after the country acquired its independence on September 30, 1966. The BPP was much more radical in its approach to government, and one of its policies included the redistribution of land rather than simply adhering to a more conservative approach of adaptation. However, the BPP did not have enough political support to win the election held on March 1, 1965 that went to the BDP (which had been supported by the British government). As a result, the BDP came to power as the government of the day electing to pursue a strategy of "adaptation" (Bruce 1998), which sought to merge "some aspects of traditional tenure arrangements with the modern, that is characterized by private ownership and the creation of the land market" (Ijagbemi 2006, 318). This strategy, manifested in the creation of the Tribal Land Act, continues to guide Botswana's governmental approach to land reform today.

Current Jurisdiction and Powers of Land Boards under the Tribal Land Act

Under the Tribal Land Act (TLA), land boards in Botswana administer customary grants of land and common law leases. Neither of these types of tenure confers ownership on the recipients, as control over the land vests in the land boards who hold it "in trust for the benefit and advantage of citizens of Botswana" (Section 10[1]). This wording reflects the 1993 amendment to the Act that opened up jurisdiction for land boards to all citizens regardless of their tribal affiliation. Although the Act does not define customary rights, these are commonly assumed to cover residence (*motse*), arable agriculture (*tshimo*), and grazing (*moraka*) but exclude hunting and gathering, which are also customary activities. As customary grants can only be given for customary forms of land tenure, they cannot be made for non-customary uses such as trading, manufacturing, business, or commerce (Section 20[2]).

With respect to these non-customary uses, land boards were given power to allocate common law rights under Part IV of the TLA. The introduction of common law leases on tribal land was designed to commercialize land rights in rural areas. Initially, the leases were intended to support the livestock industry, which was controlled by the new political elite and considered the backbone of the country's economy. In 1975, the Tribal Grazing Land Policy (TGLP) increased the scope of these leases by requiring land boards to plan and identify common grazing areas that could be carved up and individualized so that exclusive ranches could be allocated under longer leases, essentially privatizing the land. It was the expectation that lessees would "develop commercial ranches and reduce pressure on communal land" (Kalabamu and Morolong 2004, 50). The policy was based on the notion that communal land tenure inhibits individual initiative in the proper use of land resources because of overstocking of communal areas and degradation of the environment.

This negative perception of communal land tenure and its effects can be traced, as Peters (1994) points out, to Garrett Hardin's (1968) "Tragedy of the Commons," which predicted inevitable ecological disaster in allowing open access to resources for which no one is ultimately responsible. This view had an international impact and was picked up in World Bank publications. Indeed, Peters shows how it found its way to Botswana via a senior adviser for the US Agency for International Development (USAID) who was involved in the discussion promoting the 1975 Botswana government white paper concerning TGLP. Yet, as Peters reveals, an official from Botswana involved in the making of the policy told her that the "tragedy" had been unknown to the government before it was raised by the USAID adviser (1994, 162). She also convincingly demonstrates how many of the failures attributed to the operation of communal lands, in fact, came about through the application of external development policies that distorted their use and thus precipitated their collapse.

The effect of this newly adopted policy was that lessees acquired dual grazing rights; they not only had their own exclusive zones but also had access to the remainder of communal grazing resources. In seeking to advance commercial viability in Botswana, the Tribal Land Act allows for land held under a customary grant to be convertible into a common law lease that could be registered in the Deeds Registry.[19] Such an action provides title to land that can act as a form of security to raise loans, as customary grants are not regarded as marketable securities by formal lending institutions such as banks. Residential leases run for up to ninety-nine years, while the period is fifty years for commercial leases with an option of renewal.[20] When the lease terminates the land reverts to customary tenure. As part of the process of modernization of land tenure, customary grant holders are also issued certificates, but these do not contain the same detailed information as leases and consequently do not have the same status. Dikgosi of the major polities and politicians (who come from royal families or have close links with them) feature prominently among the elites who control these long-leased commercial ranches, thus consolidating earlier constellations of power in a contemporary setting.[21] These elites' preferential access to grazing land, at work under the colonial Protectorate and continuing into the postindependence era, has resulted in "a persistent narrowing in the definition of those with primary rights to land" (Peters 2004, 292) despite the global agenda to empower the poor through land ownership. Such a development is not an isolated occurrence. E. P. Thompson (1993) has documented how the wider range of rights associated with the "commons" in Britain were gradually narrowed and whittled away in favor of property owners. Resort to legal regulation in courts played an important part in this process that resulted in "the right of use . . . [becoming] not a use but a property [right]" (Thompson 1993, 135). For Peters, this process is one in which "holders of (usually) small areas of customary land in Africa are represented as 'backward,' or 'conservative' and obstacles to the 'modernization' of agriculture" (1994, 190). It was accompanied by the use of law "to force registration and titling to land,"[22] thus "converting socially managed land into a fungible property, freeing it for the market" (Peters 2014, 190). What is clear is that the agenda for change, promoting land reform around the world, deals more with policies and techniques of implementation rather than address underlying substantive concerns about redistributing land more equitably.

Contemporary Dilemmas

A major review of land policy with regard to the legal, political, economic, and social pathways just described was published in 2003; the report stated that since independence some major changes have been introduced, including "independent allocations of land to all adults, the charging of a price for the transfer of developed land between willing buyer and seller," and "the introduction of common law leases for residential, commercial and agricultural purposes and for foreign investors" (Botswana 2003b, p. 2, para. 7.). A major consideration guiding the 2003 report was the shift to an economy that was no longer agricultural (p. 1, para. 2), as evidenced by a decline in agriculture from 40 percent of GDP in 1966 to only 3 percent in 2003. The review concluded that given the shift toward urbanization, rural land was no longer vital in the way it had been in the past (e.g., as a place to retire to at the end of one's working life). Rather, urban dwellers, like those around the world, now valued safe and secure urban housing in order to provide "a home base for urban employment, and also for investment of savings, and retirement in an urban setting" (p. 1, para. 4).

This growth of urbanization and the challenges it presents are not confined to Botswana but occur across Africa and throughout the world.[23] One major problem that all sectors of society acknowledge is that due to urbanization, there is a shortage of land in the areas where people want to live and work. As a result, this trend in urbanization has led to overcrowding, which has in turn led to a very active market that produces conflict between those perceived of as squatters, those who have legitimate title to land, and government institutions and land boards who administer the land.

Based on this shift toward urbanization and its resulting conflicts, the 2003 report proposed multiple solutions. The first was the need for a more flexible policy with regard to rural land that would empower landholders to lease out residential and arable land and enter into sharecropping and share farming agreements" (p. 17, para. 64). The report also advocated protecting arable land where urbanization was "putting arable land near settlements under intense pressure for change of use" (p. 17, para. 65). With regard to rural land, the report acknowledged the policies around privatization of communal grazing land for commercial ranches were flawed, resulting in dual grazing rights and otherwise threatening the land rights of large numbers of rural people, and proposed reforms including commercial-based rents and a more transparent process of land allocation (p. 19, paras. 71–73) to reduce abuses within the system.[24]

Finally, while acknowledging the land market had flaws that needed to be addressed, the report concluded that overall, "there is an acceptance that the development of a land market is good for Botswana" (p. 53, para. 186). In reaching this conclusion it is clear that the work of Hernando de Soto and views of international consultants, like Patrick McAuslan, were highly influential and led to the observation that "by comparison with other countries in the region facilitation of the land market is relatively advanced in Botswana" (p. 52, para. 185). While recognizing that this market "creates stresses and strains" nonetheless such a market has been valuable because it "provides an opportunity for citizens to generate capital through formal acquisition of property rights" on the basis that "without access to the benefits of property ownership, people remain poor" (p. 1, para. 4). Evidence of the government's endorsement of the "market approach" to land reform can be found in the recent national Botswana Land Policy approved by the Parliament of Botswana in 2015 and in the new Tribal Land Bill 2017.

In Botswana, what becomes visible is the array of structures that the state uses in its attempts to control territory, land, and people in order to meet international expectations for a global economy. The ideological image of the state that is presented to the outside world, one of a unified coherent and accountable government, masks a whole range of entities that accommodate or resist one another in an effort to balance the international, national, regional, and local landscapes within which land is situated. It is to these multiple layers of engagement that I turn next.

Notes

1. World Bank (2003) and, more recently, in a 2016 paper by Harriet Mugera, of the World Bank Group Italy, entitled "Land Tenure Systems, Food Security and Poverty," presented at the 2016 World Bank Conference on Land and Poverty, where she emphasizes "the capacity to use land productively" and warns of the "inefficiency" of theoretical models that address the role of risk.

2. De Soto (2000). For a critique of de Soto's position, see Benda-Beckmann (2003); for a reassessment of de Soto's approach ten years after it was promoted, see Van der Molen (2012).

3. See Manji (2010) on the move toward financial services, through World Bank (2008) and United Kingdom (2009), and her critique of the assertion that such services can put an end to poverty.

4. See also Celestine Nyamu-Musembi (2007), who challenges the assumption that formalization of property rights has a causal link with the empowerment of poor people and that individual ownership is ultimately inevitable for all social contexts. The assumption that formalization of rights always has positive effects ignores the role of insecurity that such rights can also engender in their implementation.

5. See Ambreena Manji (2003a, 2003b), who critically examines World Bank policy reports on land relations, especially their promotion of rural credit that is predicated on the assumption of the availability of women's unpaid labor, for this fails to acknowledge the impact that such policies will have on gender relations.

6. Manji (2001) addresses this point, noting that what is really at stake here is not so much property rights but issues of democratization and governance.

7. See Countryeconomy.com. Accessed September 1, 2014. http://www.countryeconomy .com/demography/population/Botswana.

8. These major villages that lie at the heart of the various polities in Botswana are more like towns or small cities.

9. In Setswana, a single chief is referred to as a *kgosi*, and the plural is *dikgosi*.

10. Serfs were persons, often non-Tswana, who were treated rather like slaves.

11. For a detailed account of the way in which gender operated to place women at a disadvantage in comparison with men, see Griffiths (1997).

12. Please note that the words *native* and *tribe* were used by colonial administrators to refer to the indigenous African population during the colonial era and continue to feature as legal terms of art under the formal legal and administrative system in Botswana today.

13. Sir Peter Fawcus, one of the authors, was Government Secretary, then Resident Commissioner and Queen's Commissioner during the 1950s and 1960s.

14. Sara Berry (2009, 25) observes how elsewhere in Africa power has become consolidated in the hands of small ruling elites.

15. Within the formal legal system of Botswana, *customary law* is defined as being "in relation to any particular tribe or tribal community, the customary law of that tribe or tribal community so far as it is not incompatible with the provisions of any written law or contrary to morality, humanity or natural justice" under Section 2 of the Customary Law (Application and Ascertainment Act), No. 51, 1969. This definition, which formed part of British colonial legislation, is more generally known as the *repugnancy clause* as it gives power to the common law system to negate customary law. In contrast, *common law* (that includes *statutory law*) is defined as "any law whether written or unwritten, in force in Botswana, other than customary law" under Section 2 of the 1969 Act.

16. In April 2017, the government published proposals to repeal this Act and replace it with the new Tribal Land Bill. These proposals had not yet become law when this book was written and are beyond the scope of discussion in this book, although references to the changes that the Bill proposes may be made in places.

17. See Nancy Lee Peluso (2009), who demonstrates how establishing controls over land in West Kalimantan in Indonesia was used to rework notions of legitimacy through a reconfiguration of identity-based property rights.

18. Originally dikgosi (or their representatives) could sit as ex officio members of the land board and could, in addition, appoint one member to the board, but these rights were withdrawn in 1999 under an amendment to the TLA. Politicians and civil servants are also excluded under Section 10(3)(d) and (e). Dikgosi's rights to be appointed to the land board have subsequently been reinstated in the reorganization of appointments to the board under the Tribal Land (Amendment) Regulations of 2011. The 2017 Bill makes express mention of the appointment of three ex officio members to the board that under clause 7(1)(b)(i) include a kgosi.

19. This conversion is at the grantee's initiative and cost and on production of a diagram or plan approved by the director of the Department of Surveys and Mapping. The new Tribal Land Bill 2017 (clause 23) now provides for the registration of all customary land grants in the Deeds Registry along with a bill to amend the Deeds Registry Act.

20. Noncitizens can enter into leases limited to fifty years if they have the written consent of the ministers of the Department of Lands and Housing.

21. For a discussion of how national elites manage their positions and their contributions to the development of the state, see Werbner (2004).

22. Patrick McAuslan (1997, 2003, 2014), who dedicated his life to land-tenure reform within Africa and outside it, was a lifelong believer in and advocate for the importance of and need for the formal rule of law in land-tenure reform. He was one of the international advisers consulted by the Government of Botswana in its 2003 tenure-reform process. For a discussion and critique of his position, see Manji (2005, 2014) and Peters (2014).

23. See Ubink (2011) on the effects of a growing market in real estate in peri-urban Kumasi in Ghana; Turek (2016) on the challenges "getting urbanization to work in Africa"; and Hove, Ngwerume, and Muchemwa (2013, 1), who note that "since the early 1970s Sub-Saharan Africa had the highest urban growth rate in the world"; supported by findings from the Centre for Strategic and International Studies Project on Property and Development (Saghir and Santoro 2018). See also Habitat III (2016) for the New Urban Agenda, promoting sustainable cities and human settlements for all, adopted by a resolution of the UN General

Assembly (A/Res/71/256) on December 23, 2016, that observes that "By 2050 the world urban population is expected to nearly double, making urbanization one of the 21st Century's most transformative trends."

24. An example of earlier abuse occurred when commercial ranches were put out to tender in the 1970s. A Commission of Inquiry (Botswana 1981) looking into tendering practices discovered that many of those who were successful in their tenders were, in fact, acting as proxies for certain dikgosi who already had substantial interests in cattle and land. In this way, these dikgosi were able to consolidate their interests and expand them without having to adhere to the restrictions placed on the tendering system. The problem of fronting and speculative dealings in land is one that has long been acknowledged by the government (Botswana 2003b, 11).

2

REFRAMING THE GOVERNANCE OF LAND

Global, National, and Local Intersections

T HE PREVIOUS CHAPTER ILLUSTRATED HOW RELATIONS TO LAND in Botswana have been constituted out of a series of external and internal forces over time. Like a number of African countries that acquired their independence in the 1960s, Botswana adopted a Westphalian model of sovereignty that followed a Westminster model of government inherited from Great Britain. This model maintains a separation of powers between the executive, legislative, and judicial branches of government. Botswana is governed by a constitution and has a single legislative body—the National Assembly. The President is the head of the executive branch of government and presides over the cabinet. In recognition of the historical and ongoing role of dikgosi, a body comprising traditional leaders—the Ntlo ya Dikgosi (House of Chiefs)—advises on matters affecting custom and tradition, including reviewing draft bills before their consideration by Parliament. Dikgosi represent a number of different polities within the country, well beyond the eight hereditary chiefs and chiefdoms that were recognized under British colonial rule.[1] In recognition of the many constituencies and polities that they represent, dikgosi now number thirty-five members in the House. The judiciary is independent; the Chief Justice presides over the High Court, and subordinate courts (magistrates' courts) have original jurisdiction to try all offenses except capital offenses such as murder and treason. Some cases are heard by local dikgosi and headmen, or their representatives, and decided in accordance with customary law.

Under this model of government, Botswana has territorial borders and jurisdictional sovereignty within them. Yet, as is clear from chapter 1, the way in which Botswana operates is one in which broader conceptions of governance are at work that form part of global space, a term used by Cottrell and Trubek (2012, 362) to refer to "an evolving regulatory environment created by globalization and the increasing role international norms play in domestic settings." This space acknowledges transnational forms of law and ordering derived from diverse sources (F. Benda-Beckmann, K. Benda-Beckmann, and Griffiths 2009a, 2009b; Hellum, Ali, and Griffiths, 2011). It is one that challenges the construction of discrete domains where there is a demarcation between a state's external and internal dimensions. It is one that, as Neil Walker (2014, 13) observes, "involves the blurring of the general (internal-external) divide between the exercise of internal state sovereignty and external state sovereignty, with states increasingly pooling their capacity in international organizations, which in turn undermines the (internal-internal) sense of their uniformity and mutually exclusively divided internal sovereignty." Sovereignty affects not just how external relations shape the way in which states operate but also has an impact on a state's internal dynamics, creating new sets of relations.

Thus, there are "multiple centers of power within an exercise of government that is wider and more complex than that which is contained within traditional understandings" (Morison 2003, 188) of how nation-states govern. This chapter will explore how these broader forms of governance and governmentality are at work in Botswana. In doing so it will draw on materials from government websites and from extensive interviews with government personnel and other officials involved in land administration.[2] These data were principally acquired in 2010 and 2012. In order to coordinate comments from interviews together with stated government policy at the time in question, I was required to cite texts from websites that are no longer in operation in some cases. Where this occurs I have given the last date of access and noted that there is now a dead link. I have adopted this approach in order to highlight the dynamic processes that are ongoing and at work in promoting land administration and reform. While I consulted many of the ministries directly on their websites, they fall under the overall purview of the Government of Botswana, whose website is constantly being updated at www.gov.bw.

External Engagement: Botswana's Image on the World Stage

The international and global image of Botswana is one of a relatively prosperous, stable African state that has experienced a "rapid transition from one of the poorest countries in the world to a middle income country."[3] This transition is largely attributed to its commitment to good governance, as illustrated by the African Development Bank's rating of Botswana as the "top sub-Saharan country on all governance elements" (AfDb 2009–2013, p. 1, para. 2.1.2). Its impressive governance scores have also been confirmed by the Botswana Institute for Development Policy Analysis (BIDPA [2009]) an independent think tank operating in the country, as well as by the World Bank Group (2011). Thus it has acquired the status of being ranked "in the top quartile of various governance indices worldwide and in most cases, it is tops in the African region" (AfDB 2009–2013, p. 1, para. 2.1.2). More recently, the World Bank's *Poverty Assessment* (2015, p. 2, para. 1) acknowledged Botswana's macroeconomic achievements as being truly remarkable and emphasized that Botswana's policies led it "from independence up to the 1990s to being one of the fastest growing economies in the world." This economic growth has been underscored by the Bank of Botswana's *Annual Report* (2015), which noted "between 1981 and 1991 the real GDP increased at an average annual rate of 10.7 percent" (p. 101, para. 3.16). Furthermore, the US Department of State, in its *Botswana Investment Climate Statement* (2015), observes that "in accordance to the World Bank's rating scale, Botswana's per capita income of USD 7,730 makes it higher than most other sub-Sahara[n] countries" (3).

Botswana's real GDP growth has fallen from 5.9 percent in 2013 to 4.3 percent in 2016, a position that is attributed to a global decline in mineral prices, especially diamonds, and to a slowdown in emerging markets linked to Botswana's narrow, predominantly mining, export base and the public sector (*African Economic Outlook* 2015, 130). As a result, Botswana has been encouraged to engage in economic diversification (BIDPA 2016) and promote foreign direct investment (FDI) in sectors such as agribusinesses, clean energy, services, infrastructure, and manufacturing (US Department of State 2015). A line of credit worth USD 76.2 million has been extended to Botswana by the African Development Bank to help with this diversification, including addressing "focus on trade arrangements with other countries, both regional and multi-lateral" to address "capacity building in trade negotiations covering the WTO [World Trade Organization], SADAC [Southern African Development Community][4] and SACU [Southern African Customs Union]" (AfDB 2016). As Ben Chiagra (2012, xvi) observes, SADAC governments have been tasked with remaining "set on a path of sustainable development in order to maximize on their economic potential in an increasingly global economy." This engagement with regional and international players on the world stage cannot help but have an impact on Botswana's national development strategies.

Land plays an important part in underpinning and promoting these global spaces for development. In Botswana, land is primarily regulated by the Ministry of Lands and Housing which in 2010 comprised eight departments.[5] It is also, however, included within in the portfolios of other ministries that have an interest in or connection to land.[6] Thus, a diverse range of institutions and departments share responsibility for responding to the issues of growth in human population, changing land-use practices, technology, economic growth, and the pressures of urbanization, all of which are having an impact on countries across the globe. The resulting amendments to meet these issues as they are associated with land in Botswana have put the framework of customary law embodied in the Tribal Land Act under pressure to adapt. It is not possible to discuss all of the needs associated with these issues in detail in this book, but they include those that form part of a wider, international human rights agenda such as promoting housing and infrastructure,[7] enhancing agricultural production and preservation,[8] and conserving land and the environment as a resource.[9]

The Sustainable Global Vision's Influence on National Governance

In line with the sustainable approach to globalization, government institutions in Botswana present a vision of a seamless governance to the country's citizens and to the world at large, projecting an image that embraces sustainable and innovative policies for enhanced productivity in a competitive global market. This image is produced through government websites and published material that highlights an institution's mandate, vision, and values.[10] Echoing international agencies' emphasis on development that is sustainable (a condition of much foreign investment and aid) almost every website highlights this dimension of Botswana's current and future policy at the level of both national and local government. This emphasis on the sustainable also reflects Botswana's desire to become a world leader, as exemplified by the Ministry of Environment, Wildlife, and Tourism's vision statement that it strives "to make Botswana a world leader in the management of the environment for sustainable development."[11] (See figs. 2.1 and 2.2.)

Botswana seeks to achieve this sustainable vision of seamless governance by upholding more efficient and professional approaches to the

Figure 2.1. Aerial view of the government complex, Gaborone. *Photo courtesy of the Government of Botswana.*

Figure 2.2. Government complex, downtown Gaborone. *Photo courtesy of the Government of Botswana.*

delivery of services and upgrading technology as needed to support these approaches. For example, the Department of Lands, whose mission is "to provide competitive services in land administration," aims to achieve this objective by "using appropriate technologies and effective policies and legislation."[12] This approach is in keeping with the government of Botswana's drive "to become a society of proficient users and innovators of ICT [information and communication technology] to propel social and economic development," as stated on its website.[13] Part of the process of realizing this vision involves engaging with the private sector. For example, the Ministry of Trade and Development declares that it plans to promote the "development of globally competitive enterprises that need little or no government support" when referring to public-private partnerships.[14] And the mission statement of the Ministry of Minerals, Energy and Water Resources provides for "efficient administrative services for mineral exploitation . . . in partnership with stakeholders," including private companies and investors at home and from abroad.[15]

Underlying these aspirations are a set of expressly articulated common values that cut across ministries and departments, including integrity, openness, transparency, accountability, excellence, teamwork, professionalism, and timeliness. This expression of values is very much in accordance with those promoted by international agencies in connection with the global drive for good governance and access to justice. Additionally, in achieving these goals and aspirations, the government recognizes the need for coordination. The Ministry of Finance and Development Planning highlights its role in providing leadership in its mandate "to coordinate national development planning" that forms part of its vision for being "a world class leader and model of excellence in financial and economic management for the prosperity of Botswana."[16] The Ministry of Transport and Communications, in promoting the development of ICT and transport policies, also recognizes the need to "co-ordinate their implementation through national, regional and global collaborative efforts that harness local resources, talent and innovations."[17]

Integrating Land within the Governmental Vision

Governance around land takes place in the shadow of international goals and aspirations that are centered on a neoliberal model of economic and sustainable development. The Botswana Land Policy (BLP), approved by the

National Assembly in 2015, was formulated in the context of a broader vision for the country's development as outlined in Botswana's *Vision 2016*.[18] The BLP was also formulated as a response to changing conditions in a global arena that have presented Botswana with "challenges from global economic competitiveness, need for economic diversification, rural urban migration, food security, poverty eradication, environmental sustainability and the need for shelter" (Botswana 2015, p. 1, para. 3). In meeting these challenges, Botswana recognizes "most importantly," the need "to create a balance between the competing land use need for social, economic, and political harmony" (ibid.). Thus the government acknowledges the need to address economic concerns within the context of a broader remit that incorporates human development discourse. It also recognizes that access to land may be compromised by factors such as "market forces, gender, [and] poverty" (p. 9, para. 50). The overall policy goal to improve "land administration and management, both from a system, environment and economic perspective" (p. 9, para. 51) is based on an overall set of objectives that are very much in line with the UN's SDGs. These include protecting and promoting the land rights "of all landholders," along with encouraging citizens to retain their land rights, and ensuring that all eligible citizens "have the opportunity to access and use the land." The 2015 Botswana Land Policy also includes promoting "equity in access to land and natural resources" and "compatible and best use of land, and other land resources." To this end, it advocates establishing "an up-to-date, efficient and accessible land information centre," and improving the land management system "on customary, state land, and freehold land to make it predictable, transparent, reliable, consistent, and timeous."[19]

Internal Governance: Tensions, Contradictions, and Fragmentation

The external face of government in Botswana in these processes is overall unified and coherent. It is backed by officials whose image is one of a caring, dedicated, and motivated workforce who have the recipients of their services at the forefront of their mission. This caring image is captured on the Government of Botswana's website, which opens with the following statement: "Welcome to the Government of Botswana, Adding Value to My Life, *Tokafatso ya botshelo jwa me.*"

The rhetoric of aspiration, however, falls short of reality. While the World Bank's *Botswana Poverty Assessment* (2015, p. 16, paras. 6–8) reports that "there has been a decrease in poverty," it is nonetheless "still high." The unemployment rate continues to remain at around 20 percent (Bank of Botswana 2015, p. 98, para. 3.7), and the bank is of the view that "poverty and inequality remain widespread at levels unacceptable for a country in Botswana's position" (p. 87, para. 1.3). Zelda Okatch (2015, 1) notes that Botswana's unemployment rates at 18 percent in 2012 were higher than those for other middle-income countries for which the average was 6 percent in the same period. Indeed, it has been said that "a scratch beneath the surface will reveal . . . corruption and poverty in the midst of plenty" (Mogalakwe and Nyamnjoh 2017, 2). M. S. Ulriksen (2017, 6) observes that Botswana's "economic miracle" status "has not translated into the reduction of poverty and social equality for her citizens." She attributes this failure to "the political economy of national resource wealth, with social transfers introduced only reluctantly, in a top-down manner and only to ensure loyal support of the mainly rural poor" (ibid.).

What accounts for these two different depictions of Botswana as being, on the one hand, a prosperous land of plenty and, on the other, a land of poverty and social inequality? In part, the answer is the way in which calculations about status on the world stage are carried out. The image of Botswana as one of the highest-ranking countries in terms of development worldwide, as well as in sub-Saharan Africa, comes about through an indexed model of development based on comparative figures in relation to per capita distribution of GDP among states across the globe. This model creates a misleading impression because the income calculated on a per capita basis is derived from taking the total numerical value of the GDP and dividing it by the total number of people in the population to provide an average figure. However, many in the population may, in reality, have a far greater or far smaller income than the one represented by the average figure. A more complex image emerges when these average figures become disaggregated, one that is more fragmented and contradictory, and that can be grasped in part through messages presented by public media which juxtapose headlines such as "Land to Be Reserved for Investors,"[20] promoting a prosperous vision of the country, with headlines such as "Scramble for Land Hits Marapong"[21] and "Ngwato Land Board to Evict 102 Squatters,"[22] exposing a more problematic relationship to land.

Governmental Regulation of Land: Reality on the Ground

This more contradictory and internally differentiated image of Botswana is also evident in the current administration of land that is shared between different institutional bodies operating under different regulatory frameworks, each with its own remit and interests.[23] These bodies form part of the state, but they are not just theoretical constructs, for they are brought to life through the people who give effect to them. Officials' perceptions play a critical role in directing the way in which these institutions work, and their actions have an impact on the public's experiences of access to and control over land, particularly in relation to allocation, transfer, or change of use.

Within the Ministry of Lands and Housing (MLH), there are eight departments covering state and tribal land. The classification of land into tribal or state land gives rise to different statutory regimes of regulation. Tribal land dealing with customary land tenure is dealt with under the Tribal Land Act (Cap. 32.02) that handed over the administration of that land to land boards. State land (which came into being in 1966, when land held by the Crown under colonial rule was converted into state land) is dealt with under the State Land Act (Cap. 32.01). It covers urban land, parks, and forest reserves and is administered by central government and local government councils.

The land boards and government councils apply different rules to the allocation of land under their jurisdiction. This dual system of management makes the administration of land a complex affair, especially where differing regulatory bodies intersect with one another. When dealing with tribal land, plots allocated by the land board are free (except commercial land under common law leases), although those with allocated plots on tribal land must service the land (install electricity, water, and sewage) themselves. With state land, however, applicants must purchase the land, even if the land is sold at a subsidized rate under government incentives such as the Self Help Housing Agency (SHHA), aimed at helping lower-income families. Those who have been allocated state land acquire land that is serviced, even if such servicing was somewhat minimal in the early years of the SHHA program.[24]

Given the demand for land, authorities also regularly seek to acquire it from citizens who are willing to release it on payment of compensation; however, compensation is payable at different rates. Under the Acquisition of Property Act (Cap. 32.10) that applies to state land, it is paid at a market

Figure 2.3. Crowds gathering outside Tlokweng Land Board to await legal decision in respect of 285 plots available for allocation in Tlokweng. *Photo courtesy of the Government of Botswana.*

rate, while tribal land, which is not subject to that Act, is paid at the lower rate of an agricultural valuation based on the way in which the land is acquired (in many cases at no cost as a first allocation) and the fact that it is not held in absolute ownership. This difference in rates has given rise to enormous dissatisfaction among citizens and has subsequently led the government to acknowledge the crisis this created in Mogoditshane and other peri-urban villages (Botswana 1992, 12) where "excessive intervention of market forces led to a collapse of tribal land administration."[25] (See fig. 2.3.)

Tribal Land, District Councils, and the Town and Country Planning Act (Cap. 32.09)

Having different regulatory systems for state and tribal land, and differentiating between tribal land that is held under a customary land certificate or under a common law lease, brings a number of institutions and departments from central and local government into contact with one another. For example, the lands officer for the Kweneng Land Board (KLB) in 2010 explained that if tribal land is located in a planning area, an application for land must go to the Physical Planning Department of the District Council. Because there are two planning areas in Kweneng District (the large villages of Mogoditshane and Molepolole), the land board must cooperate with the District Council and the District Commissioner when referring applications to the Council and receiving recommendations. Whether or not the land board is bound by these recommendations depends on the route that an application takes when it is referred to the District Council. If the application remains with the physical planners at the Council, the land board can reject their recommendations and reach its own decision. However, if the application is passed on by the Council to the Town and Country Planning Board, the land board has no discretion but must accept the recommendation because, as the lands officer for KLB observed in 2010, "it is done under the Town and Country Planning Acts." This process creates problems because the land board must wait for a decision to be reached by these bodies, which can take time given the other duties they perform. Not only does this situation create uncertainty about who has authority to make decisions over the applied-for land but it can also create dissatisfaction among clients who may find that the physical planners accept the application only to have it rejected by the land board.

Even when things run smoothly, the process still takes time. It can take a month for the physical planners to assess an application. After that, it can take another month if the application is referred back to the land board because the board only meets once a month. The entire process can easily take up to a year to complete.

Change of Use on Tribal Land: Engaging with Other Institutions

Another process in which the land board engages with other institutions is in regard to applications for a change of land use. For example, in cases where an applicant wants to change their use from a plowing field to one with poultry, piggeries, or horticulture, the applicant must have a letter of support from the Ministry of Agriculture in order to make sure the land is suitable for the proposed change of use. Once again, the lands officer observed, "This takes a long time," especially when the applicant wishes to pursue an agricultural project, in which case the land board needs a management plan in addition to the letter from the ministry.

Contradictory Policies at Odds with One Another

To complicate matters, contradictory policies that come into play when dealing with tribal land cause additional difficulty. Land boards, which are autonomous institutions, have the right to determine which policies they will apply in allocating land in their district. Such policies may conflict with those of other institutions or ministries that have different expectations for and perspectives around land use. For example, in order to absorb the pressure created by the demand for land and to provide for equitable distribution to all citizens, KLB has a policy of not allocating more than ten hectares of land for agricultural purposes. This policy is at odds with organizations such as the Ministry of Agriculture or the Citizen Entrepreneurial Development Agency (CEDA), which require much larger allocations of land before they approve change-of-use plans or provide financial assistance for what they perceive to be the requirements for sustainable development.

In another case, the main land board rejected an applicant's request for thirty hectares for small-stock farming, even though CEDA required this number of hectares for funding, and he had a letter from the Department of Veterinary Services supporting his application. The Chair explained in an interview in 2010 that, despite the reasons put forward by the applicant, "We have policies and we don't want to raise people's hopes. We have to evaluate the reasons you present." When weighing these against their considerations of public policy in making land available for all, the latter won out and they rejected his application. The applicants in cases such as this one become dissatisfied with the process because they feel caught between a set of contradictory policies that impact negatively on their ability to access and develop land.

Toward a National Land Policy: Diverging Perspectives

These perspectives highlight the competing views that come into play when considering how best to manage land for the benefit of all.[26] As Lekula (formerly Deputy Permanent Secretary overseeing land boards and the Department of Lands) observed in 2012, the problem is how to deal with the fact that "Batswana feel entitled to a piece of land wherever they go." Such an attitude derives from long-standing traditions where families and households could rely on the more sustainable approach of allocation of a residential plot and land for agriculture, as well as access to free grazing under customary law. Land boards have to manage these expectations stemming from people's perceptions of their cultural heritage. According to Mana-toka (Deputy Permanent Secretary at the Ministry of Finance and Development Planning), who was interviewed in 2012 these expectations put pressure on land boards to "grab as much land as possible and allocate it" because of people "making noise." In his view, the problem is that, in making such allocations, "they have not looked at whether land is best suited to the purpose [for which it has been allocated]." From his perspective, while "Batswana still believe land should be allocated to as many people as possible," this policy is not sound because the land needs to be managed in such a way that "developments have value that will generate tax and employment for citizens."

In electing to maintain the current land-tenure systems that currently exist, the government has made a conscious decision to develop policy and legal regulation around existing institutions and regimes. A key element in this approach is how to manage land in an economically productive way that fits with the prosperous country's *Vision 2016*, while at the same time providing sufficient land for the protection and security of the country's poor and marginalized citizens. One approach adopted by the government in the Draft Botswana Land Policy (DBLP 2011) was to restrict allocations on tribal land to a maximum of two free residential plots, one of them at the applicant's home village and another elsewhere in Botswana. This policy has since been restricted to one plot under the BLP (2015, p. 11, para. 58[i]). However, in keeping with a neoliberal market philosophy, the government also proposed "that there should be no restrictions where parties are prepared to pay for tribal land that has already been allocated to be transferred to them" (DBLP 2011, p. 8, para. 2.1.2), and this philosophy, adopted in all the draft policies, has been enshrined in the BLP (2015, p. 12, para. 58[iv]), which provides for allowing additional plots to be acquired "through the private market, inheritance, or other legitimate channels recognized in law and policy."

While many officials agree with this approach to land management, others do not. One highly placed official, who had formerly worked at the MLH, who was interviewed in 2012, was critical of the 2011 DBLP stating that it was a "great disappointment" and that it represented doing "too little too late." In her view, only one residential plot should be allocated for free (rather than the two provided for in the policy at that time) because otherwise "the economically mobile will disadvantage those whose world is in a particular locality." In her opinion, the policy at the time she was interviewed "was not equitable because those with economic resources will benefit at the expense of those who do not." Although the policy was subsequently changed to only provide for one plot, this official's views signal a different approach to land-tenure reform that may be aligned with a more redistributive approach to land. This approach is associated with agrarian reform that requires "a more rigorous analysis of the social relations of land use, poverty and social inequality in interaction with the uneven processes of 'neo-liberal agrarian restructuring'" (Peters 2014, 170). It is one that would take account of the interconnection of rural social relations with the development of capitalism in national and global spheres (Akram-Lodhi and Kay 2010). It has been argued that while the BDP (2015) "stresses that equity and social justice are key to land management," nonetheless, "it contradicts itself on this" and should be taken "back to the National Assembly for revisions and amendment" (Isaacs and Manatsha 2016, 393).

Problems of Coordination and Control: Provision of Services

Despite Botswana's unified vision around cooperation, on the ground the view is not so seamless. In an interview with the Director of Housing at the MLH in 2010, a major problem was identified in terms of coordination and control and the provision of services for land. She commented that coordination was "disjointed" because, when it came to land and housing provisions, "the Ministry of Local Government would allocate plots in rural areas but Water and Transport were not part of this project and would not provide services. Wildlife and Tourism would be responsible for sewerage and they were not part of the project either." This lack of coordination has also had an adverse impact on the Poverty Alleviation and Housing Program that the Department of Housing runs. This problem is due, in her opinion, to the fact that "those participating in the programme belong to different ministries and this produces administrative and management tensions because you have functions that are the responsibility of central government that have to be replicated at a local government level that involve some overlap. There is a question about where the professionals should report. Town Planning is a national concern; then we have Town Councils and District Councils [involved in the programme]; and then there are the land boards." Moreover, difficulties arise because "it is the responsibility of housing officers at the district level to implement the project on a daily basis. They have to report back to us [the Department of Housing], but in terms of accountability they are under the auspices of the Ministry of Local Government." Attempts are being made to overcome these problems, with the government looking into streamlining the overlap of functions between ministries. How water was treated provides an example: "In the past, council water units were taken up by the Water Utilities in the town, while in the major villages this was the responsibility of the Department of Water Affairs, while District Councils had the responsibility of providing water to other settlements that were not classified as major villages."

Now the government looks to the functions that water performs so that "with regard to sources of water supply, such as dams, these fall under the jurisdiction of Water Affairs, while the provision of drinking water falls under the Water Utilities." The purpose of this focus on function "is to create a situation where we know who is directly responsible for the various functions." This reorganization will be done through a cabinet directive, but it will face "a mammoth task," as it will have to decide "who is better placed to do what."[27] What is clear is that an ongoing and continuous process of restructuring is constantly in the making. For example, land boards, which are currently under the MLH, were previously under the Ministry of Local Government and Lands and formerly allied with District Councils. According to the Chair of KLB, in 2010 this arrangement was changed because "it didn't work because of the amount of work that was involved." As a result, a wise decision was taken in his view "to make land boards operate as an independent institution." More changes are in the pipeline as the BLP (2015) envisages a restructuring of land administration that will involve "Land Authorities established at a local level to be responsible for all land tenure systems" (p. 28, para. 87[1]). What this restructuring will entail and how it will affect land boards remains to be seen.

Reviewing Global and Local Relations through the Eyes of the State and Its Officials

Botswana presents itself as a unified and prosperous nation not only to its citizens but also to the rest of the world. It does so by aligning itself with international agendas related to human rights, sustainable development goals, and land reform, and by engaging with institutions and agencies. As such, even though its national government was originally designed according to a Westphalian model, its role can no longer be addressed within this notion of a state. Indeed, as Cottrell and Trubek (2012, 374) observe, the idea of sovereignty today is much less about "territorial integrity" and more "about being recognized as a legitimate participant in the international system." The latter is clearly what the state of Botswana aspires to in its desire to be a global player and competitor in a market-driven world. Viewed from this perspective, the state can no longer lay claim to being the central, definitive standpoint from which to view and analyze its internal relationships. Another model of governance is at work, one that highlights how power in Botswana operates. This model includes global aspirations and values that can be seen to inform the local agenda; that is, state institutions have their own particular interests that may be viewed as having a local character when compared with other institutions operating within a national framework. In these processes, what becomes visible is the array of structures that the state uses in its attempts to control territory, land, and people. This outlook reveals how notions of state sovereignty become reconceived "as an effect of practices associated with law and other forms of regulation that construct relations between the state, its population and the market" beyond and within its borders (Aihwa Ong in Perry and Mauer 2003, xiv). It is one that embraces differing jurisdictions, where the remit of central, district, and local institutions often gives rise to differing priorities with regard to long- and short-term strategies for land management that may, in turn, lead to problems of coordination and control. What emerges from studying these institutions on the ground is that, far from representing a coherent and unified approach, the administration of land on a day-to-day basis is a messy business.

Notes

1. Bakwena were among one of the eight groups that were recognized.
2. These included 46 semistructured interviews conducted by myself alone or with Phidelia Dintwe between May 1 and July 31, 2010 (32) and June 15 and August 2, 2012 (14). These interviews took place at the ministries or institutions where personnel were working. They include the following: *Ministry of Lands and Housing* (30) Minister, Deputy Permanent Secretary (2010, 2012), Acting Deputy Director, legal adviser; principal officer, two officers, researcher at Land Board Services; two lands officers, administrative secretary at Department of Lands; Director (2010, 2012), Deputy Director (2010, 2012), administrative secretary at Department of Housing; Director (2010, 2012) and Acting Deputy Director (2010, 2012), administrative secretary, two technical officers (2012) at Department of Surveys and Mapping; Deputy Director and two officials at Department of Town and Regional Planning; Acting Registrar, Registrar (2012) at Deeds Registry; officer Department of Corporate Services (2012); *Ministry of Labour and Home Affairs* (8) Deputy Permanent Secretary (2010,

2012), Director (2010, 2012) and Deputy Director (2010, 2012), two researchers at Department of Women's Affairs; *Ministry of Local Government* (2) Director (2012), Deputy Director at Department of Social Services; *Ministry of Finance and Development Planning* (3) Deputy Permanent Secretary (2012), legal adviser, administrative officer; *Office of the President* (3) Deputy Permanent Secretary, one legal adviser, one officer on Poverty Eradication Programme.

    3. African Development Bank 2009.

    4. SADAC has sixteen member states including Botswana, South Africa, Malawi, Namibia, and others.

    5. These are the Department of Lands, Department of Housing, Department of Surveys and Mapping, Department of Land Board Services, Department of Town and Regional Planning, Department of Technical Services, Deeds Registry, and Department of Corporate Services.

    6. These include the Ministry of Agriculture; Ministry of Trade and Industry (incorporating what was formerly Commerce); Ministry of Environment, Wildlife and Tourism; Ministry of Minerals, Energy and Water; Ministry of Transport and Communications; and Ministry of Finance and Development Planning.

    7. Under the Botswana National Settlement Policy of 1998 (Government Paper No. 2) drawn up by the Department of Town and Regional Planning, which provides guidelines for developing infrastructure and links between settlements, and the National Policy on Housing of 2000 (Government Paper No. 2) regarding the problem of shelter and accommodation (especially in urban areas), promoting partnerships with other stakeholders, including the private sector.

    8. Botswana sought to enhance agricultural production and preservation under a National Policy on Agricultural Development (Botswana 1991) that favored those with commercial interests in cattle; through National Master Plan for Arable Agricultural and Dairy Development (Botswana 2002b) that attempted to address the pressure of human settlements by preserving scarce agricultural land to improve food security at household and national levels; and through a Revised National Plan for Rural Development, promoted by the Ministry of Finance and Development Planning (Government Paper No. 3 of 2002) that sought to provide enhanced opportunities for income generation and economic activities.

    9. Botswana's effort to conserve land and the environment is reflected in a National Conservation Strategy (Botswana 1990), put forward by the Department of Town and Regional Planning. The sustainable management of natural resources is now under the portfolio of the Ministry of Environment, Wildlife and Tourism that produced a Community-Based Natural Resources Management Policy in 2007.

    10. Most of these data were collected between 2012 and 2014, and the ministries are the ones that were in existence at that time. Thus the Ministry of Lands and Housing was in operation at that time and was only restructured into the Ministry of Land Management, Water, and Sanitation in September 2016. Other changes include forming a new ministry, the Ministry of Infrastructure and Housing.

    11. Ministry website last accessed July 8, 2012; dead link.

    12. Ministry website last accessed July 10, 2012; dead link.

    13. Government of Botswana website, accessed June 12, 2014, www.gov.bw.

    14. Ministry website last accessed July 12, 2012; dead link. This ministry has now become the Ministry of Investment, Trade and Industry.

15. Ministry website last accessed July 13, 2012; dead link. This ministry has now been restructured into the Ministry of Environment, Natural Resources, Conservation and Tourism.

16. Ministry website last accessed July 17, 2012; dead link.

17. Ministry website last accessed July 20, 2012; dead link.

18. Several drafts of this policy have been produced, in 2011, 2012, 2013, and 2014. Where these are referred to in the text they are designated DBLP 2011 etc.

19. Botswana (2015, p. 9, para. 51([i, ii, iv, v, vi, vii]).

20. See MmegiOnline, accessed January 27, 2017, www.mmegi.bw/index.php?sid=1&aid=1578&dir=2013/March/Wednesday6.

21. See MmegiOnline, accessed January 27, 2017, www.mmegi.bw/index.php?aid=50503&dir=2015/april/14.

22. See MmegiOnline, accessed January 27, 2017, www.mmegi.bw/index.php?sid=1&aid=8168dir=2012/August/Monday17.

23. Most of the data for this section were compiled between 2010 and 2012.

24. The Botswana Land Policy 2015 proposes that all land (regardless of its classification) should now be serviced before allocation (p. 24, para. 79) and that where this involves residential customary land grants these will then be allocated under subsidized cost recovery (p. 26, para. 82[iii]).

25. Under clause 32 of the Tribal Land Bill 2017 where land is acquired by the state, compensation will now be assessed on "the market value of the property at the date of service of the notice to vacate the land."

26. Most of the data derived from government officials' perspectives was collected in 2012.

27. The importance of not focusing on land in isolation but contextualizing it in relation to other aspects, such as water and sanitation, had been highlighted by Hellum and others in their book *Water Is Life* (2015). The recent reorganization of the MLH into the Ministry of Land Management, Water and Sanitation in 2016 appears to have endorsed this view.

3

INSTITUTIONAL FRAMEWORKS AND GOVERNANCE

Kweneng Land Board and the Administration of Land

THE KWENENG LAND BOARD (KLB) (SEE FIG. 3.1) demonstrates the open-ended business of intersecting domains that are configured from international and local sets of interests and values. As an institution, KLB is situated within a complex set of relations with central government ministries, as well as with departments within the central Ministry of Lands and Housing in which it is located. As with other central and district regulatory bodies, it adheres to a government template in terms of following a mandate, vision, and values that are in keeping with those of other ministries and departments. Its mandate is to "allocate and manage land in a fair, equitable and transparent manner for the benefit of Botswana."[1] Its vision is to uphold "excellence in land management," and its values include "integrity, accountability, transparency, *botho*,[2] excellence, and teamwork."[3] These are in keeping with the earlier UN Millennium Development Goals (now Sustainable Development Goals) and with Botswana's National Policy contained in its *Vision 2016* (Botswana 1997). Consequently, KLB's vision embodies global values and targets that form part of national policy agendas, which must be played out in a more local context with all the specificities entailed. The local level involves engagement with an intangible cultural heritage, as well as with a grounded territorial jurisdiction.

As a result, what emerges is a more diffuse approach to land administration framed in terms of incremental changes to existing structures and institutions, rather than a more radical restructuring as some African

Figure 3.1. Kweneng Land Board, Molepolole. *Photo courtesy of E. Wilmsen.*

states have done when formulating their policies on land.[4] Thus successive internal reviews of land tenure in Botswana have continued to follow a path-dependent approach to policy making.[5]

KLB's institutional status reflects this incremental approach to change that follows a linear trajectory in space and time. The land board has been configured to administer and allocate land that was previously vested in dikgosi. Indeed, KLB, like other land boards, derives its territorial jurisdiction from the colonial division of the Protectorate that was aligned with particular tribal authorities. In the case of KLB, its territorial jurisdiction encompasses the socio-political administrative domain of the Kwena polity discussed in chapter 1. As a result of Botswana's approach to change, KLB must meld past tradition and the implementation of present realities with the attainment of future goals that are aligned with broad global capitalist and sustainable visions of land tenure.

KLB has duties under the Tribal Land Act that involve the allocation and restriction of land, changes in use of land rights, transfers of land rights, and adjudication of land disputes and appeals. The influence of Western approaches to land have made these duties more widespread than those accredited to dikgosi in the past. As a result, KLB now allocates land for a whole range of purposes,[6] granting land rights under both customary and common law. Thus, KLB as a space of action embodies a constellation of differing configurations of interest that intersect and come up against one another.

At their introduction, land boards were intended to fulfill a number of functions aimed at improving customary land administration and ensuring that emerging economic opportunities are adequately catered for in Botswana's land management system. They were also aimed at creating capacity for handling the demanding and complex land-use issues emanating from new economic opportunities and meeting the need to democratize customary land administration (Botswana 2003a, 6). Since their inception, however, land boards have been constantly reconfigured, marking changes in their administrative structure that have had an impact on how they function. Their current institutional location is a complex one, for it involves both a recognition of their autonomy under Section 9 of the Tribal Land Act and at the same time their realignment within the purview of the Ministry of Lands and Housing and the Department of Land Board Services. What this means for KLB is that its autonomy, which allows it to sue and be sued as a corporate entity with autonomous decision-making powers, is tempered by constraints under which it can operate. In carrying out its duties, the realization of KLB's mandate and vision is shaped by the institutional structure that underpins its operations.

Governance and Governmentality in the Regulation of KLB

This institutional structure for KLB represents a model of governance that not only draws on the specificities of social and physical space in Botswana but also reflects elements that are replicated elsewhere in other regulatory models across the globe. This model is a result of "the dramatic expansion in the scope of government featuring an increase in the number and size of government calculation mechanisms" (Hunt and Wickham 1994, 76). Its development is often linked with notions of governmentality that is "about the growth of modern government and modern bureaucracies" (76). Thus while the institutional framework within which KLB operates represents a model of governance that draws on the specificities of place and space in Botswana, it also has many elements in common with regulatory models in various other nations worldwide. These common elements give rise to a form of governance that "takes account of the diffusion of micro-powers and the aggregation of such power at the level of the state and other institutional levels" (56). Such a model has, according to Nikolas Rose and Peter Miller (1992, 177), shifted discourse about the role of the state in relation to government by "no longer . . . accounting for government in terms of 'the power of the state,' but of ascertaining how, and to what extent, the state is articulated into the activity of government. What relations are established between political and other authorities, what funds, forces, persons, knowledge or legitimacy are utilised: and by means of what devices and techniques are these different tactics made operable?" This model represents a broader formulation of governance, one that acknowledges "the dramatic expansion in the scope of government" (Hunt and Wickham 1994, 76). What this approach does is to highlight "an increasing variation in the functions of governing and the diversity of institutional levels and actors included." (Sand 2004, 45). It also undermines any approach to the study of government framed in terms of top-down policy making; this type of analysis takes account of "the creation and deployment of a whole range of technologies connecting multiple centres of power" (Morten 2013, 188). Such an analysis is clearly pertinent to an understanding of how land boards operate, as the following discussion of how power is spatialized within an institutional context will demonstrate. Land boards are located within an overarching framework of institutional relations where power is exercised in a number of different forms that display both horizontal and vertical dimensions.

Setup of KLB at Date of Research

At the date of my research, KLB was composed of the main land board together with seven subordinate land boards.[7] This research was mainly carried out from 2009 to 2010, and it drew on a number of methods and sources that included archival analysis, court and land board records of both cases and meetings, and participant observation and attendance at disputes. It also involved interviews with central and district government personnel and local people from Molepolole. The interviews formed a core element, one that enabled me to acquire a perspective that is absent from more conventional and normative analyses of the relationship between national and district regulatory bodies that center on the top-down workings of the system.

In contrast, my approach is one that highlights the complex intersections of power that shape the way in which KLB and those working within it operate.[8] The interviews highlight an important perspective on how the various actors engaged with the institution perceive their roles within it, providing a dynamic account of the workings of KLB and its processes of transformation over time. For this reason, I extensively quote KLB staff and personnel in order to forefront their voices and perceptions of how land is dealt with by their institution and the kind of problems that they encounter in performing their duties.

At the date of the research, the composition of the main land board allowed for twelve members although the board was operating under par with only nine members, four of whom were women. The same was true for Molepolole sub–land board, which formed part of my study. It was operating with eight instead of ten members, only two of whom were women. At this time, these members were appointed from a range of sources including the Ministries of Agriculture and Commerce and Industry, public election at the chief's kgotla,[9] along with members appointed by the MLH.

The institutional framework within which land boards operate is a bifurcated one: its functions are split between the administrative and human resources division that administers KLB and the land board members who make decisions about the allocation, transfer, and administration of land. The administrative division is headed by the Board Secretary and Deputy Board Secretary, who support land board members in carrying out their functions by setting up the agenda for land board meetings, providing secretarial services and recording of minutes, maintaining files relating to all correspondence and disputes, keeping accounts, organizing travel. They also carry out annual personal development plans for all employees, as well as signing off on an annual performance plan for the institution as a whole.

These administrative staff are direct employees of the MLH. They provide support services to the land board members who carry out the core business of the land board—making decisions over land within the board's jurisdiction. This division of labor, in terms of administration of the board and decision-making over land in Kweneng District, is one that reflects a spatialization of power derived from KLB's institutional structure.

The Spatialization of Authority and Power: KLB Internal Relations

The institutional structure of KLB that creates a spatialization of labor in terms of a division between the core business of the board on the one hand and administration on the other, has created tensions between the members of these two groups in the carrying out of their duties. These tensions revolve round questions of power and legitimacy and how they are apportioned between the two groups. When I first met the Chair of KLB at the Land Tribunal in Gaborone in September 2009, he and his members were very supportive of my research and welcomed me and my research assistant, Phidelia, to meetings of the board. However, when it came to looking at files and correspondence, land board members were not authorized to allow this examination, and I needed to get the approval of the Acting Board Secretary (which was duly forthcoming).[10] The division of authority and responsibilities, stretching across different domains, is perceived by land board members as impeding the efficient delivery of services to the public. In my interviews with them, they stressed a number of aspects, but my discussion will focus on two areas: (1) control/input into the agenda that controls the form meetings take, and (2) file management and access to accurate information, both of which involve decision-making power over the process of land administration. These are important because they have a direct effect on how the process of decision making is exercised. Through setting the agenda and providing data on applications and cases, administrative staff members shape the conditions within which decisions over land are reached.

While administrative staff members have no control over decisions reached at board meetings, they do have power over how the meetings are structured and what is on the agenda. By these means, they have a form of indirect control over the content and direction in which the meeting will proceed. Thus the administration exercises exclusive power over the agenda and the focus of the meetings, while land board members exercise power over decision making in relation to these proceedings.

For the Chair of KLB, this division of responsibilities creates problems because he and his members only see the agenda just before the meeting and have no input into what it contains. He observed that although the public views him as a person who is "omnipotent," "who has all the answers to their problems," and "someone who can get things done," they do not realize how little power he actually has. He commented on the fact that "there used to be a war between the board and the board secretaries here." This came about because "we would come to work knowing what we wanted to do, and the secretary would not work with us." The situation is exacerbated by the fact that it is the Board Secretary who carries out the annual personal development plan for all land board members and reports back to the MLH. This assignment of this supervisory responsibility places the Board Secretary in a powerful position with regard to the career prospects of board members, especially if they wish to be reappointed by the Ministry. The Chair of KLB noted that while things have greatly improved and a much better working relationship now exists with the new Board Secretary (in 2010), because of this Board Secretary's willingness to listen to the Chair and members, it is still the case that the board has no input into what features on the agenda, including hearings and disputes.

Land board members expressed their dissatisfaction with this position, observing that they think the system would be improved by holding a premeeting where they could bring administrative staff up to date on what they have done, including matters that have been settled. This premeeting would be an improvement because putting such matters on the agenda again and again takes up space and time. As a result, members are put under pressure because "we are handling cases from the backlog." This accumulation occurs because, as one of the female members of the board explained, "we are resolving cases that have a long history from 1992." This situation has been aggravated by the number of meetings that are scheduled. As one member observed, there are "only six meetings a year, yet there are so many applicants [who are not dealt with]." In these circumstances, he observed "at the end of the day, people just allocate themselves land [without going through the formal procedures]."[11]

The importance of setting the agenda was highlighted in an interview I had in 2010 with the representative of Grace Malope, who has been in a long-running dispute with KLB. In this process, Grace could not get a hearing from the board despite repeated attempts to do so between 2004 and 2009. When her representative discussed the matter with the Chair he was advised that the Chair could do nothing because he did not have the power to put the matter on the agenda. The Chair explained that once the case was put on the agenda the board could deal with the dispute and reach a decision. Having explained his dilemma, the Chair then advised Grace's representative to complain to the Office of the President. Grace's representative was then referred to the Permanent Secretary at the MLH who called in the Board Secretary and finally arranged for a meeting to be held.

This situation highlights the central importance of having a hearing before the land board because without it a dissatisfied member of the public cannot appeal to the Land Tribunal or to the High Court. The case must have been heard first by the land board, which must have reached a decision and recorded their decision and the reasons giving rise to it, before it can go any further in the appeals process.[12] Delays in scheduling cases before the land board have given rise to a situation where members of the public have had to wait many years for the redress of their land claims or disputes.

All land board members stressed that they "still have problems with data." One who has been serving on land boards since 1999 noted that "a lot of information did not appear in our data [files], and that creates a lot of disputes." It gives rise to double allocations by the land board "because existing data from past years is not captured in the system; so this still presents a challenge." In her view: "I don't think those who are preparing are giving themselves enough time to check that all the relevant information is given in terms of the agenda. So, as a result, you will find many issues are being deferred because there is no information available while the person is appearing before the board. This causes us concern because a case goes from one board to another, and this leads to a lengthening of meetings [because they have to extend the agenda to fit in extra hearings which leads to much longer sittings].[13]

Concern over this protracted process was reinforced by another female board member who commented that it takes them "much too long to deal with cases." She explained that this happens "if there is not much preparation for hearings by administrative staff and no sketch plans." Another member made similar complaints that "[we are] never given proper information about the matters we are dealing with and that leads to a delay in assisting people." This theme was stressed time and time again in interviews (and I observed this problem in practice), leading one board member to state that the major change that she would like to see would be "the land board being able to have all the information they need to enable them to do their work."

Administrative staff are well aware of these problems and attempts to rectify them are a work in progress. With regard to disputes, a new Adjudication Department was established in the land board at the beginning of 2010. It has been created to enable the administrative staff of the land board to focus directly on the backlog of cases and the preparing and handling of disputes. Related data and file management has been a constant problem recognized by all that not only affects the content of hard-copy files but also impacts on attempts to create a computerized database. As the land Board Secretary in 2010 acknowledged, "It is hard to access data, especially from earlier years, because it is scattered all over in land board files. . . . We used to keep information [on one individual] in different files." Thus "there were separate registers dealing with applications by the public in one, documents accompanying the applications in another, and yet another where all land certificates that were issued were held."

They have now altered the system to keep all the information on one individual in one file, and they have also newly "appointed records managers which we didn't have in the past." These system changes were accompanied by a structural change whereby personnel focus on a particular area of expertise, so that the land board is now divided into acting specialist units, such as the Records and Management Unit, the Recording Unit, and the Disputes Unit, along with the introduction of in-house legal counsel. Taken together, these changes represent a reformulation of the organization of space within which KLB operates that was brought about with the aim of providing a more timely and efficient service.

This reorganization may be contrasted with what happened before 2009, about which the Board Secretary observed, "We had administrative officers heading sub–land boards, and they were doing almost everything. . . . Now, a new structure has been introduced in 2009 that is an improvement on the old one because now people are focused. Now that people are appointed to work in a particular area, we can train these people in the skills they need. . . . In the past, when officers were doing everything we did not know what training to provide for an individual. We can now institute training to suit the need of a particular department." The Board Secretary hopes that, with the introduction of the Land Administration Procedures Capacity and Systems (LAPCAS), a computerized national system for land tenure, there will eventually be a National Register for Land that will produce "one centre where we can access all this information."[14] Once again, this change is aimed at promoting a more streamlined service that takes less time to deliver services because of the instantly accessible nature of the information.

As a result of this institutional framework, power to carry out functions within the land board is shared among the different organizational units with varying forms of expertise. This is done through horizontal processes of engagement that shape these units' capacity to regulate and administer land. As a result, the organizational framework of KLB and the way it operates reflects a broader dimension of governance and governmentality associated with the growth of modern bureaucracies discussed earlier. For power is not only at work in shaping relations between administrative staff and land board members but also at play in the division of labor that exists between such members.

Spatialization of Power between Main and Sub–Land Board Members

Internal divisions not only exist between administrative staff and land board members, they also exist between land board members themselves in terms of the powers and duties that are distributed between them. The allocation and division of labor between these boards and their decision-making powers creates tensions between members of the two boards. This discord is evident from the interviews that were conducted among members of both boards.

The tensions derive from the institutional framework within which sub–land board members operate. The framework delimits the scope of their duties and powers in regard to the allocation and transfer of land under customary land tenure. For while sub–land board members have the authority to carry out certain types of customary land grants, when it comes to common law leases they can only make recommendations, which the main land board may reject. Similarly, their authority is also limited in cases concerning the eviction of squatters or repossession of undeveloped land. They also lack authorization to distribute customary land grants for the purposes of grazing land, communal land, or industrial land. In addition, the main land board has power to hear appeals from the sub–land board in which they may set aside its decisions. This vertical dimension of power at work in the relationship between main and sub–land board members is inherent in the institutional allocation and division of labor with regard to their decision-making powers.

As one main board member observed, this vertical dimension leads to sub–land boards perceiving that "the main land board is not treating them well," giving rise to a sense of powerlessness and dissatisfaction. According to another, problems arise in the relationships, because the sub–land boards "don't look at the policies, they pass the buck to us and then, when we advise them to do *x*, they feel we are being tough with them but we are not being bossy, we are just asking them to do the spade work [to enable them to implement the policy properly]." Another commented that tensions arise when the main land board does not follow the recommendations of the sub–land board. He acknowledges that they may perceive the main board as undermining them, "but we are not intending to do that. In most cases we agree with their recommendations." However, this is not the view of some members of the sub–land board who complained that members of the main board "are always against us."

Part of the difficulty lies in the interpretation of Land Board policies. According to one member of the main board, the problem is that "often they seem not to be applying the policies." In a collective interview with sub–land board members, they observed that problems arise because the boards "are working in isolation." In their view, there is a need to improve communication between the two boards.

What emerges from these institutionally structured practices are the complex ways in which power is differentially configured within KLB, which is not simply hierarchical but also engages with the "horizontal and relational nature of contemporary processes that stream across space" in the constitution of KLB (Low and Lawrence-Zuniga 2003, 26). It is brought about through the interactions and regulatory mechanisms that are at work in the institutional configuration of KLB. Thus the challenges posed by the local and district administration of KLB are located within an institutional framework that reflects a broader and more global dimension structured around processes of governmentality and corporate governance present not only in Botswana but on a more global scale.

The most visible instance of this confluence is through a monitoring process that engages with transnational values, embodying access to justice, good governance, and accountability measured through indicators, targets, and audits. For these values not only form an essential element of the UN's Sustainable Development Goals but also form part of Botswana's Vision 2016 and National Land Policy.

KLB as a Corporate Entity: Indicators, Targets, and Audit Culture

Like all land boards, as an institution, KLB is a corporate entity.[15] As such, it has to provide annual accounts that are subject to audit and certification by the auditor general.[16] Looking at the balance sheet and accounts for the years ended March 31, 2004 and 2008,[17] it is clear that Kweneng Land Board is a substantial organization with considerable assets and liabilities[18] that have increased steadily over the years, although it still finds itself short of resources.

Corporate forms of governance are very much associated with audits, targets, and indicators that are "fundamental to modern forms of governmentality," and balance sheets and accounts provide classification and representation of the corporate enterprise through figures (Merry 2011, S83). Over time, these figures have become associated with KLB's endorsement of principles of fairness and transparency because the promotion of these principles—including accountability, along with associated notions of efficiency and service delivery—have become equated with the meeting of targets and performance indicators set out for land boards in their annual performance agreements, the terms of which are reached in discussion with the MLH. This kind of monitoring represents a type of governance that is based on statistics, a model of accountability that is often referred to as the "audit culture"[19] that is transnational in scope. It represents a results-based approach to management, centered on a set of techniques applied on an international scale to rank nation-states' progress in relation to one another. It is one that informs KLB's approach to land management and forms part of the process of applying and implementing an audit culture through the use of specific forms of knowledge production established in accordance with global standards.

The most obvious example of the audit culture is demonstrated by the World Bank and other international agencies' ratings and ranking of countries comparatively in terms of calculations of GDP, which is "one of the most widely used and accepted indicators" of national standing (Merry 2011, S83). Along with indicators evaluating the rule of law or human development index, these indicators are used as data to rank countries, especially in terms of GDP, as "developed or less developed" (Morten 2013, 10).

As Merry has argued "this growing reliance on indicators provides an example of the dissemination of the corporate form of thinking and governance into broader social spheres" (2011, S83). Thus corporate forms of governance become more widely applicable and mark a transfer of power from the state to organizations as evidenced by the audit explosion, "an idea which has become embodied in a wide range of programmes for accountability and control" (Power 1997, 7). As part of this process, indicators "are a technology of not only knowledge production but also about governance." They are used to manufacture "evidence-based policy" feeding into "results based management" (Merry 2011, S84).

These measurement techniques not only generate a form of expertise and knowledge production but also represent a form of governance "that employs policy arrangements that emerge outside the administrative system of a single nation-state (government) but which, nevertheless, have a comparative impact on a globally or regionally designed set of recipients" (Bernstorff 2004, 251). They engage with governmentality that reflects an approach suggesting "that power exists beyond the state and that the centres and levels of governmental power, like its techniques and objectives, are multiple and differentiated" (Morison 2003, 162–163).

As my study demonstrates, this results-based approach is not only applied on an international scale, to the ranking of states in relation to one another, but also applies to monitoring the performance of KLB.

What Does Monitoring Involve?

For KLB, monitoring involves the Chair and Board Secretary signing off on an agreement annually with the MLH. In the 2010 Annual Performance Agreement, this involved choosing "six to eight commitments [out of the] 21 Point Agenda priority areas" and listing "the output(s) and outcomes you will be responsible for delivering during the next twelve months in relation to these priority areas." In the annual agreement, KLB under the heading of Visionary Leadership, signed up to do the following:

- Optimize land use
- Improve timely delivery of land
- Improve customer relations
- Improve financial and asset management
- Improve project management and service delivery
- Improve information management and communication

Under the heading for internal processes and under Human Resources Management, KLB elected to

- Increase staff competency
- Enhance staff welfare and motivation

In addition, it also elected to increase Information Communication Technology capacity.

In performance of these targets the performance agreement involved setting deadlines, which entailed, for example, that disputes should be processed within a three-month period, along with any appeals. These kinds of targets feature, more generally, in relation to government services provided throughout Botswana, reflecting a temporal approach to the spaces they inhabit that is linear in form.

Probing Beneath the Surface: What Does Monitoring Signify?

All these targets and deadlines are aimed at improving service delivery to the clients of KLB, but what do they reveal about the product that is the outcome of these processes? Resolving disputes in a timely fashion, for example, is important but does not speak to the quality of the decisions that are reached. Although disputes may be heard within an allotted time period, this practice says nothing about the decision-making processes and value judgments that are applied. In other words, as Jerven Morten has observed, indicators and targets are used to create an impression of certainty and objectivity that creates "a dangerously misleading air of accuracy where the resulting numbers are used to make critical decisions that allocate resources" (2013, xi). Thus these mechanisms "create an aura of 'objective' truth" that, according to Merry, conceals "their political and theoretical origins and underlying theories of social change and activism" (2011, S84).

As Richard Rottenburg observes in an international and global context, "these models and technologies acquire an agency of their own precisely because they are disseminated and duplicated and in this process come to be endowed with an authority to define the best solution to a particular problem" (2009, xxvi–vii). Yet what they actually represent is "an assertion of power to produce knowledge and to define or shape the way the world is understood" (Davis et al. 2012, 8).

The world of certainty and the representations that give rise to it depends on the data that are incorporated into the systems that provide for its foundation. In the case of KLB, a computerized national land register may create greater certainty over defining the physical and spatial features of land, but it still leaves open the question as to whose claims to these territorial demarcations of land should be acknowledged and whose ignored or rejected, with all the consequences that ensue from such a decision. For the outcomes appear as forms of knowledge rather than as particular representations of a methodology and particular political decisions about what to measure and call it. In other words, "the political process of judging and evaluating is transformed into a technical issue of measurement and counting by the diligent work of experts" (Merry 2011, S86). This process is important for, as Rottenburg points out, "the daily struggle for access to and control over social development occurs through the creation of objective representations," and indicators represent "a consolidation of power in the hands of those with expert knowledge" (2009, xxv).

The complex considerations that underpin these representations are highlighted, for example, by the cases dealing with squatters that will be discussed in chapter 7. To be termed a *squatter* is to question the legitimacy of that person's relationship to the land s/he is occupying, making way for eviction and the land board's repossession of that land. Yet for some people, their designation as *squatters* is a contested issue because they claim the land they are occupying has been in their family for generations. Nonetheless, they face challenges from the land board's or state's designation of their occupation of land as illegal because of their families' failure to follow prescribed procedure for certification established by land boards, or because of the board's or the state's desire to acquire such land for development purposes. As one land board member explained, part of the problem with squatting is that "you find some people have been here so many years without regularizing the land [i.e., going through land board procedures]. Some have been staying there before land boards were established. They will resist relocation saying, "No, I was born here, why can't you establish a settlement here?" Then they are brought into conflict with the National Settlement Policy that requires a certain number of people [for a settlement to be established], and they fall below this number.

Governance as a Self-Reflexive Process: Aspirations and Change

What emerges from interviews with those working for KLB is the self-reflexive nature of the process evidenced by the degree to which land board members and administrative personnel engage in internal self-inspection and notions of accountability. Thus, the process of auditing, which forms part of the governance structure of KLB, can also be viewed as representing "an idealized normative projection of the hopes invested in the practice, a statement of potential rather than a description of actual operational capability" (Power 1997, 4).

The process is not simply a matter of technical expediency. In redesigning the process of government, auditing represents a practice that is not simply a question of meeting set targets but forms "a system of values and goals" that can lead to positive transformational change (Power 1997, 7). This system is one that "makes possible ways of redesigning the practice of government" that do not simply reflect "a choice between centralisation and decentralisation" but gets to grips with "regulating relationships in complex systems" (Power 1997, 11).

The self-reflexive process provides the transformative potential for creating "new forms of governance and power" that allow people to monitor their own behavior for themselves (Shore and Wright 2000, 57). This ability gives rise to a situation where governments can now simply check indicators of performance without carrying out substantive investigations. What emerges is "a transfer of regulatory terms from direct inspection of compliance to the indirect systems of self-checking" (Aalders 1993, 88). Consequently, a form of governance arises "that engages the person in governing himself or herself in terms of standards set by others" (Merry 2011, S90). Thus, the process can allow individuals to engage with aspirations for change and transformation that go beyond merely meeting set targets and the technical accomplishment of meeting their objectives. Engaging in the process can also enable those taking part to reassess forms of accountability and the practices that they adopt in order to achieve this goal.

This aspect of self-reflexivity and awareness is very important and is at work in KLB as evidenced from discussions involving board members and administrative staff outlined earlier. One board member recalled a former Board Secretary with praise, noting that "he made us plan" and that "he made us budget by objectives," which she perceived as contributing to an improved system of land administration. Another member recognized that while problems with filing might be attributed to the administration's failure to keep adequate records, land board members were also at fault "because most of us don't prepare for meeting prior to the client's attendance," and this lack of preparedness led them to place too much reliance on overworked technical officers to supply the details. Yet another talked about the importance of self-reflection. He observed "if people appraise themselves and give themselves a chance to read and understand [the TLA and its policies], they can improve [their service delivery]." This male board member, a surveyor, was never without his copy of the Tribal Land Act, which he regularly consulted at meetings, with the result that Phidelia and I nicknamed him "Mr. Tribal Land Act." From another perspective, a female board member observed in her interview: "The job is very challenging and I like challenges. I hate a job that is predictable. I went to work for Barclays [Bank]. In the accounting system you just work with figures and they are fixed. [In this job] you are opening your mind and you see life as it is. You see people dreaming and you start dreaming yourself. It urges you to do something."[20]

This reflective process was at work in learning about access to justice, which the Acting Board Secretary noted had promoted "real change [in land board procedures that] came about after the introduction of the Land Tribunal[21] who pointed out to land boards where they were going wrong. Before the Land Tribunal an applicant would apply, we would look at the sketch plan and if we decided we could not allocate we would just reject the application. The Land Tribunal made us aware of the principles of natural justice and said we must call the applicant to a hearing." Failure to do follow this procedure in the past has in her view "created a situation where those past decisions are still coming back to haunt us."

Regulatory Power: Soft Law and Legal Pluralism

All these dimensions of social relations and how they are constituted in relation to land not only draw on formal laws engaging with legal pluralism associated with customary and common law[22] but also embrace the normative power of regulatory decision making that forms part of a broader system of governance. This system of governance differs from the juristic or weak model of legal pluralism that was promoted by colonialism, whose approach not only embodied a Western or European notion of law but also provided a lesser degree of recognition to local systems of customary law. Instead, the governance of KLB represents a social unit that generates and maintains its own norms in interaction with a broad range of sources. It can be viewed as an example of Sally Falk Moore's *semiautonomous social field*, based on fieldwork carried out in the garment industry in the lower east side of New York City. Moore recognizes that a social field "can generate rules and customs and symbols internally, but that . . . is also vulnerable to rules and decisions and other forces emanating from the large world by which it is surrounded. The semiautonomous social field has rule-making capacities, and the means to induce or coerce compliance, but it is simultaneously set in a larger social matrix which can, and does, alter and invade it, sometimes at the invitation of persons inside it, sometimes at its own instance" (1973, 720). Thus what is at work in Botswana, as well as in settings elsewhere in the world, is a form of *soft law* (because its norms do not derive from formal legal sources associated with the state) that may be associated with a strong or social-scientific perspective on legal pluralism.[23] An example is provided by Markus Weilenmann's work on what he terms *project law* in the context of international development aid cooperation (2009a,

2009b). At an institutional level, he explores the law-making capacities of development projects and of international and national development agencies. Based on practical experience as an adviser to the German Agency for Technical Aid, he traces how project ideas are turned into feasible development plans through chains of translation that weave through executive policy-making agendas, international rules of negotiation, and finally to the practices of local partner organizations. What emerges is a view of legal pluralism that is not confined by territorial or geographic markers but rather is multidimensional in nature and derived from networks or webs of relations. It addresses a more nuanced understanding of how power is constituted and operates that will be explored in subsequent chapters.

Some Concluding Observations

What emerges from my study of KLB is the extent to which the context within which it operates represents a set of connective threads embodying international, national and local dimensions at work in the administration of land within its jurisdiction. In managing and negotiating these interests, KLB's maneuverability is constrained by the institutional structure within which it is located. This location is one that requires it to engage with central government ministries, as well as with departments within its own MLH. It is also one that features an internal set of divisions within the land board itself that derive from the division of labor within the institution that spatially constructs relations between administrative staff and land board members, as well as among land board members themselves. Thus, the way in which KLB is structured demarcates zones of authority and power apportioning responsibilities and duties among its personnel, according to the divisions to which they belong. In this context, power is deployed by administrative staff and land board members in different ways, yet in ways that make them interdependent in the handling of the overall process of land management. What is evident is the extent to which duties and responsibilities are apportioned among different organizational units through horizontal processes of engagement. At the same time, however, power also operates in the form of a vertical axis, with main land board members exercising control over recommendations and appeals from the sub–land board.

Such power derives from the institutional space that determines the division of labor and remit of authority that is accorded to main and sub–land board members. In this way, both horizontal and vertical dimensions of power are brought to bear in different ways, thus illustrating the complexities of the bureaucracy at work in KLB. Its institutional structure reflects the intricate interplay of both centralized and decentralized district authorities that reflect a more global dimension of governance and governmentality. This model is one that is found more generally in countries across the world, where the state withdraws from adopting a direct regulatory role within its jurisdiction, in a top-down hierarchical manner, in favor of a more transnational engagement with accountability and regulation.

I now leave the world of bureaucratic and executive regulation and policy making to explore access to and control of land through another lens. This lens centers on a more bottom-up perspective derived from individuals', households', and families' perceptions, practices, and experiences of the allocation, transfer, and administration of land in their daily lives.

Notes

1. KLB website, accessed on August 1, 2015, www.kwenenglandboard.gov.bw.
2. According to Vision 2016, *botho* refers to one of the tenets of African culture—the concept of a person who has a well-rounded character; who is well-mannered, courteous, and disciplined; and who realizes his or her full potential both as an individual and as a part of the community to which he or she belongs (Botswana 2009b, 5).
3. Ibid.
4. E.g., Zimbabwe and South Africa.
5. See Botswana (2002a, p. 2, para. 1.05).
6. These include residential, industrial, commercial, civic and community, arable fields, game ranches, commercial and arable farms, tourist camps and lodges, hunting and photographic concession areas (Botswana 2003a, 6).
7. KLB's subordinate land boards are Molepolole, Mogoditshane, Thamaga, Letlhlakeng, Lentsweletau, Lephepe, and Matokwe.
8. The KLB interviews that took place between May 8 and June 20, 2010 included eight main land board members and seven Molepolole sub–land board members along with eleven administrative personnel, including the Board Secretary, a Senior and an assistant adjudication officer, two lands officers, two Acting Deputy Board Secretaries, two principal technical officers and one land surveyor.
9. The chief's kgotla forms part of Tribal Administration but is also at the apex of the Kwena sociopolitical administrative structure, formally referred to as Tribal Administration.
10. I am enormously grateful to all the members, staff, and personnel of KLB who so generously allowed me to observe their daily activities and gave up their time to explain their activities and to be interviewed from 2009 to 2010.
11. The problems that these informal allocations give rise to are highlighted in chapters 6 and 7.

12. The problems this process causes are highlighted in chapter 6 dealing with the Land Tribunal.

13. My own experience attests to this problem as I have been at hearings that started at 8:30 a.m. that were still going when I left at 6 p.m. at night and were scheduled to go on until 9 p.m.

14. While a centralized database aims to resolve many of the problems that the land board faces, for example, with regard to double allocation, it does still leave the question of how decisions will be made about who qualifies for inclusion on the register and who is excluded. Thus further questions are raised about the legitimacy and authority of the decision-making process in terms of which rules and norms will prevail over claims to land as exemplified by the adjudication of disputes discussed in chapters 6 and 7.

15. Section 9(1) of the TLA.

16. Under Regulation 32(2) of the TLA.

17. Accounts for other years were not readily available from government databases.

18. For example, in 2004, KLB had an income of BWP 1,760,867 with investments of BWP 7,027,297.26 (Botswana 2007b, 2). The pula (P) is the basic monetary unit of Botswana, and the currency abbreviation is BWP.

19. See Power (1997) and Strathern (2000).

20. This board member revealed that she had been motivated to join KLB for the following reason: "I wanted to know why people coming after me [in my application for land] were being allocated while I was not so I wanted to know about the system." She applied for land in 2004 and had only just been allocated land in 2010.

21. The Land Tribunal was established under Section 40 of the TLA in 1995 and officially commenced operation in 1997.

22. Customary and common law are discussed in chapters 1 and 2 and exemplified by the formulation of the text of Customary Law No. 51 of the Application and Ascertainment Act, passed in 1969.

23. For discussion and debates over the meaning and scope of legal pluralism, see J. Griffiths (1986), Merry (1988), and A. Griffiths (2002, 2013).

PART II

THE BOTTOM-UP IMPACT OF LAND ON DIVERGING FAMILY LIFEWORLDS AND GENDER RELATIONS

4

FAMILIES, NETWORKS, AND STATUS

Grounded Perspectives on Access to and Control over Land

THE FOCUS IN CHAPTERS 4 AND 5 SHIFTS from the state's many institutions and regulatory mechanisms for dealing with land to one based on individuals', households', and families' relationships with land. This approach provides a more micro form of analysis that operates on a different scale from that of the national and district forums and their administration of land discussed in previous chapters.

Within this framework, I highlight the links that land creates between persons and space that are both territorially and socially grounded. The two families who feature in my discussion are descendants of two brothers, Makokwe and Radipati. They not only live within the jurisdiction of the Kweneng Land Board (KLB) but are also genealogically linked over a number of generations to the Kwena polity and the place where they live. Their relationships with land share a space that is not only a physical place but connects with a more intangible universe that embodies social relationships. Thus these families can be said to form part of local space in terms of community based on territorial and genealogical relations. Yet, at the same time, tracing their life histories over generations reveals that their life courses are shaped by wider processes beyond their boundaries that have had and continue to have an impact on their daily lives. These processes reflect ways in which forms of global governance, dealing with land at differing historical moments, filter through and are experienced by families and households in Molepolole. Local and global spaces become intertwined, but they do so in ways that have different consequences for the life trajectories of these families and households compared, for example, with state or district institutions. These differences are not just a result of individuals' varying capabilities but are the product of their historically constructed lifeworlds that have been wrought over time, creating differentially configured social relations among the current generation.

What is crucial to the account of these life histories are the factors that contribute to differential life trajectories that become visible through an in-depth, ethnographic study of people's lives. This provides for a more nuanced analysis of family relationships that goes beyond general, abstract classifications that so often appear in international agencies' agendas for empowering the poor, where policies in relation to women and children are presented as if they were an undifferentiated and homogenous group. The value in adopting an ethnographic approach is that it involves a thorough investigation of the factors that come together in the construction of such persons and how they have an impact on the extent to which these persons can gain access to and control over land. Thus, it provides for a more comprehensive understanding of the way in which these persons are positioned with regard to land and the strategies that they may, or may not, be able to pursue in respect of it.

In engaging with these families' life histories, global and local spaces become interwoven in ways that create structures of social inequity. What emerges are the uneven ways in which distribution of resources, such as land, are apportioned. These are not simply produced through local conditions but are also caused in part by wider processes of political, economic, and social disbursement. This has implications for the ways in which upward mobility may become open to some individuals and families while constraining others in ways that perpetuate social stratification and inequality. The concrete effects of these processes do not derive from random chance but come from particular and specific conditions that may challenge more general and abstract propositions on which prescriptions about land and its development are established.

The data on which these particular life histories are based form part of a larger ethnographic study[1] that builds on Isaac Schapera's field notes centered on Mosotho kgotla from 1937, which he generously gave me. My oral accounts collected from 1980 to 2010 extended these histories for two generations into the nineteenth century, so that the total research now covers five generations, documenting continuities and differences across a landscape of precolonial, colonial, and postcolonial dimensions. Key features of these life histories will be highlighted to illustrate how their differing life trajectories took shape.[2]

Diverging Lives: Life Trajectories of Makokwe's and Radipati's Families

Makokwe and Radipati were brothers who shared a father, Koosimile, but had different mothers because their father was a polygamist. The brothers were the founding members of Mosotho kgotla, part of the chief's ward, Kgosing, established in 1937 when Bakwena moved from Ntsweng to establish their polity in Molepolole. What emerges from these life histories are the differing resource bases on which each family's livelihood are founded that have had an impact on their relationship with land. Makokwe's descendants had access to a resource base revolving around subsistence agriculture, raising livestock, and migrant labor of an unskilled nature on an intermittent or contract basis. These characteristics, shared by many other families in Botswana, associate them with what Jack Parson (1981) termed the *peasantariat*. The members of this kin group are increasingly distanced from elite cattle owners and higher income wage earners (Botswana 1985, 8), and the activities in which they engage have links to those associated with precolonial and colonial settlement patterns discussed in chapter 2.

In contrast, Radipati's descendants have focused on attaining education and the acquisition of skilled and secure employment, which among the earlier generation was predominantly government based but has now branched out to include commercial and corporate activities. This approach has set them apart from other families and placed them among those whom David M. Cooper (1982) has referred to as the *salariat*. The salariat represents a growing middle class—an urban elite in Botswana that no longer engages in subsistence agriculture or insecure migrant labor. Their lives reflect a different form of temporality from that of the Makokwe family, being more closely instantiated within powerful institutions forming part of a nexus for national and urban development.

Makokwe Family Group

Ramojaki (age seventy-three in 2010)[3] is the youngest son of Makokwe and has been living in Lekgwapheng ward in Molepolole for many years. He is the only one of six brothers who is still alive. Ramojaki moved with four of his brothers from Mosotho kgotla to Lekgwapheng, where their relatives provided them land because of lack of space in Mosotho kgotla. This family land has since come under the administration of KLB, and the family now hold the land under customary land certificates that have been transferred from one generation to another. When interviewed in 2010, Ramojaki was attempting to earn a living as a subsistence farmer, having spent most of his adult life working in South African mines before returning to work as a borehole mechanic for the district council in Molepolole before his retirement. His protracted employment at the mines (thirty-three years) was common to many of his generation, including his brothers.[4] Work at the mines was already taking place during Britain's colonial overrule (1885–1966) when Botswana was known as the British Bechuanaland Protectorate. During this period, the Resident Commissioner introduced taxes that forced many men to seek employment beyond the Protectorate's borders, principally at the mines in South Africa. Dependence on European imports, ecological constraints (vulnerability to drought and diseases, especially those decimating cattle such as rinderpest, an infectious viral disease), and the need to meet obligations in cash newly imposed by colonial administrators contributed to the escalation in migration that set the context in which Kweneng, like many other southern African regions, acquired the status of a labor reserve.

Ordinary people's lives became entangled with regional and international patterns of consumption and labor relations that created a dependence on a cash economy (Schapera 1947; Kerven 1982). These patterns of consumption set the context in which social relations, regulated through kinship and mafisa,[5] played out within the broader context of political and economic change. Although Batswana embraced colonial overrule and new labor relations; the country nonetheless continued to favor powerful elites, such as dikgosi, who were able to manipulate this situation to their advantage (Ramsay 1991).[6]

Caught up like many in his generation in migrant labor, Ramojaki remitted money home to pay taxes, provide support for his family, and pay for substitute labor required for subsistence agricultural activities on which families left behind depended for their existence. Under these conditions, when Ramojaki's and his brothers' sons were old enough they went to the mines and their fathers retired home to work at the land and at the cattlepost. This pattern reflects a lifestyle based on fluctuations in income and instability deriving from temporary contract labor linked with diminishing returns from subsistence agriculture and small-scale livestock production.

In 2010, Ramojaki lamented the position he found himself in, observing that sickness had deprived him of "a good lifestyle."[7] In addition to his reduced ability to engage in subsistence activities, he bemoaned the fact that "only two children and grandchildren are keen to take care of livestock." This marks a departure from precolonial and colonial times when families worked cooperatively across households, pooling their labor. When Sechele I (c. 1833–1892) transformed the Kwena into a regional power and made land a central feature of a settlement pattern based on agro-pastoral activities (requiring families to move between the village, the land, and the cattlepost), the need for labor and access to resources beyond those of individual families led to a situation where Kwena society was bound together in a system of mutual, if somewhat unequal, series of exchange relationships (Griffiths 1988). Current practices may be attributed in part to changes in these labor patterns within familial and household networks. In the 1930s, the Makokwe family were linked into cooperative networks that extended across several households and contributed to the livelihoods of individuals and family members through the pooling of resources among and between generations. These networks evolved to include staggering contracts at the South African mines in order to acquire money to invest in livestock and seeds for subsistence agriculture.

In recent years, however, given the lack of access to the South African mines and the fact that other options for maintaining livelihoods have come into being, these cooperative ties and dependencies have diminished. The widow of Ntlogelang, one of Makokwe's sons, observed in 2010 that her grandchildren "are not keen to work jointly like their parents used to do" and that "they are only interested in taking care of their immediate families." Her experiences are reinforced by Ramojaki's sister-in-law who explained that "Nkadikang [her deceased husband] and his brothers used to help each other plough their fields using their livestock." This shared practice no longer takes place, partly because of the "advent of modern technology." When "the brothers resorted to the use of tractors . . . they stopped helping each other." According to Nkadikang's son, Ranko (age fifty-two), now "everyone fends for his [own] family." Although the extended family still comes together for events like funerals or births, its extended networks are smaller, more nucleated family units where support is concentrated among fewer members (see figs. 4.1–4.3). This pattern is especially the case where resources are scarce.[8]

Figure 4.1. Author interviewing at the Lands Beyond Lekgwapheng outside Molepolole. *Photo courtesy of E. Wilmsen.*

Figure 4.2. Makokwe family compound. *Photo courtesy of E. Wilmsen.*

Figure 4.3. Feedback on research to Makokwe family members, by author and Boineelo Borakale in one of the family's compounds. *Photo courtesy of E. Wilmsen.*

According to Ramojaki, "times are hard" because land, which is central to providing shelter and a resource for individuals' and families' livelihoods, is becoming more difficult to acquire. His son, Ranko, worries for his children's and grandchildren's future because "it is not an easy thing to acquire plots within the area as it used to be." This land shortage is the result of increased demand for land in populated areas and an amendment to the Tribal Land Act in 1993 that permits all citizens to apply to land boards anywhere in the country, regardless of tribal affiliation. For example, waiting lists for those seeking land allocation amounted to 149,500 people as of January 8, 2010, in Mogoditshane,[9] the peri-urban area adjacent to the capital Gaborone, and to 37,354 people in Molepolole itself.[10] In 2015, the situation was so serious nationwide that the *Sunday Standard* newspaper reported sarcastically, "The number of Batswana on the land allocation list is more than the population of Botswana."[11] Such pressure has come about because of a shift in the economy away from a predominantly agricultural base that has resulted in the majority of Batswana seeking to make a living in urban areas.

Thus land, especially in Kweneng District with its close connections to the capital and its proximity to the South African border, has become an extremely valuable resource. Although tribal land cannot be sold as it vests in the Land Board "for the benefit of citizens of Botswana," it can be transferred, and developments on it can be sold to a transferee.[12] Thus those with financial resources can invest in land and operate in a market system, whereby they can purchase as many developments as they can afford—a system in line with a transnational, neoliberal approach to land management. However, those without resources are placed at a disadvantage and cannot compete in this market for the following reason: although residential plots allocated by the land board are free, once they have been developed, selling these developments on land can yield substantial sums of money, particularly where these are in areas close to the capital. The pressure has been such that this market in land has fostered speculation and illegal dealings, activities that have been the subject of public inquiries[13] and court cases over the years.[14] Even the government has acknowledged that land has acquired a capital value that has led to its commoditization through the sale of developments on it.[15]

For families like the Makokwe's, it is hard, if not impossible, to enter or participate in this commoditized land market. They may be viewed as reflecting a status that Pnina Werbner (2014) has termed "the making of an African working class." In her analysis of the Manual Workers Union, this group of workers represents a largely uneducated workforce comprising 50 percent of women (7). She observed that these workers were among the lowest paid in government employment including cooks, cleaners, storekeepers, and drivers. They represent a group of citizens for whom "the class gap between the elite salaried and manual workers in Botswana's public services is evidently huge" (14). This gap has developed because the disparity in remuneration is such that top civil servants earn "ten-fold the salary of industrial class workers and often a good deal more," and it "has continued to widen" (14).

As a result, families like Makokwe's lack the resource base that would enable them to make investments in land. Also, a lack of education has meant that they have been unable to pursue higher income–producing employment. Ramojaki and his brothers never went to school, having instead herded cattle as young boys until they left for work at the mines. Among the younger male generation who have had the opportunity to go to school, poor educational attainment has limited their opportunities at a time when jobs even for those with a tertiary education are hard to come by.

Although female members of the family generally have a higher level of education (as girls they were able to attend primary school in the village while their brothers were herding cattle at the cattlepost), they have had difficulty acquiring remunerative employment. The women in Ramojaki's generation focused their labor on domestic and agricultural activities that provided little surplus income. Among the younger generation of women, attempts have been made to expand their income-generating activities. Ramojaki's daughter, Akohang (age forty-seven), for example, has found work from time to time as a cook or cleaner when not engaged in agricultural activities. Her cousins, Koketso (n.d.b.) and Mmopi (age fifty-one), have also worked briefly as a domestic and a shop assistant, respectively, when they were younger. Where women in this family group have found employment, however, it tends to be low paid and generally of an insecure and intermittent nature.

The same is true for the men in the family, who had to shift from external migration to internal employment following retrenchment at the South African mines. Where they find work, like Rammutla (age forty-three) who is employed in construction in Jwaneng (a mining center in Botswana), or Kgangwana (age thirty-six) who works at a grocery in Gaborone, or Tumelo (age twenty-nine) who works for a bakery, it continues to be contract based and lacking in stability. Although the informal sector provides work for many in Botswana, especially women, who, for example, make a living selling food at kiosks along the road, only Ranko's daughter, Malebogo (age twenty-five), has managed to find work in this sector selling air time for mobile phone companies. The low-paid and intermittent nature of the work available to the family means that its members cannot afford to invest in land, for even though plots are initially allocated for free, the family does not have the resources to develop them within the required five-year period, thereby leaving them vulnerable to dispossession. As a result, many of the younger unemployed generation, both female and male, remain living at home.

This situation exacerbates the problem of poverty, as adults who would normally be absent continue to live at home with their siblings, along with their own and their siblings' children. In the past, marriage provided an impetus for establishing new households. Makokwe's sons did this, acquiring land through their father's maternal relatives and establishing new households in Lekgwapeng. However, the prolonged labor migration caused postponement of marriage, which in turn resulted in many unmarried women with children remaining in their natal household. This pattern, established during colonial times, has continued into the postindependence period (Griffiths 1988, 295; Gulbrandsen 1980, 29–30; Kocken and Uhlenbeck 1980, 53; Molenaar 1980, 12). As a result, many women in Botswana today have children but remain unmarried. It is among this group, consisting of female-headed households, that the government of Botswana acknowledges poverty is most prevalent.

Among Makokwe's family group, out of the thirteen women in the younger generation (ages twenty to thirty-four) only one is married, although seven others have children. Accommodating all these children within existing households is not easy and can lead to conflict. While some, such as Ramojaki's unmarried niece, Mmupi (age fifty-one), have managed to acquire a residential plot and to raise children despite lack of support from the children's fathers, Mmupi believes that her children are facing an even greater uphill struggle than she did because "the youth of this generation [face] a very big challenge of finding both residential and plough field plots due to the land shortage that has affected most of the big villages in Botswana." Their situation is compounded by the fact that they face another "major challenge [that] is the lack of employment."[16]

Under these conditions, the Makokwe family lacks resources to benefit from the acquisition and development of land under the neoliberal approach. Their predicament, like that of a number of families in Kweneng, stems from their location within an accumulated set of social relations over time that has limited their scope for action. For their history reflects "a product of layer on layer of linkages, both local and to the wider world" (Massey 1994, 156) that has shaped their lifeworlds from a structural standpoint beyond their control.

Returns on the Makokwe's investment in subsistence agriculture have been unpredictable and largely unproductive because of diseases affecting animals, climatic constraints including drought, and poor soils that produce variable results. Although government subsidies exist to assist farming at this level, they do little to lift the family out of poverty. The United Nations (2007, 8) has recognized "the chronic weakness of agriculture as a source of income" in Botswana, noting that "there was no evidence that poverty-focused agricultural support schemes such as ALDEP [Arable Land Development Program] and ARAP [Accelerated Rainfed Arable Program] had ever succeeded in raising anybody out of poverty, and . . . were unlikely ever to do so" attributable to "problems of diminishing agricultural income and activity related to, and compounded by, environmental degradation."[17]

The Makokwe family also faces another problem because Kweneng District spans an area "where only 5 percent of the total land is suitable for arable agriculture" (Botswana 2003/04–2008/09, 18). The implications are that "increases in population will result in more industrial and residential construction as well as construction of physical infrastructure" (18). Unfortunately, the younger generation's attempts to alter their livelihoods and move out of farming have not met with much success, given the obstacles they face. This circumstance is in direct contrast to that of their cousins in the Radipati family.

Radipati's Family Group

Such problems do not appear to confront Radipati's descendants, who have experienced very different life trajectories. Maintaining good connections to those Bakwena dikgosi in power, as Radipati did, contributed to a situation in which his descendants were able to pursue a different life progression from those of the Makokwe family. Although born into Koosimile's third house, Radipati regarded himself as being more senior in status to Makokwe, given his mother's connections to the Kwena ruling family, which led to him being adopted as a kind of nephew to Kgosi Kgari Sechele II (1911–1918). This prominent position resulted in his receiving an education, which was unusual among men of his generation. He sought to educate all his children, including his daughters, and after his death his widow, Mhudi, continued to fund their education through the sale of cattle acquired through her labor. Cooper has noted that having cattle to sell was crucial to a family's ability to finance education (1982, 18). Mhudi had access to this vital resource, and as a result, all of Radipati's sons and daughters acquired an education, an unusual attainment for the time. Two of his sons, David (age sixty-seven) and Moses (age fifty-five) acquired university degrees in law and agriculture, respectively, outside the country because at that time there were no facilities for higher education at home.

Their education empowered Radipati's descendants to follow a different career path from most of their contemporaries. David set up his own business, a bar/bottle store and disco, before moving to Boputhatswana, the Setswana-speaking "Homeland" in apartheid South Africa, to work as a law lecturer. In 1989, he returned to Molepolole to work as a freelance lawyer and to pursue an entrepreneurial lifestyle, taking an active interest in local and national politics. His brother, Moses, went straight into government employ as an agricultural officer in the Ministry of Agriculture, where he continues to work to this day and uses his income and expertise to build up a cattlepost while still benefiting from full-time employment. He is fortunate because for those in government or public service a retirement pension is available from the age of forty-five. This income provides an opportunity for individuals to invest in a business of their own, becoming self-employed and more commercially self-sufficient at a later stage in life, an option that a number of salaried Batswana in this position pursue.

Another brother, Pelonomi (age sixty), did poorly at school, so he did not have the options that were open to his brothers. He went, like many of his generation, to work at the mines, coming back to the village to find work as a hospital orderly. He is fortunate, however, because his family network has supported him, and his employment has been consistent. He retired at sixty and now lives in a residential plot in Goo-Thato ward that he acquired from the land board.

Radipati's daughters are also unusual. They have all been formally employed for most of their lives, which has provided a degree of independence and made them less dependent on male networks for support. Goitsemang (age seventy-two), the eldest daughter, recalls that her mother's contemporaries were very surprised by her mother's attitude. "Many people asked her why she spent money from plowing on education when tomorrow you may have nothing and your children may do nothing for you." As a result of education, Goitsemang was able to train as a nurse and work in South Africa "because there were no jobs in Botswana before Independence." She left nursing in 1969 and returned home to help look after her sick sister Salalenna. She then found employment in Gaborone with a construction company during the construction boom taking place in postindependent Botswana. Over the years, the company promoted her from store worker, to wages clerk, and finally to personnel officer, a position she held until leaving in 1984 to care for her mother in Molepolole. By this time, she had acquired two plots of land in Gaborone—one of them through the company she worked for—which enabled her to provide accommodation for her daughter Eva and Eva's husband in 1989, when Eva was working as a teacher. The other plot was acquired through the Self Help Housing Agency (SHHA) and was and continues to be rented out.

Like many of her generation, including her two sisters, she has children but has never married. Unlike other female-headed households, however, she and her sisters do not find themselves in the impoverished circumstances of many of their contemporaries. Through her position with the company, Goitsemang was able to get a job for her younger sister, Olebogeng (age sixty-six), who has also been able to purchase an SHHA plot that she rents out.

Among their daughters in the younger generation, all four have been employed as teachers, in government service, or in business. Their children are pursuing tertiary education at the University of Botswana, predominantly in business studies. They have all been successful in acquiring residential plots from KLB, as well as land in urban areas that they have developed.

Radipati's descendants very much fit the profile of those whom Cooper (1982) refers to as the *salariat*. None more so than Olebogeng's eldest son, Bongi (age forty-two) who exemplifies upward social mobility. Like his uncle David, he completed a law degree at the University of Botswana (UB), followed by an LLM at the University of Witwatersrand in South Africa in 1994, after which he was appointed law lecturer at UB in 1997. Also, after working in private practice, he went to Columbia University in 1999 and spent a year at Harvard as a visiting researcher. He then returned to UB. From there, he became a legal adviser to the Office of the President in 2007. In 2011, he moved to the Attorney General's Office. He has been in professional, consistent, and pensionable employment throughout his adult life. As a result, he has been able to invest in land; he and his wife, Adelaide, bought a residential plot in Phakhalane, a highly sought after and expensive suburb of Gaborone.[18]

Aware of the problems the younger generation is facing with regard to land, Bongi and his wife have acquired land from land boards for all three of their daughters, the eldest of whom was in her first year at UB in 2010. They have been able to take advantage of the amended Tribal Land Act that no longer links allocation to tribal affiliation in order to acquire two plots in Ramotswa and Mmankgodi, both of which are in desirable locations close to the capital but outside Kweneng District. They also have land about ten kilometers from Letlhakeng, gateway to the Central Kalahari Game Reserve, where tourism is actively being promoted. While this plot is still a field and they "have not done anything with it [yet]," it has the potential for future development, especially if tourism is successfully established there.

Power and the Construction of Social Inequity:
Transnational and Local Domains

Over time, the Radipati family has become an upwardly mobile social group for whom land represents an opportunity for advancement. They have the resources, knowledge, and contacts to pursue more entrepreneurial projects in line with the government's Vision 2016, a vision that is beyond the reach of the Makokwe family. For as the life histories of these families' descendants demonstrate, access to resources varies according to affiliation within varying types of networks that produce differing lifeworlds for their members. This structural inequity, created through the complex relationship between international, transnational, and local influences on space, gives rise to dimensions of class created out of a constellation of factors that contribute to the accumulation of human/social as well as economic capital. As Botswana's history shows, it has long been dependent, first, on South Africa and, second, on Europe as markets for its cattle, as well as on global market prices for diamonds that have underpinned its economic prosperity to date.[19] These markets are subject to the vicissitudes of fluctuating world demand and wars (Parson 1981; Murray and Parsons 1987; Wilmsen 1989, 105–129). The Government of Botswana (1991–1997, xxi, 95, 145) itself acknowledges the ways in which the country's development is inextricably tied to decisions, processes, and events that take place at regional and international levels beyond its borders. Indeed, publication of its last development plan was postponed beyond its normal six-year cycle so that government ministries could recalculate their forecasts for growth and development in light of "the effects of the just ended global financial and economic crisis."[20]

For families such as Radipati's, their lifeworlds are the product of an accumulated resource base that has positioned them to benefit from laws and policies relating to land. Their upwardly mobile status has enabled them to diversify their livelihoods in ways that have given them enhanced access to land and control over it. Also among this group, women have largely managed to overcome the constraints of gender through their access to resources such as education and employment, which have enabled them to develop their capacity as individuals to be proactive in the acquisition and development of land. Makokwe's descendants, however, have not been as fortunate as those of Radipati, for their lifeworlds are the product of a diminishing resource base that has denied them financial and skills-based resources that would enable them to move away from the peasantariat by investing in more commercial ventures, such as raising crops for sale to large chains, developing an agribusiness, or extending production of livestock to sell cattle to the European Union. Such commercial activities are in keeping with the government's drive toward development of "globally competitive enterprises that produce goods and services that comply with local and international standards" creating an "entrepreneurship culture."[21] Although social mobility, as Radipati's family illustrates, is attainable, what facilitates this capacity to rise to a higher social or economic position are social structures made over generations that provide a resource base on which they can draw. Radipati's descendants were able to negotiate their upward mobility by creating spaces for their advancement. These spaces, revolving around education and employment, created opportunities for advancement at the time they were pursued, but they no longer have the same purchase today. For example, university graduates are no longer guaranteed a job for life, as they were in the past, and instead find themselves among the ranks of today's unemployed. This situation makes it even more difficult for Makokwe's family members to create spaces for enhancing their resource base, for although their educational attainment has progressed over generations, it has not progressed sufficiently within the evolving social structure to provide alternative options for improving their livelihoods.

What emerges from these life histories are the ways in which Makokwe's and Radipati's networks and resource bases build diverging lifeworlds, for the differences they embody derive from constituent parts that reflect the ways in which social stratification is created and maintained. Understanding what shapes these networks is crucial if governments, international agencies, and NGOs are to move beyond global and national rhetoric around poverty reduction, land administration, and access to justice, to a more concrete understanding of the specific factors that render certain sections of the population vulnerable when it comes to land. A more nuanced understanding is needed regarding how individuals, households, and families relate in terms of status, age, and position within the life cycle, and how these relationships intersect with current government and land board approaches concerning the allocation and transfer of land.

Although all relationships are important, the role of women features prominently in global visions. For example, goal five of the UN Sustainable Development Goals seeks to "achieve gender equality and empower all women and girls" (United Nations 2015a, 15). Thus chapter 5 takes a closer look at how women in their various manifestations, including their location within the life cycle and social networks, intersect with government approaches to land. This survey necessitates an evaluation, not only of economic considerations that play into regional, national, and transnational perspectives on managing land but also of those factors that are central to the recognition and creation of justice for women. It also requires an understanding of conditions under which women can gain access to and control over land, including an appreciation of the role that gender plays in constructing social relationships, and the distribution of resources among family members, to be explored in the subsequent chapter.

Notes

1. The results of which are documented in Griffiths (1997).
2. For more detailed life histories, see Griffiths (1997, 2014).
3. All ages in brackets represent the age of the person referred to in 2010.
4. His brother Nkadikang, for example, worked at the mines for forty-two years and his brother Ntlogelang for thirty-five years.
5. As discussed in chapter 2, under a mafisa arrangement, cattle are lent out in patronage to individuals who become clients under obligatory conditions that include mortgaging the clients' assets against the safety of the patron's property and interests.
6. Dikgosi were able to continue to consolidate their power through the accumulation of wealth that was newly acquired through their collection of taxes on behalf of the British (Wylie 1991).
7. Many who return from working at the mines become sick because of the poor working conditions to which they were subjected.
8. Pnina Motzafi-Haller (1986, 259) notes how, in extreme cases of poverty, families abandon members, leading to a truncated set of relationships within families and households.
9. Mogoditshane now has a population of 56,139 people that makes it the second-largest village in Botswana after Molepolole. See the Population and Housing Census (Botswana 2011b).
10. Molepolole has an estimated population of 63,128, according to the Population and Housing Census (Botswana 2011b, para. 2.4).
11. See *Sunday Standard*, June 7–13, 2015, p. 1, where Phaladi Letswamotse observes that the population of Botswana currently stands at 2.1 million and that "the government would have to spend more than the total national budget to allocate land to citizens on the waiting list."
12. Section 10(1) of the 1968 Tribal Land Act.
13. See, e.g., Botswana (1981); see also Botswana (1992b).
14. *Kweneng Land Board (KLB) v. Matlho and Another* (1992) BLR 292; *KLB v. Mpofu and Another* (2005) 1 BLR 3; *KLB v. Selaki* [and Sekgome] (2004) 1 BLR 154(HC); *KLB v. Molefhe and Another* (2005) 2 BLR 155; *KLB v. Murima* (08) (CA) CACLB-034-07.

15. Botswana (2002, 2003). See also the Draft Botswana Land Policy (Botswana 2011a) that refers to a land values market and capitalization of land (p. 20, para. 4.1).

16. The government of Botswana acknowledges that these problems represent a big challenge, see Botswana (2012b, para. 34:12). See also Botswana (2010–2016, para 2.14:19), noting that according to the Demographic Survey of 2006, 66% of those aged 15–19 were unemployed, along with 55% of those aged 20–24. In their presentation to the 64th Session of the UN General Assembly on October 6, 2009, Botswana Youth Delegates Bogolo Kenewendo and Yolisa Modise observed that "youth unemployment is a big challenge in Botswana" and that "poverty also remains a problem especially in rural areas, affecting particularly women, youth and the elderly" (Botswana 2009c).

17. See United Nations (2007).

18. This plot is on state land that had to be purchased.

19. See African Development Bank (2007, 137). Note the concern over the need for economic diversification given "the declining per capita earnings from diamonds and slow growth of non-mining exports of goods" (Botswana 2012b, p. 4, para. 8).

20. Botswana (2012b, p. 2, para. 2).

21. Ibid., p. 10, para. 28.

5

TRANSFORMATIONS ON THE GROUND

The Changing Position of Women in Relation to Land

OVER TIME, THE GENDERED DYNAMICS OF LAND TENURE have shifted, so that women are now gaining access to and control over land in ways that eluded them in the past. As recently as the 1980s, women faced difficulties in gaining access to property, including land, under customary law (Griffiths 1997). This circumstance derived from the gendered position they occupied in kinship networks, combined with the economic, political, ideological, and social spheres shaping the world in which they lived.

Although women in Botswana primarily interacted with customary law, Western-style law cannot be ignored, for the two are mutually constitutive and together create the framework within which approaches to land must be considered when studying women's relationships with land. This mutually constitutive relationship in law is often overlooked by policy makers pushing for land reform because of the influence of Western-based statutory law, which promotes registered title to land without understanding the social dynamics of what the process entails.[1] Although recognition of the need to take account of informal, traditional, or customary law is growing, this awareness has less to do with perceptions of its benefits and more to do with its perceived failure by international donors to meet human rights standards, especially with regard to women.[2] Thus its recognition is premised on a need to bring these forms of law within these agencies' control in order to reform their perceived deficiencies. This approach can have unintended consequences. In examining the effects of land reform in Kenya, Celestine Nyamu-Musembi (2002) observed how government policy (promoted by international agencies) in formalizing rights in land had an adverse impact on women. Women accounted for less than 5 percent of registered landholders in Kenya, the result of a practice in which land became registered in the name of the male heads of households as sole owners, even though sole ownership was not a requirement of registration.

International concern over women's vulnerability is often linked with the gendered power relations at play in the world that women inhabit along with their subjugation to customary law. This concern has led to the creation and promotion of international instruments, such as the UN Convention on the Elimination of All Forms of Discrimination against Women (CEDAW) by the General Assembly in 1979, the Southern African Development Community's Gender and Development Declaration in 1997, and the Protocol to the African Charter on Human and People's Rights relating to the Rights of Women in Africa in 2003. These documents which seek to reduce women's vulnerability and provide for their empowerment have worthy aims. However, what constitutes vulnerability is a matter for empirical investigation. It involves addressing how questions of land, poverty, and access to justice are handled in specific contexts. Simply asserting that women's vulnerability is a function of customary law is too vague and imprecise to be meaningful. Yet this assumption is often taken at face value and used to dictate international agencies' policies and regulatory frameworks, despite attempts to challenge these abstract assertions. For what is at work in their approach is a reliance on a particular Western-style paradigm of law that underpins a temporal notion of linear progress. In this paradigm, informal or customary law is presented as representing a less-evolved legal system that is located in the past, that looks backward rather than embracing the present and looking to the future.[3]

Kweneng Land Board: Research Findings in 2009–2010

To gain a broader picture of women's evolving relationship with land, I needed to acquire data beyond the life histories of Makokwe's and Radipati's descendants discussed in the previous chapter. Thus I incorporated a study of land certificates and leases from Kweneng Land Board into my 2009–2010 research.[4] My study was the first of its kind to investigate land certificates and leases under the Tribal Land Act, providing much-needed data on land transactions. For as Professor Ng'ong'ola, an expert on land at the University of Botswana, observed in 2004, "There is not much information on how women have been faring in their dealings with Land Boards."

Table 5.1. Land certificates—Molepolole Sub–Land Board

Land Type	Men	Unclear/Other	Women	Total
Residential	1,061	22	1,347	2,430
Arable/Agricultural	880	15	716	1,611
Total	1,941	37	2,063	4,041

The study of these transactions indicated that a shift in practice had oc-curred, leading to women's increased participation in them. This shift was due to several factors: enhanced education, informal and formal sector em-ployment, and changes in law that reflected social changes on the ground. Understanding the social dimensions of change is a vital, yet often over-looked, component in international donors' policy-making frameworks, which often focus on reforming laws and institutions without acknowledg-ing the impact that the social environment has on their reception.[5] Such knowledge, however, is crucial if rhetoric is to be distinguished from reality. Otherwise, a danger exists that these policies will give rise to unexpected outcomes and detrimental effects that are contrary to the intentions of those promoting them (Weilenmann 2009a, 2009b).

My study examined 4,041 certificates and 1,200 leases over a ten-year period from 1999 to 2009. It also featured women and men appearing as claimants and appellants before Kweneng Land Board (KLB) for all types of land use.[6] That women were featuring in the processes of acquiring cer-tificates and leases is clear from table 5.1.[7]

Overall, about half of the land certificates were registered in women's names, including certificates for residential plot and field allocations, regis-trations, transfers, and extensions. Fewer women (44 percent) feature when it comes to agricultural fields. This finding departed from earlier research indicating that where women were accessing land they were doing so by in-heriting fields from their mothers or grandmothers. Faustin Kalabamu and Siamsang Morolong (2004) noted that women were more likely to acquire fields than men, as the latter were more interested in other types of prop-erty like cattle. However, discussions in 2010 with government personnel, NGOs, and local people suggested that women may be giving their fields to men because of inadequate resources to work them and/or fears about per-sonal safety. As the Deputy Director of Social Services in 2010 explained, "Women are not really into farming because fields today are so far from the village that when they go there they have to live alone. There have been

Table 5.2. Leases—main land boards

Land Type	Men	Unclear/Other	Women	Total
Residential	305	3	292	600
Commercial	347	57	196	600
Total	652	60	488	1200

a number of cases reported of older women being raped at the farm lands, and women are scared. In the past, old people were used to farming, but for a poor single mother who will be alone at the lands, it will not be safe for her."

In addition to certificates awarded through the Molepolole sub–land board, women also feature in leases awarded by the main land board (see table 5.2). Out of 600 residential leases, 292 were awarded to women and 305 to men (with only three applicants whose sex was unclear or who represented another category such as a company). Fewer women featured in the 600 commercial leases (196 women and 347 men). Nonetheless, they were present (with only 57 in the category representing bodies such as corporations).

Women not only possess certificates and leases but also represent over 50 percent of those on the waiting list for land in Kweneng District as a whole. For example, in May 2010, in Gamodubu (formerly a plowing area near Molepolole), 10,856 names were on the waiting list, consisting of 5,944 women and 4,901 men (plus 11 where the sex was not indicated). Thus my findings indicate that women of all ages (from 21 to 84 years) are acquiring land through certificates and leases to a much larger extent than has generally been recognized.

Access to and Control over Land through Inheritance: Customary Practices

Although certificates and leases provide a lens into women's interactions with tribal land, they do not capture how land transfers operate within families, particularly with respect to women. In cases of inheritance, the kgosi or his representatives play an important role in handling land transactions under customary law unless a written will supersedes its application or some other factor negates its operation. Thereafter, the matter is remitted back to the land board to make any necessary amendments to the land certificate.

In the case of inheritance, customary authorities apply customary law to the distribution of an estate. It is generally accepted that daughters inherit fields and that the family yard goes to the youngest son. At the five kgotla meetings held in Molepolole in 2010, some discrepancies arose as to the treatment of these assets, with some maintaining that the family yard went to the youngest child regardless of sex (Mokgopeetsane and Ntloolengwae wards) while others were firmly of the view that it went to the youngest son (Dikoloing, Lekgwapheng, and Mokgalo wards). With regard to fields, some said these assets went to the eldest rather than the youngest daughter (Dikoloing and Ntloolengwae wards), but all agreed that she had to be unmarried. Where an additional field belonged to the father, consensus was that this property went to a son, although, once again, some disagreement took place regarding whether the eldest or the youngest son inherited and depending on whether the property was situated in the north or the south of Botswana. Such discussions reveal the local nature of people's understandings of customary law.

In this process, transmission of property among families is focused on maintaining future generations and preserving assets for children (Griffiths 1997, 161). Given the patrilineal nature of traditional Tswana society, tracing descent through the male line—through the man's father where the parents are married, and through the woman's father where they are not—privileged males over females regarding inheritance under customary law, with the eldest son receiving the greatest share of all the property in recognition of the responsibilities that he adopts as head of the family. In that role, he was not only his children's custodian but also had responsibilities for representing and maintaining extended kin as the senior male among his family group. Under this system, daughters inherited less than their brothers because it was envisaged that they would marry and then live among their husbands' relatives, with their husbands establishing the *malwapa* (residential yards). Through marriage, these women's children would be affiliated with their husband's family group, tracing descent through the male line where property devolves from father to son. Daughters tended to inherit their mothers' personal property such as clothes and domestic utensils. They also sometimes inherited fields worked by their mothers. In contrast, brothers inherited the plow, cattle, any guns that their father may have had, and any other family property, including land. Among siblings, property was not shared equally but was dependent on their sex and birth order within the family.

These formulations of customary law derived from archival and oral sources but were never rigidly adhered to (Griffiths 1997, 46). For example, in 2010, a married daughter, Kgomotso, was allocated a family plowing field but gave it to her older brother Ranko because she had acquired another plowing field from a *rakgadiagwe* (patrilineal aunt). Similarly, her aunt, Olebeng, Makokwe's youngest child, was given control over the natal household in Mosotho kgotla in the 1980s when she was unmarried because her older brothers had all married and established their own households elsewhere in Molepolole. She lived there until she married in 2001 (in late middle age) and moved to her husband's homestead. In some cases, however, families follow established norms. For example, Rammutla, who is Nkadikang's youngest son, inherited his parents' residential yard when his father died. He had the certificate transferred into his name even though his mother is still alive and living with him and his wife in the yard.

Inheritance Data from Customary Land Certificates

To explore how far families recognized women as beneficiaries, I examined land certificates at Molepolole sub–land board (transferring residential/arable land) from 1999 to 2009. Inheritance involves a land transfer requiring certification by the land board through an amendment to the land certificate. It was not possible to conduct a random sample of certificates for each year because of the patchy state of the board's records. Many were unavailable or lacked information, including data specifying the sex, age, and marital status of both transferor and transferee, and whether or not they are related. This incomplete status was especially the case with records from earlier years. Inadequate record keeping featured in discussions in chapter 3 has been a complaint leveled against land boards ever since they were established, and the problem repeatedly surfaces in appeals to the Land Tribunal and other legal forums.

Out of the 4,041 certificates, 629 involved residential transfers and 367 dealt with fields. In addition, I examined 259 appointments dealing with administration of deceased persons' estates in the chief's kgotla for the year 2009 in order to ascertain the sex of the administrator and whether or not there was a family relationship between the deceased and the appointee. Given concerns over property grabbing in the past—especially by brothers and uncles of the deceased—knowing who acquires authority as an executor is important, although it may not prevent de facto seizing of assets.

Table 5.3. Residential transfers according to relationship data

Year	Wt-re	Mt-re	Tr-W+M	Wt-no	Mt-no	Tn-W+M	Tt-W+M
2009	41	26	67	62	61	123	190
2008	15	10	25	23	20	43	68
2007	17	13	30	14	15	29	59
2006	12	15	27	7	8	15	42
2005	20	20	40	18	19	37	77
Total	105	84	189	124	123	247	436

Key	
Wt-re	total number of transfers to women where parties related
Mt-re	total number of transfers to men where parties related
Tr-W+M	total number of transfers to women and men for the year where parties related
Wt-no	total number of transfers to women where no information on relationship
Mt-no	total number of transfers to men where no information on relationship
Tn-W+M	total number of transfers to women and men for the year where no information on relationship
Tt-W+M	total number of all transfers to women and men for the year

Residential Transfers

While customary land itself cannot be sold, developments on it can be, subject to approval by the land board. So, not all the residential transfers included in the data set involve inheritance cases. Of the 629 residential transfers, sufficient information was only available on 436 transfers from 2005 to 2009. Out of these transfers, it could be established that 189 involved inheritance compared with 247 transfers where there was no data to support this view. Out of the 189 involving inheritance, 105 were to women transferees compared with 84 male transferees. These break down in terms of table 5.3.

These records demonstrate women transferring land alongside men, and while the number of transfers where parties are not related is higher, this finding is not surprising because people increasingly sell or transfer residential plots for money, especially in an area close to Gaborone where a tremendous demand for land exists. Among related parties, the number of transfers to women and men appear to be more or less equal, with a slight increasing trend toward women from 2005 to 2009, especially where the parties involved in the transfer are related.

Table 5.4. Field transfers according to relationship data

Year	Wt-re	Mt-re	Tr-W+M	Wt-no	Mt-no	Tn-W+M	Tt-W+M
2009	21	20	41	21	45	66	107
2008	17	18	35	6	17	23	58
2007	10	4	14	6	7	13	27
2006	0	7	7	8	12	20	27
2005	3	4	7	8	13	21	28
Total	51	53	104	49	94	143	247

Key

Wt-re	total number of transfers to women where parties related
Mt-re	total number of transfers to men where parties related
Tr-W+M	total number of transfers to women and men for the year where parties related
Wt-no	total number of transfers to women where no information on relationship
Mt-no	total number of transfers to men where no information on relationship
Tn-W+M	total number of transfers to women and men for the year where no information on relationship
Tt-W+M	total number of all transfers to women and men for the year

Field Transfers

Of the 247 field transfers for the years 1999 to 2009, transfers to men made up 60 percent. However, data on fields was more difficult to access, as many of the records had been lost in the sub–land board's move to their new premises. Finding women less represented than men was surprising given earlier findings from life histories that implied fields were one type of property that women did appear to inherit and pass on. Out of these certificates, it could be established that 104 transfers involved inheritance compared with 144 where there was no data to support this view. Out of the 104 transfers involving inheritance, 51 involved women transferees compared with 53 men. These break down in terms of table 5.4.

Where parties were related, the majority of field transfers (as with residential plots) were to sons and daughters (70 percent of cases), with overall numbers of women and men almost equally split between 51 women and 53 men. Most transfers were postmortem. This observation more closely mirrors previous ethnographic data on family land transfer. Regardless of the apparent decline in field inheritance, however, figures show that women are inheriting residential plots and, to a lesser extent, fields. This finding is in line with more general findings from KLB discussed previously.

One last note of interest: in transfers, women are not only featuring as transferees but are engaged in transferring property as transferors. Out of the 439 residential transfers from 2005 to 2009, on the data provided, 191 were to women and 195 to men (there was insufficient information to form a view on the remaining 53 transfers). Out of the 246 field transfers, on the data provided 130 were women compared with 86 men (of the remaining 30 transfers there was insufficient date to form a view).

Customary Land Tenure and Records: Compliance and Change

What these certificates show is that, despite the norms of customary law favoring male inheritance, women are inheriting land. In large part, the reason is that their siblings agree to a different form of property distribution and document this agreement through affidavits submitted as part of the transfer process. Families are clearly negotiating their own forms of distribution regardless of normative customary expectations. This change marks an important finding because what occurs in daily life often passes unnoticed in a system where more emphasis is placed on the study of conflict or disputes. It also acts as a corrective to normative assertions about customary law, that is, that it is backward-looking and divorced from current social practices that prevail within in the community at large.

What is crucial to an understanding of what is happening here is the recognition that consensus among families is central to reaching a decision on how property is to be distributed (Griffiths 1997, 2012). In Ntlooengwae ward, for example, the headman explained that one reason why women possess certificates today is because "sometimes when one of the siblings looks after the other siblings or parents, the plot will be transferred to the person who was looking after other family members, and women often take on the caring role." Or, it "may be the yard was developed by that particular person and having invested a lot [of effort] in that plot the certificate will be transferred to the person who developed the plot." Much emphasis was made in ward meetings of how much it costs to develop a residential plot today; buildings are no longer huts made of mud and may represent substantial investments. For example, Radipati's daughter, Goitsemang, found herself in this position in the 1980s, having rebuilt the family homestead, and in the process she incurred costs to make a house where a hut once

Table 5.5. Appointment of executors chief's kgotla, 2009

Relationship	Women	Percent	Men	Percent	Total
Wife	54	23			54
Daughter	45	20			45
Son			29	13	29
Mother	25	11			25
Sister	18	8			18
Brother			16	7	16
Uns relative	16	7	9	4	25
Husband			6	3	6
Father			3	1	3
Gdaughter	3	1			3
Niece	2	1			2
Other			2	1	2
Nephew			1	1	1
Aunt	1				1
Gson					0
Uncle					0
Total	164	71	66	30	230

stood. Although she never had a formal land certificate in her name, Mosotho kgotla members supported her over her brother David's attempt to take
control of the family household in part for this reason.

These attitudinal shifts toward women are supported by the number of
women's appointments to deceased persons' estates recorded in the chief's
kgotla records for 2009. As shown in table 5.5, of the 230 cases where the
appointee's sex is known, 71 percent of the appointees were women (that is,
164 women). Also out of the total number of appointments, wives accounted
for 23 percent (that is, 54 women). These findings mark a change from past
research where wives did not appear in these appointments (Griffiths 1997).
Today, however, they are present, and headmen now acknowledge that
when husbands die wives may take over the property. Even though statutory law has recognized women's rights to inheritance as a surviving spouse
for some time under the Succession (Rights of the Surviving Spouse and
Inheritance Provisions) Act (Cap. 31.03), the Act's provisions do not apply to
estates that are under the control of customary law.[8] This changing norm in
relation to women is not surprising given the mutually constitutive nature
of law that extends beyond the boundaries of institutional settings.

Table 5.6. Women involved in appeals, 2009–2010

Land Use	Women	Men	Total
Residential (Res)	70	79	149
Commercial (Com)	59	308	367
Water Point/Borehole (WP/B)	32	159	191
Agricultural (Agr)	34	97	131
Tribunal Order (T.O.)	23	117	140
Civic and Community (C&C)	0	5	5
Miscellaneous (Misc)	4	29	33
Unclear (Unc)	10	36	46
Total	232	830	1,062

Table 5.7. Breakdown of women's appeals by land board, 2009–2010

Gaborone Tribunal	Appeals	Palapye Tribunal	Appeals	Total
Kweneng	32	Ngwato	64	
Kgatleng	20	Tawana	20	
Malete	42	Tati	6	
Rolong	14	Chobe	2	
Ngwaketse	3	Ghanzi	7	
Tlokweng	17	Unclear	1	
Kgalagadi	3			
Tawana	1			
Total	132		100	232

Note: Tawana Land Board appears twice because land boards are not confined to one jurisdiction, meaning that appellants are not restricted regarding where they can take their cases.

Women as Appellants

Although the majority of transactions involving women and land operates on a consensual basis, women are also featuring more often in disputes at the Land Tribunal, although not at the same level as men. The amount of data was not sufficient to analyze the total number of appellants who were women throughout the period 1999–2009. However, it was possible to do an analysis for one year, 2009–2010.[9] As tables 5.6 and 5.7 demonstrate, out of the 1,062 cases lodged during this period, 232 appeals were lodged by women, amounting to 22 percent of appeals in that year. Out of these appeals, 132 of them were lodged by women in Gaborone and 100 were lodged by women in Palapye. Table 5.7 shows that the highest number of women appellants fell within Ngwato, Malete, and Kweneng Land Boards.

Factors Enhancing Women's Participation in Land Transactions

What then accounts for these transformations that have taken place over time? Local people, land boards, government personnel, and staff from NGOs attributed women's acquisition of land to a number of factors. These included legal developments such as the Abolition of Marital Power Act (Cap. 07) and the Deeds Registry Act (Cap. 33.02). The former Act abolishes the husband's marital power over matrimonial property where the marriage is in community of property. Under this law, married women can now acquire land certificates and leases in their own names. Additionally, an amendment to the Deeds Registry Act under Section 18 enables married women to register land in their own names.

Another factor contributing to women's increased presence in land transactions has been pressure by international human rights instruments on the Botswana government to pursue gender equality. Some of these instruments include the Convention on the Elimination of All Forms of Discrimination against Women (CEDAW), as well as cases such as *Attorney General v. Unity Dow* (concerning discrimination against married women and the citizenship of their children)[10] and the *Student Representative Council of Molepolole College of Education v. Attorney General* (where a policy excluding pregnant female students from college for a year was held to be discriminatory).[11] However, while Botswana has ratified CEDAW and its Optional Protocol,[12] it has so far failed to ratify—or even sign—the Protocol to the African Charter on Human and Peoples' Rights on the Rights of Women in Africa.

Yet another factor contributing to women's increased presence has been the development of women's awareness of their rights through enhanced education and employment; much of which has been brought about through the work of NGOs over the past twenty-five years, such as Emang Basadi (Stand Up Women) and Ditshwanelo (Center for Human Rights).

Under these improved conditions, analysis suggests that three types of women are acquiring land. First, unmarried, proactive female household heads who have children and are employed or run small businesses. Second, unmarried caregivers within their family group whose siblings agree to their inheriting the family yard because of their lack of resources or because of their economic investment in the home. Third, women whose married male lovers assist them in setting themselves up in small houses (as *dinyatsi*, or mistresses).

Proactive "Can-Do" Women

Women outnumber men in Botswana, a situation that has been the case for a number of years (Van Klaveren et al. 2009, 34). In Kweneng District, the female population, like in the rest of the country, is just above that of males at slightly over 52 percent,[13] and like in much of the world, women in the district generally outlive men.[14] More distinctive of Botswana, however, is that many of these women remain unmarried but have children. The 2006 Demographic Survey records 64.6 percent of the population as never marrying and 46.6 percent of all households countrywide as headed by women.[15] This phenomenon is publicly acknowledged. As one female land board member observed, "Most women are not married, so they go ahead in applying for land [because they have no husband to depend on]." She also commented, "Batswana women have children before marriage. Then they think of having their own place. They don't want to stay in the family home [because this may cause quarrels]." Indeed, according to the Acting Deputy Land Board Secretary, "Even if women are married, we recognize that divorce rates are high and that a woman might [apply for land because] she might be chased away and obliged to return to her family home." Although many female-headed households are among the poorest in the country, some have escaped poverty and succeeded in maintaining themselves and their families.[16] Kakanyo Fani Dintwat (2010, 284) noted that the large-scale entry of women into education and paid employment provided them with alternatives to marriage by giving them a wider range of choices than they had previously had. When unmarried women are successful, it is usually through one of four circumstances: education, formal employment, informal sector employment, and/or self-help/proactive engagement.

EDUCATION

The NGO Ditshwanelo acknowledges that "women get an education in Botswana because it is open to all." The Deputy Director of Social Services similarly recognizes that "more women have gone to school" than in the past. However, she also observes that "there is still a problem for uneducated and poor women." For example, the Education Statistics Brief (ESB) for the country in 2009 records that school enrollment for girls accounted for about 50 percent of enrollments, but at the secondary level girls represent 61.1 percent of those dropping out of school.[17]

FORMAL EMPLOYMENT

Today "more women [are] entering the employment sector," according to the Director of Housing, "so they can take up more opportunities than previously." The Women's Finance House, an NGO, also observes that women no longer "only engage in unpaid work or producing food in fields" where they are "bogged down by perishables so that they accumulated nothing." Although the 2006 Demographic Survey found that unemployment is higher for women at 19.7 percent compared with 15.3 percent for men, overall women in formal employment accounted for 47.7 percent of those employed, which indicates a marked improvement from the past.[18] A high percentage of these women (74.3 percent) are employed in the service industry in hotels and restaurants. Other sectors where women predominate include education, finance, wholesale and retail trade, and health. The 2006 survey found that only 25 percent of women who were employed worked in agriculture compared with 64 percent employed in services.[19]

INFORMAL-SECTOR EMPLOYMENT

The majority of informal sector businesses is operated by women, most of whom work from their homes or along the roads. The majority of these women sell sweets, airtime, and vegetables. Other activities include sewing; making textiles; providing food at lunch; trade kiosks (tuck shops); hair salons; raising poultry; selling coffee, jam, and floor polish; and horticulture. Women account for 67.6 percent of the informal-sector workforce, a sector perceived by the Deputy Permanent Secretary at the Ministry of Trade and Industry to play a major role in creating employment, production, and income generation, with an increase in growth of 72.3 percent since 1999.[20] This growth is attributed in part to government programs promoting these developments. Thus, the Deputy Director of Social Services sees women "empowering themselves through trade encouraged by government, for example, baking bread and selling it to schools and, during the harvesting season, selling home-grown watermelons to schools."

Government programs whose purpose is to empower "women to access credit for small businesses" have been established through the Citizen

Entrepreneurial Development Agency (CEDA). However, according to CEDA officials, most projects that are funded are run by men. Nonetheless, women can access more modest loans through the Women's Finance House, an NGO that assists low-income women without other sources of support. It only deals with women in groups of three or more, who are between 21 and 65 years old and have a preexisting business with a turnover of less than BWP 1,000 (about USD 100) per month. Its officers report a lot of activity in the informal sector where women seek to make a living and pay for their children and grandchildren to go to school.

MOTIVATION FOR SELF-HELP/PROACTIVE ENGAGEMENT

The Director of Housing notes that "there has been a move to women being more proactive [in land] . . . because women have to fend for their families." The Deputy of Social Services agrees, commenting that "more and more women are applying for land now." She sees "women becoming more independent. In the past, women held marriage as an ideal, but now over time women have seen other single women who have made it in life without a man. They can see that they can make it without a man." She notes that "there are many independent women who are now doing well on their own, even those with low-literacy levels. Perhaps they are doing well with small businesses and their success can motivate other women." These proactive approaches are endorsed by a female land board member who attributes the increase in women in land transactions to the fact that "many women are unmarried." Given that "most of the women in Botswana are single," they "apply for plots [because they can't rely on a man to provide one]."

In a collective interview, sub–land board members acknowledged that most of the younger, unmarried generation tend to apply for land on their own behalf. One noted that "women tend to apply for land at an early age, unlike their male counterparts." Thus "a man may only get started at thirty-eight, maybe after getting married." They wait "until, at a late stage, they realize now [that] I'm a man, I want to go out on my own [i.e., away from my parent's yard]." A female colleague agreed, stating "most Batswana men are very slow [off the mark]; they don't react like women. Maybe men enjoy staying with their parents. They wake up late [when they get married and then apply for land]." In her experience, "Unmarried men applying for land is rare."

Despite these developments, the NGO Emang Basadi observes that while "things have changed, men resist this." They caution that men are frustrated because "their voices are now faint" and that this loss of predominance leads to gender-based violence. One of the reasons for this reaction, they argue, is because as women become more proactive, "men may feel displaced from their roles and responsibilities," including their role as breadwinner. They maintain one reason for this change is "because women never used to work formally." As the Deputy Permanent Secretary at the Ministry of Labor and Home Affairs acknowledges, "The lifestyle has changed in Botswana." He attributes this change to the number of programs that provide assistance, so that "when you look at women and economic empowerment, there are so many packages [available] that you see many women coming up." Concerning married women, a female senior adjudication officer of KLB explains, "Married women used not to own properties; the husband owned them, but this is no longer the case." She observes that more women today are educated and "have the ability to hold their own money." She attributes women's advancement to their access to education and their ability to "stand on their own."

The Acting Deputy Land Board Secretary recognizes the crucial role that NGOs such as Emang Basadi and Ditshwanelo have played in educating the public: They "have promoted women's empowerment, and the government seems to be supporting them." As a female land board member observed,

> Ditshwanelo have made a contribution to women featuring in land certificates and leases because they run workshops. One of their recommendations was that having a spouse should not be a hindrance for women to acquire land. The land board adopted that recommendation. At the time I joined the land board, women had to acquire their husbands' consent to apply for land. This was also the case for transfers. Now there is no problem related to women acquiring land [in their own right], unless you make it a requirement that they have to prove that they have the resources to develop that land. That might be a hindrance, but we haven't gone that far yet, except with advertised plots and commercial plots because they are limited.

Family Caregiver Investors

Another group of women acquiring land represents those whose siblings agree to their inheriting the family home. This agreement is primarily due to their (1) lack of resources, (2) role as caregivers for family members, and/or (3) economic investment in the premises. As discussed previously, the land board provides flexibility in allowing for distribution of property based on consensus that may allow women to inherit land contrary to customary practices. Although women have always acted as caregivers within the family, this role has acquired a greater degree of recognition than in the past. Such recognition forms part of a reassessment of changing gender roles within the society as well as a more egalitarian approach to inheritance rights.[21]

In discussions and interviews in 2010, kgotla members perceived daughters as being more reliable than sons in providing caregiving services as well as economic support. This perception was attributed to sons outsourcing resources to unmarried women and children beyond their family circle. These attitudinal shifts may be perceived as an example of Eugen Ehrlich's ([1913] 1936) *living law*, where siblings are reaching their own agreements on distribution of property by signing affidavits submitted as part of the transfer process that must take place before the land board can certify an amendment to a land certificate. Headmen and land overseers now acknowledge that families often make their own arrangements regarding the distribution of the family home and fields. For example, Dikoloing ward members comment that "due to modernization, it happens a lot." The headman of Mokgopeetsane ward, kgosi Benjamin, noted that where an inheritance is concerned the families "come to me bringing all their names, and I must write a letter to the land board."

Such agreements among family members are not confined to Kweneng District. The Senior Adjudication Officer for KLB, from outside the district, is one of eight children in a family of six girls and two boys. She and her siblings have done well in life. In her case, she and her husband, a senior police officer who died in 2006, managed to acquire residential, commercial, and agricultural land throughout Botswana in the course of employment transfers. She is, therefore, not worried about having sufficient property for her children to inherit. Most of her siblings are in a similar position. However, one sister did not do well in school and has not managed to find a job. This sister now cares for their elderly parents. All siblings support her caregiving by each contributing BWP 200 (about USD 20) a month for her upkeep. They have agreed that when their parents die, she will inherit the family yard because of her straitened circumstances.

Small House Women

Obtaining information on the third category is difficult: unmarried women who receive financial assistance to acquire land from men, many of whom are married. A male land board member drew attention to this issue, stating that although he did not wish to detract from women's achievements because "women are working and sweating for themselves," he did "know of a few women who are involved with married men. [These men] get fed up of going to motels and lodges and encourage the women to get a plot and develop it so they can visit them there." He stressed that this arrangement does not apply to all women, but "there are a few like that. If you were to check, you would find that they don't have the means themselves to develop the plot, but there are developments going on [paid for by the men]."

These relationships may represent a long-standing tradition of *bonyatsi*, relationships between unmarried women and married men that have some social recognition but are not legal marriages. In these cases, the woman (referred to as a *nyatsi*, or concubine) has no legal status, but the man may voluntarily provide financial assistance during the relationship by building her a house or developing land she has acquired, as a form of security for her and their children in the event of their relationship terminating. The subject of small houses features regularly in the Botswana press, highlighting family conflicts that arise in relation to the distribution of resources among family members. As a matter of interest, while the women associated with these houses are often taken to task in the media for exacerbating family breakdown, almost nothing is said about the men who engage in these relationships.

Women and Land: Relationships and Intersections

Dynamic changes in social, physical, and legal processes have given rise to women's differing spatiotemporal relations to land. In the case of inheritance, a diverse set of beneficiaries inherit land through negotiated consensus among family members. Although disputes may arise,[22] for many families the process represents a voluntary exercise, free from legal intervention except with regard to the formal processes of land transfer. It demonstrates what ordinary negotiations in daily life can achieve, highlighting spaces for action that mark a shift in attitudes that not only intersect from the top down but also from the bottom up, attaining common ground in the communities in which they operate.

These intersections reflect changes in women's relationships to land that have come about through numerous factors, including enhanced education, informal- and formal-sector employment, and legal reforms. Education, employment, and legal reforms have enabled women to become more proactive in their pursuit of land, but only within the social structures of their respective resource bases, accumulated over generations, on which individuals and their families can draw. Where resources are sufficient, room for negotiation and consensual decision-making among family members is greater. However, where resources are limited, conflicts are more likely to arise.

Such conflicts embody diverging social conceptions of norms and rights in relation to land. Thus claimants in disputes may draw on competing norms in their presentation of claims over land. Where such cases arise and cannot be settled by the family, they are referred to the local kgosi or wardhead and/or KLB for adjudication. The KLB is also called on where disputes arise more generally, over contested claims to land between parties who are unrelated, as, for example, in the case of conflicts over double allocations, boundary disputes, or a transferor's legal capacity to transfer land to a third party. If these disputes cannot be settled satisfactorily by KLB, claimants have a right of appeal to the Land Tribunal and possibly to the High Court or Court of Appeal. Consequently, I turn next to law. Once again, the lens through which relationships to land is viewed alters to a focus on disputes. In dealing with conflict, I engage with the spatial and temporal dimensions of law as applied to legal arenas in the form of the Land Tribunal, High Court, and Court of Appeal. While these forums share certain characteristics in common, they also display differences that derive from their spatial and temporal configurations that, as I demonstrate in the two subsequent chapters, shape the ways in which they administer law.

Notes

1. Exceptions to this approach exist; see, for example, the work of the International Institute for Environment and Development (Cotula 2015a, 2015b, 2016).

2. See, for example, one project call issued by the UN in 2008 for a study of informal justice worldwide that I was invited to participate in repeatedly associated informal justice (including customary law) with what it referred to as deficits in the democratic process.

3. See Hellum (1998) and Griffiths (2001) who argue against this blanket assessment of customary law and who document, for example, the circumstances where polygamy under customary law operates to protect rather than disenfranchise women who would otherwise be disenfranchised under the application of a Western paradigm of law.

4. I am indebted to Phidelia Dintwe for her perseverance in tracking down land board records.

5. See Manji (2010) on the difficulties of drafting legislation to protect women's access to land in the face of opposition from commercial lenders and the problem of reconciling financial inclusion with the aim of international development to end poverty.

6. Given the state of the records, it was not possible to sample a set number from each year or to conduct a random sample from the records. Accordingly, we utilized the records that were available.

7. While information was incomplete in a number of cases, especially for the years 1999 to 2005, it was possible to identify the sex of the certificate or leaseholder from their Omang identity card. The fifth number on the identity card signifies sex: a man if it is 1, and a woman if it is 2.

8. Section 3 of the Succession (Rights of the Surviving Spouse and Inheritance Provisions) Act (Cap. 31.03).

9. Up to February 2010 for Palapye and up to May 2010 for Gaborone.

10. Court of Appeal, Civil Appeal No. 4/91 or 1992 LRC (Const) 574.

11. Civil Appeal No. 13 of 1994 [1995] (3) LRC 447.

12. See Griffiths (2010, 737–761).

13. Botswana (2003–2009, 7).

14. Ibid., 11.

15. Botswana (2006, 26).

16. Thus these independent women have been described as "can-do women," the term used by one of my male interviewees to describe his female relatives.

17. Botswana (2009a, 10).

18. Botswana (2006, 33).

19. Ibid., 31.

20. See Botswana (2007a, vii).

21. See Kalabamu (2006, 2009).

22. See *Molefi Silabo Ramentle* v. *Edith Modipane Mmusi and Others,* Court of Appeal, CACGB-101–112, where a court of five judges ruled on September 3, 2013, that the Ngwaketse customary law of inheritance does not prohibit female children from inheriting their deceased parents' intestate estate that was the family homestead.

PART III

LAW AND SPACE: NEGOTIATING LEGAL PLURALITY IN BOTSWANA

6

NEGOTIATING CONFLICT

The Handling of Disputes in the Land Tribunal

From Consensus to Conflict: Dealing with Disputes

Parts 1 and 2 have mapped the contours of varying perspectives on land, from institutional interplay between regional, national, international, and transnational actors, to local social actors' different perceptions and challenges. These varying lenses, through which relations to land are viewed, highlight the interrelationships between global and local domains and the differential consequences that these intersections may embody for the diverse range of social actors caught up in them. These configurations invariably give rise to disputes, and so I now turn to examining how conflict over land is handled within the formal apparatus of Botswana's legal system, first at the level of the Land Tribunal, and then at the level of the High Court and the Court of Appeal. These formal legal forums adjudicate on competing claims to land using the power of law to determine which claims have legitimacy and which do not. Thus they operate on an exclusionary basis, through negating one claimant's assertions of legitimacy in favor of another's with regard to access and control over land. These claims may, as Sara Berry (2002) notes, represent a broader domain of contestation, for "struggles of land in postcolonial Africa have been as much about power and the legitimacy of competing claims to authority, as about the control of property per se" (639–640).

Claimants working through the legal system as a whole may move from one forum, such as the Land Tribunal that aims to build consensus in decision-making, to another, more formal court-like process that focuses on regulating conflict through adjudication. This shift in approach raises questions about how to conceptualize justice, fairness, transparency, and efficiency that exist as somewhat abstract terms in the transnational domain, into more concrete manifestations applicable in national and local legal contexts that are constantly evolving over time. This shift is highlighted in chapter 7, where the tensions between approaches to assessing property and authority in relation to land, in terms of social processes, or alternatively, on the basis of a particular construction of "legal" facts, become abundantly clear.

The relationships that inhere in land as social space and that exercise power over it are also pertinent to the legal spaces that law inhabits. Both involve aspects of temporality that hinge on interpretations of the past. Berry (2009) demonstrates how claims to land in West Africa deploy strategies that turn on narratives of origin or ancestry because, as Christian Lund (2013) observes, "conflicts over land . . . are characterized by an intensive reference to the past as the source of unadulterated legitimacy of claims to the future" (14). The appeal to the past, however, may generate competing constructions when social and legal spaces intersect. In the case of Ghana, for example, Lund presents a characterization of the past in terms of tradition "as a timeless past, a reservoir of 'how things have always been done' in the constant flow of time" (14). A number of African countries, including Botswana, have deployed this characterization of time in challenging what they perceive to be European or Western representations of their law and culture.[1] However, an alternative interpretation acknowledges the role of "significant historical events, of transactions that are involved in various vindications" (14). These interpretations are different from one another because the former "justifies claims to the future as a seamless construction of the past," while the other "justifies them as the result of salient fortunate events" (14). How the past is invoked in relation to land (viewed as property in legal contexts) depends on how property is perceived. These differing conceptions of property relations with regard to land provide for legal contestation based on space, where one group of actors lays claim to property on the basis of *social* space, which perceives time as an enduring, traditional past, while the other lays claim on the basis of *legal* space, which perceives time as an evolving, linear past. In this process, as Franz von Benda-Beckmann and Keebet von Benda-Beckmann (2014) have observed, temporality plays a key role, for not only must a decision be made in accordance with the dominant ideas about the relationship among the legal property regimes *at the time it is taken* but also according to ideas about what this relationship entailed that prevailed when *past* decisions were made. Thus the way in

Figure 6.1. Land Tribunal, Gaborone. *Photo courtesy of Stefannutti Stocks.*

which law sets property relations into time not only facilitates or constrains social actors in their pursuit of property claims but also has an effect on the "temporal strategies" that they pursue (20). The role of temporality is very much in evidence in the case law discussed in chapter 7.

In elaborating on the working of the Land Tribunal (see fig. 6.1), I draw on materials derived from archival research, Tribunal records, and, in particular, on participant observation of disputes at the Land Tribunal in both Gaborone and Palapye, as well as on extensive discussions and interviews with Land Tribunal personnel in 2010 and 2015. These sources have enabled me to acquire a dynamic picture of the Land Tribunal in action and to develop a more informed understanding of the ways in which the Tribunal's institutional structure both facilitates and impedes the work of its staff through the spatial dimensions of power that shape its operations.

Space as Legal Domain and Territory in the Land Tribunal

Within the formal legal system of Botswana, the Land Tribunal was introduced in 1995 to handle disputes that could not be settled by the land boards and that had previously been referred to the Minister of the former Ministry of Local Government and Lands.[2]

According to members of the Land Tribunal in Gaborone, the Tribunal was created because appeals to the Minister proved unsatisfactory for three primary reasons.[3] First, appeals took a long time to be heard because they had to be scheduled around the Minister's other duties, leading to a substantial backlog resulting in great dissatisfaction among appellants. The appellants' complaints were corroborated by government's own comments in the National Development Plan (NDP9) that the introduction of the Land Tribunal "was meant to address the problem of lengthy procedure for processing of appeals plus the increasing number of appeals resulting in long delays."[4] Second, the Minister was not the best-placed person to handle these appeals, as ministerial appointments are political, and the incumbent does not necessarily have expertise in land law and management. Third, the establishment of a Land Tribunal helped to bring about the impartiality and openness that the Final Report of Review of Botswana National Land Policy in 2002 stressed was necessary. It noted at the time that principles of "openness, fairness and impartiality will be met by open hearings before an impartial body which gives reasoned and published decisions rather than no hearings or closed hearings before officials acting on behalf of the Minister"[5] (Botswana 2003, para. 92). Over time, the steady backlog of cases and appeals led to the Tribunal's eventual expansion to include four branches with a headquarters in the capital city, Gaborone, and with divisions between branches being administrative (as opposed to jurisdictional), so that any branch can hear cases from any part of the country.[6] In addition, provision was made for a new Chief Land Tribunal President to oversee the administration and workload of all branches of the Tribunal.[7] Thus the Tribunal has come to represent a legal domain that encompasses national, district, and local arenas within a national framework of governance over land. Its territory and sphere of control form part of an infrastructure that acts as a bridge uniting the administrative determinations of land boards and the application of customary law with a more internationally or globally oriented type of legal proceedings that adopts a particular form of legal regulation at work in Europe and elsewhere, and which is applied by the High Court and the Court of Appeal in Botswana.

Constitution and Role of Land Tribunal

In creating the Land Tribunal, the government envisaged a body that would be easily accessible to the public. Such accessibility necessitated that appellants not be required to have formal legal representation or to pay high fees to use its services. The Tribunal was also intended to function in such a way that members of the public could understand its rules and procedures. To this end, the Tribunal was empowered to regulate its own procedure and frequency of meetings, with express acknowledgment that the Tribunal "should not be bound by the rules of evidence or procedure applicable in civil or criminal proceedings."[8] This leeway in creating the rules for its regulation extended to the recognition that the Tribunal "may disregard any technical irregularity which does not, and is not likely to, result in a miscarriage of justice."[9] Thus the Government of Botswana's website (http://www.gov.bw), setting out conditions of access to the Land Tribunal, notes that "while the decisions made by the Tribunal are final and legally binding, the process has been designed to be less formal and easier to access than the general court system."[10] The success of this design is acknowledged in the 2002 review of the Botswana National Land Policy where reviewers observed, "the Tribunal has been a universally welcomed development."[11] Reviewers attributed the success to the fact that the Tribunal "combined openness, fairness, impartiality, economy and informality. Insofar as there is any problem with the Tribunal, it is that it has difficulty in keeping up with its caseload."[12] The Land Tribunal's caseload has expanded considerably from 394 cases over twenty-five years (from 1971 to 1996), to 3,723 cases over thirteen years (from 1997 to 2010).[13]

The informal organization of the Land Tribunal allows for a more open-ended conception of law that lives comfortably within social space, in contrast to the more regulated legal space that operates in the High Court and the Court of Appeal. Thus its approach to law is more in line with that associated with the strong form of legal pluralism referred to in chapter 3, where a greater scope exists for hearing a wider range of arguments in support of claims made by the appellants appearing before it. This approach is in contrast to the more juristic or weak form of legal pluralism that is at work in the High Court and the Court of Appeal, where very clear restrictions determine what can and cannot be admitted in court. Yet, despite its greater scope, the Land Tribunal cannot do as it pleases; it is subject to regulation. Before turning to how the Tribunal operates on a day-to-day basis, I briefly discuss the appointment of tribunal members and the appeals process.

Appointment of Tribunal Members and Appeals Process

The Land Tribunal consists of three members with a President at its head, and appointments to the post are made by the Ministry through an open application process. The President must have a law degree, have been in the legal profession for not less than ten years standing[14] (formerly five years),[15] and have been working in public service. The two members who serve under the President are usually people who have been in public service for some time and qualified in a land-related profession such as estate management, surveying, agriculture, or land administration. In January 2010, two forums were holding sessions in the Land Tribunal Gaborone, the main Tribunal and the ad hoc Tribunal (the latter set up to resolve the backlog of cases); and two other forums were sitting in Palapye, the main Tribunal and the ad hoc Tribunal.[16] The members came from different backgrounds, including a planner, an estate agent, a geography teacher, and a land-use officer. The President of the main Tribunal in Palapye, Mr. Nare, had been a magistrate overseeing criminal, traffic, and maintenance cases for twelve years before he joined the Tribunal. Members of the Tribunal work under contracts that are governed by provisions in the Public Service Act (No. 30 of 2008) (Cap. 26:01).[17] These contracts provide for an initial appointment of three years and can be renewed every two years up to a limit of nine years.

These appointed officials, both with and without backgrounds in law, hear citizens' appeals. Appeals to the Land Tribunal can be brought by any person disputing a decision made by a land board, as well as by land boards themselves for enforcement of their decisions (often dealing with the eviction of squatters).

Phase One: PreTribunal Hearing

The appellant must draw up a Notice and Grounds of Appeal, which may be in letter form and which must be written in one of the two official languages of Botswana: Setswana or English. Three copies of this document, together with the necessary supporting documentation and the registration appeal fee of BWP 10 (about USD 1.00) must be lodged with the Registrar of the Land Tribunal at Gaborone, Palapye, and also now Maun, or Francistown. The minimal fee makes the Tribunal accessible to most appellants. This action must be taken within one month from the date on which the appellant first became aware of the decision of the main land board, planning authority, or Minister.[18] The appeal is registered when the registration fee is paid, after which the Tribunal then writes a letter to the appellant stating that s/he is free to get a lawyer or friend to support the case, and also to call witnesses, but it does not give a specific date for the hearing. All parties who have been cited in the appeal must be served with a copy of the appeal documents. The Tribunal then writes a letter to respondents asking them to respond to the appeal.

Next, it is the duty of the Land Tribunal to file the documents and put the case on the Tribunal's roll, issuing a notice that provides a date for the hearing. A critical criterion is that the Land Tribunal can only hear appeals where a land board has written a resolution giving reasons for its decision.[19] This requirement has proved to be a major hurdle, especially in cases associated with a land board's backlog of cases that has caused further delays in issuing decisions despite constant requests and orders for such documentation by appellants and the Land Tribunal. Since the Land Tribunal has no jurisdiction to reach a decision on the case or to make a judgment on the allocation or transfer of land in place of the land board, appellants are without recourse until the land board provides sufficient documentation. In many of the cases observed during the course of this study, the matter had been going on for years with the cases going back and forth between the land board and the Land Tribunal, a state of affairs that caused a great deal of resentment among appellants and tribunal members. An example is provided by Eva Aaron's case. My research assistant Phidelia and I first met Eva Aaron at the main Land Tribunal in Gaborone in November 2009.[20] She had been in dispute with Kweneng Land Board (KLB) since 1994, and after the Land Tribunal hearing in 2009, she had three more hearings at KLB in 2009 and 2010, followed by a subsequent case before the Land Tribunal before she was finally issued a land certificate in 2011.[21]

Phase Two: Tribunal Hearing[22]

On the set date, all parties appear before the Tribunal. They mingle quite freely in the Tribunal hearing room, where the atmosphere is generally informal before proceedings begin. In some cases, this gathering provides the opportunity for parties to reach an amicable agreement without proceedings having to take place.[23] Proceedings are normally in English but can take place in Setswana if parties have difficulty understanding English. Indeed, during the hearings, the parties often switch between a combination of English and Setswana, giving rise to a form of what I call "Setslish." While the Tribunal sit on a raised platform (like a court), every attempt is made to ensure that parties feel free to speak unhindered by the formal requirements of a court, and for those who cannot speak English, an inter-preter is provided. In practice, the court clerk often undertakes this task.[24]

When the Tribunal President (TP) and members enter the room, all who are present stand up. The clerk of court then calls the case and presents the files to the tribunal members. Proceedings then follow a script similar to the one included below (LT 103/2006).

TP: Are the parties here?

SERWALO I. VALASHIA: Yes my Lord, I am Serwalo Ivy Valashia.

TP: Are the other appellants here?

SERWALO I. VALASHIA: I am representing them, my Lord.

TP: Are the respondents present?

MR. BOTLHOKO: Present. my Lord. I am David Botlhoko, chair of Kweneng Land Board assisted by Mr. Oduetse Lekoko, principal land surveyor of the same institution.

TP: Are the parties ready to proceed?

Although this exchange follows a more formal legal tradition, the ap-pellant or appellants then present their case for appeal in a much less formal way. This presentation may be done in person or through legal represen-tation. In the seventeen cases that Phidelia and I observed at the ad hoc Land Tribunal in Gaborone, only five involved appellants who were legally represented, and out of these, three involved borehole syndicates.[25] In in-terviews with personnel, we were told that appellants are informed before they come to the Tribunal that they can bring a lawyer or a friend to assist; however, "not many appellants bring lawyers [compared with] land boards [who] have lawyers to represent them."[26]

Before appellants begin to testify, the Tribunal asks if they want to do so under oath or not. The advantage of taking the oath is that an appellant's testimony is given greater weight than it would otherwise carry, and also the appellant has the right to cross-examine the respondent or respondents and their witnesses. If they are not under oath, they cannot cross-examine, although they can do so indirectly by posing questions to the presiding panel. After the appellant has presented his or her case, the respondents are asked to present their arguments together with the testimony of any witnesses they may have. The Tribunal also asks whether they wish to do so under oath. During the process, proceedings may be adjourned for a period to see if parties can reach an amicable settlement. However, where parties fail to resolve their disagreements, the Tribunal will resume the hearing. Tribunal members seek to assist appellants by making sure they understand what is happening. For example, in case LT 23/2003, the appellant was a seventy-two-year-old female farmer who had difficulty reading written documents, including a sketch plan that her lawyer had provided her. In this case, the Tribunal President intervened to say, "Mr. Bakhuma, I think the appellant does not understand," leading her lawyer to move on to a simpler line of questioning.

In this process, difficulties often arise, especially in ad hoc cases, because of the long-standing nature of the dispute that has taken place over many years and for which little or no information and documentation is available. In some cases, the Tribunal must deal with the appellant's lack of knowledge of Tribunal procedures, as well as the land board's ongoing failure over a number of years to provide the necessary documentation. This creates problems for current land board members who are often asked to speak to the handling of disputes that began long before they took office and for which no adequate written information exists regarding what took place. An example is provided by an excerpt from case LT 176/2003, which involved an appellant representing himself in his application for the setting aside of a judgment made in KLB's favor. In making his case, the appellant explains,

App: I applied because at the time the case was on I was ill, and that is why I have applied for this rescission.

TP: You just mentioned you were ill. Do you have any supporting documents [to prove this].

App: No. I was ill. I had flu. I did not go to the Post Office [where a letter calling him to a hearing was waiting for collection]. I found slips but no letters as they had been returned to your office.

[*TP explains to App that he needs to come up with a good explanation for his absence (i.e., that he needs to back up his story).*]

App: Yes, your honor . . . after I was informed of the rescission, I wrote a letter to the Land Tribunal saying I could not attend.

TP: What happened after you received the slips?

App: I went to the Post Office but the letters were not there. I had the slips.

TP: So what action did you take? I believe from the slip you could see that it was from my office?

App: I then got a letter saying that a decision had been taken in my absence. I wrote a letter to the Land Tribunal saying that I was not able to come because of illness.

TP: In terms of the matter, do you have a strong case?

App: Yes, madam.

TP: Why do you say so? You do not seem to have a strong reason for your default, so we need to explain this.

App: This case has been dragging on for a very long time, since 2001.

TP: What is the basis of your claim? Why do you have a strong case against the land board? I am not getting a satisfactory answer from you. We need to probe further to see if we can grant the rescission.

App: I would say. . . .

TP: You don't need to go into details.

App: I have been trying to talk with the land board, but they are not willing to do that, and that is why I have to come here.

TP: You are not coming up with issues [i.e., with a good explanation].

[*KLB is called on to respond, and the Chair responds.*]

KLB Chair: The appellant has not come up with any convincing reason why he failed to turn up. The second point, my lord, is about the allocation made by the sub–land board. It had no authority to allocate a commercial plot.

TP: But sub–land board should not have written to him [allocating plot].

KLB Chair: Section 5 [of the TLA] [It is in fact Section 20(2) of TLA that] states, "No Land Board or subordinate Land Board shall grant any land under this Part for trading, manufacturing or other business or commercial purposes." This provision invalidates his claim. [*Chair says matter should have been referred to the main land board for a decision.*]

TP: But the problem lies with your [the land board's] process. The appellant was told he was allocated land by the sub–land board. The letter is written by [one of your] officers. Don't you think you need to determine [look into] this?

KLB Chair: Be that as it may. We would like these matters to be resolved.

Ironically, it appeared that the Chair, who had moments earlier been pressing for the case to be resolved, had been given the wrong file, and therefore did not have the necessary documentation to facilitate such resolution. Indeed, to complicate matters, the sketch map drawn by the technical office was useless as the plot sketched did not have dimensions on it. Given this situation, all the Chair could do was to say, "I apologize," to the Tribunal.

Under these circumstances, the Tribunal President suggested that the case should be remitted back to KLB for a decision. This step was necessary because the sub–land board was not legally empowered to make an allocation. The appellant was very unhappy with this decision:

APP: This business of going back to the plot has cost me so much time. When I wrote to the Land Tribunal I was asked to go and get personnel from the Land Board to see the development. We are going there for the third time . . . they don't keep records, the personnel keep changing. [*He is aggrieved that their records are not in orde*r.]

TP: If they don't grant [your application], you can appeal the decision. The court orders as follows: The respondent's resolution contained in the Minutes of February 2, 2003, are hereby set aside, and this matter is remitted to the land board to reconsider the case and make a decision within a month. The respondent is asked to consider all matters including the principles of natural justice.

Phase Three: Disposal, Judgments, and Appeal

Once the Tribunal has heard all the parties, the matter is reserved for judgment. However, in cases like the one just presented, there was generally a short adjournment for the Tribunal to discuss the matter, and then the Tribunal president rendered its judgment there and then. All parties subsequently stand as the Tribunal members exit the hearing. Where a case is remitted, the appellant is informed that if dissatisfied with the land board's decision, s/he can appeal to the Land Tribunal. An appellant can also appeal to the High Court on a question of law, where s/he can represent herself or himself, in contrast with the land board, that must as a statutory body be legally represented.[27] The High Court has power to remit the appeal back to the Tribunal (as the Tribunal did with respect to the land board).[28] However, appellants may also appeal from the High Court to the Court of Appeal within six weeks of the High Court's judgment.[29]

Tribunal Members' Perceptions of Their Work and Challenges

A major problem that tribunal members highlighted is their challenges in dealing with land boards because "they don't have the right attitude. They just appear and are unprepared." All tribunal members agree that this challenge arises because accessing minutes with written resolutions, which are crucial to their jurisdiction, "poses a real problem." The tribunal members are not unsympathetic to the problems faced by the Chair of KLB, but they consider that these difficulties should have been dealt with by now, as "land boards have had plenty of time to get their act together. They have been established since 1970." They recognize that many of the problems derive from "human resources and how they [i.e., the persons running the human resources department] operate at land boards," but observe that "where there are problems," the Chair "should take the matter to the Minister or to the Office of the President. He should not just go on making excuses for the situation." Although they acknowledge that "the Land Tribunal is the first to admit it is not the best in record keeping," at least "the public can access our files."

Many problems also arise, in the opinion of tribunal members, because land boards lack respect for the Land Tribunal. One member noted, "When they appear before the High Court they have everything—the files, the records, etc."[30] However, land boards do not prepare for appearing before the Land Tribunal because "to them [the land board] this is not a court. They don't respect us like a court." Tribunal members attribute this attitude to the structure within which the Tribunal operates, where land boards and the Tribunal fall under the authority of the Ministry of Lands and Housing that oversees them. In their opinion, this arrangement leads to land boards viewing the Tribunal as being on the "same footing as themselves," and as such they "see appearing before the Land Tribunal as being in the nature of another meeting where they can make excuses about not having files or records or about being late for court because of the traffic. This is not acceptable."

In the view of tribunal members, "This attitude brings the Land Tribunal into disrepute" because "the land boards' incompetence rubs off on us." As a result, tribunal members report that public confidence in the Tribunal has been eroded. Members report that "appellants say openly in court, 'This is a very terrible land board.' Then the Chair of the land board will say, 'Yet again, we are sorry but we don't have the minutes,' and the appellant will say to the Tribunal, 'See, I told you.'"

The tribunal members consider that land boards need to be included with the Tribunal's education program because "land boards have given customers a lot of bad advice, for example, telling people to apply to the

Land Tribunal when they have not in fact reached a decision so that an appeal is not competent." These concerns make the Tribunal feel that there is a need to "take drastic action [in relation to land boards] but we can't, we are powerless." All they could do in 2009–2010 was to fine parties who failed to carry out their orders.[31] An attempt was made to imprison land board officials for contempt of court, but this action was held to be incompetent by the High Court. In 2010, the Tribunal observed, "We have asked for powers to enforce our decisions," reasoning that "we should have full powers of contempt, including the power to send people to jail in order to maintain our integrity as an institution." Such powers have since been granted, in the new Tribunal Act 2014, so that the Tribunal now has powers not only to fine but also to imprison those who fail to attend proceedings after having been subpoenaed, or who are in contempt, although they view this remedy as a last resort.[32] The 2014 Act has also extended the Tribunal's jurisdiction, so that it is no longer restricted to customary land matters, but can now cover state and freehold tenure with planning matters and surveying.[33]

In 2010, tribunal members forcefully argued that the Land Tribunal should be "treated as being part of the judiciary," with "Tribunal Presidents being appointed by the Judicial Services Commission or by the President as is the case with the Industrial Court." Tribunal members take this view because they feel that their association with the ministry "means there is no separation of powers." In this view, the Tribunal forms part of the executive in its administrative capacity. As a result, the public view the Tribunal "as being an extension of land boards." To rectify this situation, tribunal members feel they need to form part of an independent institution set up by an Act of Parliament. An independent institution sanctioned by Parliament, would, in the view of the tribunal members, be akin to having "branches like the High Court, enabling us to reach out to the people." They also observed that having a Tribunal in Gaborone is not sufficient "because it is a long way for people to come and it is expensive." In order to take services to the people, "We should always be traveling around. We need to be in the field." The Tribunal does travel, but in 2010 it could not do so as much as it would have liked because of a restricted budget from the ministry over which it had no control.

Tribunal members viewed a lack of resources as curtailing their ability to do their jobs "more effectively," particularly [with regard to] legal resources. In 2010, members had to resort to using the law library at the University of Botswana to do research. This practice was inconvenient because they could only do this when they could find time to go there. They also mentioned the problem of retaining personnel, such as registrars, who are hard to keep "because the salary is not attractive due to low grading." Therefore, they "can't keep people in post as these are the kind of people who are active in the market." It remains to be seen whether the requirement of a law degree for a registrar will lead to better remuneration and retention of staff.[34]

Part of the problem of the Land Tribunal remaining within the ministry is that Tribunal Presidents are viewed as administrators, which conflicts with their role as judges. This conflict arises because "if you are the head of a Tribunal, you are an administrator, and the ministry takes the view that we are administrators like anyone else. But we do the core business of adjudication. Elsewhere, administrators just sit in the office and are available for meetings, but here [at the Land Tribunal] the core business of adjudication is affected because every time the President of the Tribunal has to attend a meeting s/he can't hear cases. As a result, the public suffers. We want to be able to be able to focus on hearing cases." They maintain that if they were autonomous, they would like their structure to follow that of the Industrial Court: "There would be a director who deals with administration," which would "enable the judges to deal with cases." Over the years, tribunal members have repeatedly submitted requests to the Ministry to make it an independent body, but these attempts have come to nothing. In tribunal members' views, the Ministry is concerned that autonomy "will lead to more lawyers having control over the Tribunal, and [thus] give rise to more legal technicalities and sophistry." In the tribunal members' opinion, this view is unfounded, for as one Tribunal President observed, "Over all the years, we have been operating, no one has yet complained that we are too technical."

Spatializing Law: Its Plural Dimensions

These debates have resonance with KLB's observations on the complex dimensions of spatializing power. However, what I would like to emphasize here is the extent to which the tenor of proceedings in the Tribunal follows that of the customary system in general (Griffiths 1990–1991, 223; 1997). As Ornulf Gulbrandsen (2012) has observed in another context, the values of consensus "have been appropriated in the governing apparatus of the Botswana nation-state" (xi). Thus, while there are formal legal requirements that the Land Tribunal must observe, they are embedded within an approach to dispute processing that is geared toward getting parties to reach consensus (as discussions in dikgotla in chapter 5 illustrate), rather than honing in on findings of fact that are used to uphold one legal argument over another. The latter approach is more commonly associated with a Western legal model based on adversarial proceedings that, although the product of a particular historical convergence, has come to have a global outreach in its deployment in countries across the globe. This ethnocentric model creates winners and losers and operates within a highly regulated, hierarchical legal framework.[35] It is one that represents a juridical or weak form of legal pluralism, which characterizes a lawyer's view of law embodied in the High Court or the Court of Appeal. Rather than following this approach, the Tribunal allows parties to air their grievances without concern for technical legal rules that involve, for example, the exclusion of hearsay evidence.[36] In allowing oral argument and disputation, the focus in the Land Tribunal is on all aspects of the dispute and how these may be dealt with to the satisfaction of the disputing parties. While this striving for consensus is not always achieved, and in those cases, adjudication comes into play, nonetheless every effort is made by the Tribunal to encourage the parties to reach an accommodation. Its approach to conflict is one that is deeply embedded in Tswana culture. Thus, it stands in marked contrast to the form of proceedings that takes place in the High Court and the Court of Appeal, to which I turn in the next chapter. In these forums, another approach to legality is upheld, one that is spatialized in terms of limiting legal discussion to a very technical set of legal issues that must be addressed in a particular manner. As a result, the legal spaces within which land is debated and adjudicated in the both the Land Tribunal and the courts represent a form of pluralism that not only allows for alternative perceptions of law but that also acknowledges the complex intersections between them.

As noted earlier, while the Land Tribunal has greater leeway in its legal approach to dispute resolution, it nonetheless finds that its freedom of action is curtailed through the organizational framework in which it must operate. Because both the Tribunal and the land boards are under the overarching control of the Ministry of Lands and Housing, they are placed on the same institutional footing. So, although the Tribunal has power to adjudicate appeals from land boards, it perceives itself as being on the same horizontal plane in relation to land boards and their decision-making powers. As a consequence, others view the Tribunal's legal role as just an extension of the administrative power exercised by land boards. The result, according to tribunal members, is that its legal role has become conflated with administration, and this conflation has had an impact on the way in which they can carry out their duties. In arguing for greater autonomy, tribunal members are seeking a different spatial configuration for the Tribunal, one that would place it firmly within a judicial setting, aligning it with courts and the independent functions they embody, rather than remaining within the purview of the MLH. The structure that the members envision is one that would acknowledge a complete separation of powers, with the Tribunal operating as an independent entity with power to control what takes place within its jurisdiction. This proposed change would provide the Tribunal with more authority, but in its efforts to gain authority on par with the High Court and the Court of Appeal, the Tribunal risks losing its more open-ended approach to law. It risks becoming more specialist in nature, with all the consequences that that specialization entails, which I explore in the next chapter.

Notes

1. Scholars have drawn attention to the different ways in which culture and its association with customary law have been deployed in an African context: either on the part of some feminists who, as Fareda Banda (2004) argues, challenge the universalism of human rights on the basis that it represents an idealized, northern male perspective on rights that is ethnocentric; or, as Martin Chanock (2002) observes, on the part of self-interested male elites from the South, who refer to the past as a means of promoting African culture as being inimical to a rights-based discourse of the North, centered on the individual.

2. The Tribal Land (Establishment of Land Tribunals) Order No. 59 of 1995 was enacted under powers contained in Sections 14 and 27(2) of the Tribal Land Act as amended by Section 40 of the Tribal Land (Amendment) Act of 1993.

3. Interviews were held on October 12, 2009, January 13, 2010, June 14, 2010, and July 14, 2015, with the following personnel: Mr. Baruti, President, Main Tribunal, Gaborone (who left to go to the High Court and who has been replaced by Mrs. S. Kaisara [formerly Ms. S. Chuma]); Ms. S. Chuma, President, Ad Hoc Tribunal, Gaborone; Ms. Moremong, Registrar; Mr. Motlogelwa and Mr. Manase, Principal Clerk of Court; Mr. K. Rutherford, Mr. S. Rapinyana, and Mr. G. Tobedza, colleagues, all at the LT Garborone; as well as with Mr. Nare, president, Main Tribunal, Palapye, and Mr. Mareng, Acting Registrar, Palapye.

4. For NDP9, 17.10 at 333, see Botswana (2003/04–2008/09).

5. While these comments were made with regard to extending the remit and jurisdiction of the established Land Tribunal, they are also applicable to the need to bring the Land Tribunal into existence in the first place.

6. This expansion was effected under Section 4 of the Land Tribunal Act (LTA) 2014, which received assent on January 23, 2014.

7. Section 4(1) of the 1914 Act.

8. Under the Tribal Land Order No. 59 of 1995, para. 6(1), and also under Section 8(5) of the 2014 Act.

9. 1995 Order, para. 6(3), and Section 8(1)(c) of the 2014 Act.

10. Website last accessed July 31, 2016; dead link.

11. Botswana (2002a, para. 840).

12. Ibid.

13. These cases were compiled by Phidelia and myself from a number of sources, including registers from the Ministry of Local Government and Lands (the MLH in 2010), individual registers for the twelve land boards, as well as the Consolidated Land Tribunal Register that came into effect in 2005. For details, refer to the appendix.

14. Section 4(2) of the 2014 Act.

15. 1995 Order, para. 3(1)(a).

16. The ad hoc Tribunals dealing with the backlog of cases have subsequently been disbanded.

17. The Public Service Act is a direct result of the ratification of three International Labor Organization (ILO) Conventions by the Government of Botswana in 1997.

18. This period was originally four months under the 1995 Order, para. 4(2).

19. Section 7(1) of the TLA states that "subject to the provisions of this Act and to any regulation made under the provisions of section 37, a land board may regulate its own procedure: provided that no grant of land shall be of any effect unless the land board by resolution approves such grant and a record of the substance of such resolution is recorded in the minutes of the meeting at which the resolution was passed."

20. LT 67/2008.

21. This information was acquired from personal interviews with Eva Aaron in 2010 and 2015.

22. All transcripts quoted in this section are taken from proceedings that Phidelia and I attended at the Land Tribunal.

23. LT 6/2005.

24. LT 6/2005 and LT 52/2008.

25. The other two cases involved female appellants, one of whom was involved in an agricultural dispute and the other who was appealing against KLB's refusal to regularize her plot. As the appellant was subject to an eviction order, the case was dismissed from the Land Tribunal because it involved criminal proceedings.

26. Only six of the cases we attended actually involved legal representation for land boards, However, the other eleven cases featured KLB, and lawyers may well not have been present because, as discussion of the cases will show, the land board did not have the correct files, minutes, or resolutions or the necessary sketch plans, and so the case could not proceed. When we began our research at the Land Tribunal, KLB retained the firm of Monthe Marumo and Company to handle all their cases. However, during the research period there was a shift toward attempting to deal with legal issues by using an in-house lawyer; nevertheless, in important cases the board still resorted to private attorneys.

27. Section 5(11) of the 1995 Order.

28. See LT 23/2003.

29. As with the Land Tribunal, the appellant must file the Notice and Grounds of Appeal with the Registrar of the Court of Appeal. The costs of this involve BWP 6 for leave for application and BWP 15 for the appeal fee.

30. From High Court records, one can see that preparedness is not always the case.

31. Under the 1995 Order, paras. 6(10A) and (10B).

32. Under Section 9(3) of the 2014 Act.

33. This recommendation was made by the consulting team who drafted the Final Report of the Botswana National Land Policy for the purpose of promoting "efficiency" and "administrative justice" (Botswana 2003b, p. 27, para. 93).

34. Section 20(1) of the 2014 Act.

35. Because of this Western legal model, Simon A. Roberts (1979), in his classic book *Order and Dispute*, declined to use the term *law* for the reasons set out in his discussion of how societies regulate themselves across the world; see his chapter entitled "Why Not Law?"

36. Hearsay evidence is oral testimony that has its roots in a statement made by a person who is not present in court. It is hearsay because the person who makes the statement in court is relying on the testimony of someone who is absent from court and therefore not available for cross-examination. Therefore, there is no independent verification for the veracity of what is being said.

7

CONSTRUCTING LEGALITY IN THE HIGH
COURT AND THE COURT OF APPEAL

W HERE LAND DISPUTES CANNOT BE SETTLED BY AGREEMENT or adjudication by land boards, Tribal Authorities, or the Land Tribunal, they
proceed through legal system to the High Court, and in some cases, on to
the Court of Appeal (see fig. 7.1). This process brings them into a more formal legal regulatory framework that shapes the spatiotemporal domain in
which they are heard. Disputes may progress straight from the land board
to the High Court (who may remit the case back to the Land Tribunal for
adjudication), whereas appeals from the Land Tribunal can only proceed
to the High Court on a point of law. This requirement considerably limits
the scope for legal argument in the court and narrows the focus for discussion. Unlike argumentation in the Land Tribunal—which has a substantial
degree of latitude owing to its lack of restrictions on rules of evidence and
procedure of the type that apply in ordinary civil and criminal courts—
when a case goes before the High Court, it must proceed on the basis of
written legal pleadings put before it. However, at the Court of Appeal level,
the facts of the case are not open to discussion or reinterpretation—it is
only the interpretation of the law[1] applied to them that can be challenged
in this arena.[2]

Thus claims to land must be articulated within a particular organizational form that shapes legal space. This space, which involves contestation around social actors' relations with land and the ways in which these
must be presented in a legal forum, reflects a temporal dimension that is
predicated on a linear understanding of time. This linear form is one that
engages "with its continual juxtaposition of equivalent intervals" (Greenhouse 1998, 1637). These set periods of time determine how a case must proceed at each stage of its presentation within a hierarchical court structure.

Figure 7.1. Court of Appeal and High Court complex, Gaborone. *Photo courtesy of the Government of Botswana and Wanderingscot (wanderingscot.com).*

Thus, they operate in a *time-space* dimension in structuring the routines of the court's everyday life.

What this dimension means for litigants and how their claims are processed will be examined through case law that involves statutory interpretation of the Tribal Land Act (Cap. 32.02). Thus the focus of this chapter revolves almost exclusively around an analysis of written texts.[3] Particular attention will be given to Section 10, which delineates land boards' powers with respect to land in their tribal areas. This section has given rise to a number of questions about the nature of rights under customary land tenure and their relationship with other laws that has provided the impetus for land reform embodied within Botswana's current National Land Policy.[4]

Such an investigation reveals how varying notions of social space structure claims to land, resulting in differing forms of entitlement. These, in turn, give rise to competing projections of what constitutes legitimate control over land. Such projections involve reconstructing logics from the past to fit present and future interests that, from a Western perspective on law, must fit into a seamless, ongoing, linear temporality that results in a form of timelessness or what Carol Greenhouse (1998, 1650) has referred to as an "all-time" perspective. This temporal viewpoint forms part of what Peter Fitzpatrick (1992) has termed "the mythology of modern law." In this process, contestation between distinctive temporal logics may arise when conceptions from different legal systems with distinct perspectives of time and space become embedded in one and the same property, giving rise to countervailing claims over it. As becomes evident from the case law, these logics have become crystallized around concepts of communal and individual property rights.

Historical Context of Land Rights in Botswana

As earlier discussions have highlighted, the Tribal Land Act attempted to redesign established customary land tenure by transferring powers held by dikgosi over land (in precolonial and colonial times) to land boards in the following provision: "All the rights and title to land in each tribal area . . . shall vest in the Land Board . . . in trust for the benefit and advantage of the tribesmen of that area and for the purpose of promoting the economic and social development of all the peoples of Botswana."[5] The relevant powers transferred included the following:

a. the granting of rights to use any land;
b. the cancellation of any grant, including a grant made prior to the coming into operation of this Act;
c. the hearing of appeals from, confirming, or setting aside any decision of any subordinate land authority;
d. the imposition of restrictions on the use of tribal land.

This transfer raises the question, however, of what was the nature of these land rights?

The nature of rights attached to customary land tenure historically were not homogenous, but rather depended on the purpose for which the land was allocated and the productive use to which it was put. Its status as residential (*lolwapa*), agricultural (*tshimo*), or grazing land (*moraka*) had an impact on the rights that accrued under it (Botswana 1992a, 2–7). Although customary law did recognize individual rights to residential land as exclusive, permanent, and inheritable, this concept of rights was not as applicable to agricultural land, for once cultivated land was harvested, it reverted to the status of grazing land to which all members of the morafe had communal rights (5). Thus rights were acquired and divested according to a cyclical nature of time that coincided with agricultural practices over the seasons. This approach to rights—which marks a continual motion between rights accorded to a particular household or family and those rights associated with communal grazing vested in the morafe as a whole—is predicated on a particular spatiotemporal composition. This approach to rights differs radically from those rights whose existence depends on a more exclusive and linear form of transmission.

In recognizing the variegated nature of these rights under customary tenure, the government noted the difficulty in "finding the correct pigeon hole of its [customary land tenure] concepts" (Botswana 1992a, 5). Indeed, it expressly warned against subjecting "the content of the customary land tenure to common law analysis and therefore supplanting the system from its natural setting" (6).[6] Although it noted that "comparisons are legitimate," it also stressed that "the absence of . . . private ownership in the customary land tenure does not imply insecurity of tenure." The government also warned against simply characterizing rights under the system of customary land tenure as communal because the system does recognize that "private rights exist in residential and arable land," although "the concept of individual ownership as understood in the common law [of Botswana] has no parallel in customary land tenure" (6).

Land Rights: Intersection and Conflict

Contemporary competition for access to land where people wish to live and work has created a market in land over time. This competition has led to conflicts about the nature of rights conferred on those operating under customary land tenure that have been hotly contested in the courts, especially in peri-urban areas such as Mogoditshane in Kweneng District. Because of Mogoditshane's location, right next to the capital city, people have been flocking there for many years to seek employment but have had problems finding somewhere to live. Local people who had access to plow fields in the area saw an opportunity to capitalize on this need by transferring or subdividing their fields and selling the subdivisions to those who wanted to convert them into residential property. Given that this land formed part of Bakwena Tribal Territory, it was under the control of Kweneng Land Board (KLB), who should have been overseeing and controlling its allocation, transfers, and any authorizations required for change of use.

Unfortunately, the land board was very slow to act, and when it did act, local people perceived it as being biased (if not corrupt)[7] in its decision making, as the board seemed to favor some applicants well ahead of others who had been on a waiting list for years.[8] As a result, local people took matters into their own hands, exercising what the 1992 government report refers to as "traditional ingenuity" in employing their own methods of transferring and selling land (Botswana 1992a, 16).

Such activities gave rise to questions about the status of such land and the rights attached to it. The case that projected the interpretation of these rights into the limelight was *Kweneng Land Board v. Matlho and Another.*[9] In this case Pheto Motlhabane sold a piece of land that he had acquired in Mogoditshane through inheritance from his forefathers for BWP 1,500 to Mr. Matlho. Mr. Motlhabane had been in possession of this land since 1960, before the introduction of the TLA. The sale was by verbal agreement and Mr. Matlho, after making a partial payment of BWP 500, took occupation of the land and began building a house whose construction had cost BWP 15,000 by the time the case went to court. The land in question was located in Bakwena Tribal Territory in Kweneng District. KLB sought an order from the High Court restraining Mr. Matlho from occupying that land, arguing that it had been unlawfully acquired from Mr. Motlhabane. KLB argued that as ownership of tribal land was vested in the land board under Section 10(1), Mr. Matlho had no right to acquire, develop, or occupy the land without a certificate issued by the board. Mr. Motlhabane, however, argued that as the land had been in his possession before the introduction of the TLA, the terms of Section 10(2), which stated "nothing in this section [that is Section 10(1)] shall have the effect of vesting in a Land Board any land or right to water held by any person in his personal and private capacity" applied to him. The Attorney General, who appeared as an amicus curiae, complicated matters even further by suggesting that some land could be granted in a "personal and private capacity" and by noting that sales in agricultural and residential land had regularly been taking place among tribesman[10] for at least twenty years. He also argued that as land was available and free to all tribesmen, the rule that land could not be sold must have been aimed at sale to nontribesmen. The High Court accepted this argument and held that Section 10(2) applied to Mr. Motlhabane, with the result that the land at issue had not vested in KLB. This decision meant that the land was owned and was the private property of Mr. Motlhabane's family, and because one of the hallmarks of such ownership was the right of the owner to dispose of it as he saw fit, Mr. Matlho had legitimately acquired the land and could not be restrained from occupying it.

In adopting this interpretation, the court was aligning the notion of personal and private capacity with an individual right of ownership upheld by a Western type or European model of law that draws on a framework of rights accorded to freehold and registered title to land.[11] Thus the logic of one type of legal system became transposed, at a later date in time, onto another dealing with customary land tenure. Also at issue in this case is the assumption that practices such as sales of land between tribesmen automatically represent legal or lawful claims. Indeed, it was this very informal market in land, bypassing the control of land boards, that the Kgabo Commission was set up to investigate in order to address problems posed by what was viewed as illegal acquisition and/or uses of land. In its response to the commission's report, the government adopted the view that Section 10 "simply transferred existing rights and obligations from one authority to another—from the Chief to the Land Board," and that it "did not create any new rights with respect to Customary land" (Botswana 1992, 7). Notably, the government's interpretation was directly at odds with that of the court, which incorporated an evolutionary, linear temporality in its interpretation of the section.

In the meantime, the KLB went to the Court of Appeal on a point of law. KLB argued that the court had erred in holding that Section 10(2) acknowledged customary ownership of land acquired and possessed before the introduction of land boards and in holding that an attribute of such ownership was the ability of the owner to sell land without the authorization of the land board.[12] In its judgment, the Court of Appeal upheld the High Court's decision by a majority judgment based on the opinion of two judges, with one judge dissenting. Their written opinions reflect the extent to which notions of temporality about law played an important role in their interpretations of Section 10.

In his judgment, Aguda J. A. set out the parameters of the dispute, noting that all parties accepted that "the land in question is governed by customary ownership of land in Bakwena Tribal Territory."[13] What was in dispute "are the consequences which flow from the acceptance of the concept that the land falls under customary law, at least until the Tribal Land Act was passed."[14] Amissah P., in his majority opinion, explained what, in his view, lay at the heart of discord among the judges, which he attributed to "competing philosophies with regard to the character of customary law.

On the one hand there is the view which stems from a conception of customary law as a developing body of law. Concomitant with this is a desire for the protection of private rights."[15] This interpretation of customary law represents an evolutionary perspective in adopting a notion of development as representing a form of linear progress that leads customary law to a recognition of private rights. What is highlighted here is the affirmative power of linear time "in its ability to resolve tensions among priorities, loyalties, and accountabilities" (Greenhouse 1998, 1638). This comes about through its "single principle of selection" (1636) that, according to its hierarchical nature, rejects any plurality of views that may be simultaneously in existence, in favor of one particular approach that acts to the exclusion of all others.

In contrast, Amissah P. highlights an opposing position (that was adopted by Bizos J.) that "stems from a concept of customary law which makes it static in character." He credits this view as having had its roots in a number of books written "primarily not from the point of the lawyer but from the point of view of the sociologist or anthropologist. Where the considerations of the law come in, customary law is equated with the well-known English legal concept of custom. . . . One of the essential elements emphasized in these definitions is the element of ancient origin."[16] What was at issue here was not the facts, but whether customary law could have evolved to accommodate private ownership, that was the view of the majority on the court, or whether it was fixed and unalterable in a way that would not permit sale to a third party, the view that the dissenting judge, Bizos J., adopted. According to Amissah P., reasons for supporting this interpretive approach include the need to uphold legal certainty (with regard to the past, present, and future). This view accords with the perception of temporality with regard to law's timelessness that endorses "neutrality in a linear time idiom" (Greenhouse 1998, 1642). For the temporality of law under this interpretation follows a linear trajectory in that it ascribes an unalterable past to customary law that continues to apply in the present.

Amissah P. rejected this interpretation of African customary law because, in the majority's view, customary law should "apply to the changing situations of the people whose lives it regulates, it must have been and should be living law. . . . Just as the English common law, as distinct from custom, has evolved with the development of the people, so must African customary law in the areas in which it governs in African societies develop to meet changing situations."[17]

Both interpretations put forward by the court, however, were predicated on a linear notion of temporality that was ascribed to customary law. The majority took an evolutionary approach whose trajectory was based on moving forward and displacing past prescriptions with current developments. This approach may be contrasted with that taken by Bizos J., the dissenting judge, who adhered to a linear and temporal perception of customary law that remained founded in past prescriptions that were to be applied in the present. These debates highlight one of the dilemmas for law in general in terms of its temporality. On the one hand, law presents itself as timeless in order to lay claim to neutrality in terms "of being capable of balancing competing interests and in engaging in a value-free discourse" (Greenhouse 1998, 1642). On the other hand, its temporality also entails legal decision making that involves a determination at a particular moment in time, thereby acknowledging the cumulative nature of law in terms of past decisions that inform the present and future in order to accommodate change.

In his dissenting judgment, Bizos J. also declined to find that the land in question had devolved under customary rights to Mr. Motlhabane. In his dissent on this point, he considered that the evidence tendered to the court was biased because it was based on hearsay; that is, evidence that is based on what a witness has heard from another person rather than on that witness's direct personal knowledge or experience. This testimony was given, in his opinion, by parties who had an interest in the dispute. His approach to legal analysis here is one that is directly informed by Western understandings of law. This approach to evidence fails to take into account the fact that oral testimony, which the common law system treats as hearsay, is often the only kind of available evidence within the structure of the customary system where judgments need to be made about events that took place a long time ago and for which there are no written records.[18] Bizos J. also maintained that Mr. Motlhabane had failed to satisfactorily explain how what was family property came to be held by him in his personal and private capacity *apart* from the rights of other family members.[19] This point was valid because, although there may have been a subdivision in Motlhabane's favor, it would not necessarily have given him private rights over the land to the exclusion of other family members whose consent may well have been required for its transfer. The question of family ties to and rights over land lies at the heart of many disputes that regularly feature as cases brought to land boards, dikgosi, and the land tribunal, where one family member seeks to assert his or her rights to the exclusion of all others.

The final point raised by Bizos J. was that if customary law had changed to accommodate the sale of land, then there needed to be "clear, convincing and consistent" evidence to establish this change.[20] It should not be "made out on ambiguous statements in hurriedly drawn affidavits by persons who have a pecuniary interest or by a person closely connected with those who have such an interest."[21] Bizos J.'s finding was directly contradicted by Ammisah P.'s observation that the "affidavits were sworn by persons who were in a position to know the history of the land in question."[22] These divergences mark a difference in approach toward the way in which the evidence in the case was assessed. For Bizos J., the oral testimony was viewed as hearsay and therefore unacceptable based on an understanding of Western and Cape Colonial law that emerged from the colonial encounter. Ammisah P., on the other hand, did not view the evidence in this way, but rather acknowledged the provenance of those testifying and their position in Kwena society, placing a value on local knowledge of the land and people's relationship with it.

These divergences mark differing logics that have a temporal base. Bizos J.'s perspective on evidence, which requires impartiality, is one that is a feature of the common law devolved from the colonial encounter and Roman-Dutch law; while Ammisah P.'s perspective, derived through the office of the chieftainship, places a value on local knowledge of the land and people's relationship with it. In this structure of local knowledge, which has its roots in a precolonial past, relationships between people are central to a morafe's existence from the past through the present and into the future and cannot be avoided.[23]

Even though the High Court ruling was upheld, the Court of Appeal has been criticized for its judgment by Siamisung Thoki Morolong and Clement Ng'ong'ola (2007, 156) for failing "to provide a satisfactory elucidation of [Section] 10(2)" and for "attempting to hurry along the transformation of customary land tenure rules" (2007, 157). Indeed, in dismissing the appeal, Amissah P. concluded by asking, "How may the rights acknowledged by legislation be determined?" and by responding, "This is a matter to be determined by the trial court from all material before it. In this case the court decided that the respondent's claim was justified. Holding the view of customary law as I do, I do not think I should disturb that decision."[24] His conclusion highlights the spatial dimension in line with common law (i.e., a

European/Western legal model) where the remit of Appeal Courts is highly restricted to a determination of a very narrowly defined set of legal issues.

Post Court of Appeal Decision in *Matlho*

Following the Court of Appeal decision in *Matlho*, the government stepped in, and Parliament made amendments to the TLA. These included deleting Section 10(2), substituting "tribesmen in the area" in Section 10(1) with "citizens of Botswana,"[25] providing land boards with enhanced powers under Section 17, and replacing Section 26 with Section 38, which expressly provides that "any rights conferred upon any person in respect of any grant or lease of tribal land . . . shall not be transferred, whether by sale or otherwise to any other person without the consent of the Land Board concerned."[26] However, in order to not overburden the system and to ensure that legitimate transactions were not affected, the land board's consent is waived in cases where (1) land is developed to the satisfaction of the land board; (2) it relates to a sale in execution to a citizen of Botswana; (3) it involves hypothecation by a citizen of Botswana;[27] or (4) it represents devolution of land on inheritance.

However, these changes did not put the matter to rest. Although the 1993 amendments to the TLA made it clear that from that date onward there could be no claims made under Section 10(2), what remained open was the question of how to deal with claims raised under this section before the amendments came into effect. Regarding the temporality of law under general principles derived from a Western or European perspective, amendments to it are deemed not to have effect retrospectively. As a result, before the 1993 amendments came into effect, rights under Section 10(2) were still being successfully pursued in the courts[28] until the case of *Kweneng Land Board v. Mpofu and Another.*[29]

The facts of this later case were very similar to those of *Matlho*. The applicant Mpofu applied to the High Court to prevent the respondent, KLB, from demolishing her home in Mogoditshane, which was built on what had once been part of an undeveloped field and on which she had spent BWP 300,000 in constructing a home.[30] KLB made a counter-application for an order that the purported allocation to Mpofu by the second applicant was unlawful. KLB also applied for an order to cancel the second applicant's customary rights, if any, over the piece of land in question. The second applicant argued that she had inherited the land from her mother, who had inherited it under Bakwena customary law from her mother, who had been allocated the land by Kgosi Pule around 1910, long before land boards came into existence. Over the years, the family subdivided the field for use by children and relatives, and before 1989, the second applicant and her husband occupied the land in question. In 1989, the second applicant transferred the land, by way of donation, to Mpofu, who was a Zimbabwean national but related to the second applicant's family through marriage. Mpofu built a fence around the plot and a few years later proceeded to build on it. When she took possession of the property she had an understanding with the second applicant that she would apply to KLB for formalization of her occupation of the plot. She filed an application but never heard anything from the land board. In 1994, on being informed that KLB had lost her original application, she filed a second application. She heard nothing until May 2000 when she was called to the Mogoditshane sub–land board to discuss her occupation of the plot and her alleged illegal building operations on it. The judge, Collins J., who had visited the property under dispute, observed the following:

> The plot upon which the first applicant's residential dwelling is erected, alongside others which are similar, was once part of an undeveloped grazing or cultivated field (*tshimo*). During the course of the material time-frame, the field ceased to be pastoral and a homogeneous unit. Instead, the burgeoning urbanization that grew around Gaborone in the late 1980s (Mogoditshane in particular) resulted in pastoral lands losing their function as such and becoming "available" for human urban settlement lawfully and unlawfully. This tshimo was no exception. This judgment must be understood against that background. What was once a pastoral field has in a very short time become a subdivided urban residential village ward.[31]

Collins J. went on to hold that, given the confirmation of the second applicant's hearsay evidence[32] by an elderly ninety-year-old witness and given KLB's failure to respond to the historical allegations regarding disposition of the land, "the second applicant's rights of occupation of the tshimo, and hence of the plot forming part of it, was lawful in terms of the customary law."[33] Having established that the second applicant's rights of occupation were lawful, he then felt bound by the Court of Appeal decision in *Matlho* to find that the second applicant held this property in her private and personal capacity and that the transfer to the first applicant was therefore lawful. However, while he was bound to follow *Matlho* on the basis of precedent and the doctrine of stare decisis, he clearly rejected its rationale, including the onus put on the land board to prove that every occupier of tribal land does not possess or occupy it in a personal or private capacity, as being "tantamount to a negation of the whole basis of our tribal history and organization."[34] He explained his objections to *Matlho* as follows:

> The whole purpose of the [Tribal Land] Act was to vest tribal land in land boards. Botswana had become sovereign and independent in 1966, and the first Tribal Land Act was enacted into law two years later. I do not think anyone can doubt that the primary purpose of the Act was to blend together or sublimate the interests of tribal society in relation to tribal land with national interests in respect of such land. In essence the land boards stepped into the shoes of the chiefs but without disturbing the character of either tribal society or tribal law including tribal land heritage, occupancy, distribution and management. The fact that land boards became accountable in a vertical direction to a new civil administration has never, to my mind, meant that there was any abrogation of pre-existing tribal land law.[35]

Indeed, the government's response to the Court of Appeal's ruling in *Matlho* was to "snuff it out immediately" by repealing Section 10(2).[36]

Mindful of the legal limitations placed on Collins J., when the case went to the Court of Appeal, the court convened with five instead of the normal three judges in order to deal with the issue of precedent. The court unanimously held that the stare decisis[37] rule that operates in Botswana can be overturned where a later Court of Appeal "is satisfied that the earlier decision, and particularly the *ratio decidendi*[38] of it, was incorrect."[39] The court also held that the majority in *Matlho* erred in interpreting Section 10(2) as creating a class of private ownership within customary law. In delivering the judgment, Tebbutt J. P. commented,

> I have no doubt that the interpretation of the words "land or right to water held by any person in his personal and private capacity," in the context of the Tribal Land Act, is obscure and fairly and equally open to diverse meanings. For instance, were there plots or pockets of land within a tribal area which did not belong to the tribe but were owned by persons who were not tribesmen? Or did churches and other places of religious worship fall outside the ambit of tribal land, although situated within a tribal area. One can conceive of many instances of which the above are but some examples. Again, did the legislature know of the private sales referred to by Bizos J. A. as having taken place because of "traditional ingenuity having found its way around the restriction," particularly to non-tribesmen . . . and decide not to interfere with them? Whatever lay behind the object of the legislature in enacting [Section] 10(2), I cannot accept that it intended to create a class of private ownership within the customary law. It would fly in the face of all the tenets of customary law, which from all the authoritative text writers specifically excluded it.[40]

The court also felt justified in reaching this decision on the grounds that not long after the Court of Appeal ruling in *Matlho*, Parliament deleted Section 10(2) and made amendments to the TLA that indicated it had never intended to convey ownership of customary land through Section 10(2). It also held that where Section 10(2) was invoked, the onus was on the party claiming rights under it to provide proof of this, and not on the land board to prove that the land in question was not held in a private or personal capacity.

As a result of these findings, the Court of Appeal held that the second respondent could not hold the land in her personal and private capacity, and so did not have the right to alienate it to Mpofu, whose occupation of the land in question was consequently unlawful. However, the court did acknowledge that the land had been passed down to the second respondent under customary law. It therefore ordered that Mpofu had to vacate the plot within thirty days and that occupancy of the plot should revert to the second respondent. It also granted KLB an order to demolish the residential house on the plot should it so desire.

Government Initiatives for Dealing with Squatting

During the time period that *Matlho* and *Mpofu* hearings were working their way through the courts, the Government of Botswana observed that problems caused by the occupation of land in Mogoditshane and other peri-urban areas was getting so out of hand that it set up a Commission of Inquiry in 1991 that gave rise to the Government White Paper No. 1 of 1992.[41] This government paper made recommendations about how to deal with those occupying land in the area who did not have land certificates issued by Kweneng Land Board. It included the establishment of a task force to investigate the claims of existing occupiers, to see who could be identified as squatters involved in the illegal occupation of land. The government imposed a BWP 5,000[42] fine on illegal occupiers with substantial buildings on their land with the understanding that occupiers could then acquire legal rights to the property and an official land certificate from the land board. This proved to be unworkable, however, with Collins J. A. observing in the *Murima* case[43] that the "decision backfired in their faces almost immediately. Illegal occupants lined up to pay their 'fines' in the knowledge that their illegal acts were now sanctioned and that they had security of tenure henceforth. For those occupants, it was not a 'fine' but a 'purchase-price' (and well worth the money considering the alternatives)."[44] In recognition that the situation was out of control, the government then issued Presidential Directive (No. CAB 28(b)/2000), which adopted a more hard-line approach, pursuing the eviction of illegal occupiers of land and the demolition of buildings on that land in order to prevent "a complete breakdown in law and order."[45]

Within the legal domain, however, to which I now return, the Court of Appeal decision in *Mpofu* put an end to *Matlho*, even if it did not expressly overrule it. However, apart from establishing that Section 10(2) did not convey private ownership in customary land, it did not provide any definitive interpretation as to why it had been enacted or what fell within its remit. This leaves open the possibility that a Section 10(2) claim could still arise in respect to tribal land that was acquired before land boards came into existence and before the 1993 amendment to the TLA took effect, although Morolong and Ng'ong'ola (2007, 117) note that the shift in burden of proof to the claimant in *Mpofu* "would probably make such a claim unsustainable."

For example, an attempt was made to resuscitate a Section 10(2) type of claim in the *Malan* case, but the Land Tribunal[46] held that there was insufficient evidence to uphold it. This finding was subsequently upheld in the High Court[47] and the Court of Appeal.[48] In its judgment, the Court of Appeal stressed that *Mpofu* "emphatically and definitively laid to rest the spectre of tribal 'ownership' of tribal land by individuals."[49]

The other matter left undetermined by the *Mpofu* case was whether or not buying or selling of tribal land was legitimate. Although customary law has been held to not encompass ownership of tribal land by individuals, the question of money changing hands in relation to it has received a somewhat different treatment. In the Court of Appeal case *Charlotte Marokane and Others v. Joel Sello Kereng*,[50] the issue arose as to whether the sale of a portion of a plowing field by Barnett Pakoeng Seboko Marokane to Joel Sello Kereng for BWP 60,000 was valid. After protracted litigation, the parties agreed to proceed by way of a special case for adjudication by the court of the legal issues to be addressed. In other words, both the High Court[51] and Court of Appeal could only adjudicate on these issues. In essence, the family of the late Mr. Marokane, including his widow, challenged whether the land could be subdivided and sold without their consent and that of the land board. While nothing was expressly stated, the family implied through their pleadings that the deceased's actions amounted to the kind of actions associated with individual ownership. They argued that the rights, title, and interest in tribal land held in terms of a certificate of customary land grant "are incapable of subdivision at the instance of the grantee"[52] and that such rights "are not transferable without the consent of the land board" because the sale was unlawful and invalid.[53] The plaintiff disputed these claims, arguing that the sale was valid because there is no statutory or other prohibition on portions of tribal land irrespective of tenure being subdivided or transferred.[54] He also alleged that "rights of possession, occupation and use of tribal land are sold all the time" and that he had purchased "the deceased's right to the possession, occupation and use of this land," paid a price for it, and was therefore "entitled for the rights in it to be transferred to him."[55]

The High Court judge, Walia J. held that "tribal land in Botswana is routinely divided and subdivided" and "cut up" to create leases and subleases over defined portions.[56] He also observed that "there is no statutory prohibition on the division or transfer of tribal land provided the consent of the land board is given."[57] He gave the example of *Rutang v. Rutang*, a divorce case where the High Court ordered a piece of tribal land to be subdivided to enable each spouse to have a defined portion.[58] He also acknowledged the subdivision of tribal land in relation to boreholes.[59] As a result of these findings, he held that customary land is divisible, whether held under a customary or common law grant, and ordered the land board to excise from the plowing field in question the portion that was sold to the plaintiff by the deceased and to issue a certificate of customary land grant in his favor.

The land board in *Marokane* was a party to the action, but chose not to actively engage in the dispute. Although it has been held that what is prohibited under Section 38 is not the sale of tribal land, but its transfer without the consent of the land board, the terms of Section 38 as they applied to this particular case were never discussed, possibly because it appeared that the land board did not intend to contest the transfer.[60] In effect, the decision appears to recognize something that resembles individual ownership rights by acknowledging that the deceased had power to alienate part of his property without the consent of any family member, his wife,[61] or the land board. This ruling appears to contradict what Section 38 was intended to prevent, namely, unregulated sales in land.

The Court of Appeal upheld the High Court ruling in *Marokane* on a basis of interpreting the sections of the TLA, primarily Sections 10(1) and 38, in accordance with the view that "the legislature does not envisage the law in this area to be static but to be subject to development as circumstances in Botswana develop."[62] It went on to state, "The approach of the courts to interpretation and application of the [Tribal land] Act should recognize such development."[63] This perspective is very much in line with the approach to customary law that Aguda J. adopted in the *Mathlo* case in the Court of Appeal.

This interpretation of law once again marks a linear form of temporality involving evolutionary change. It is a perspective on customary law that the Court of Appeal endorsed in ruling that "in the light of modern development and the requirement to bear in mind the need to promote the economic and social development of all the peoples of Botswana, there is no policy reason against allocations of tribal land being divisible and every policy in favour of their being so."[64] So, despite challenges from time to time, the push to "move with the times"[65] increasingly moves the courts and the legislature toward a Western or European model of law in its definition of the contours of legal space.

Temporality and Space: A Linear Trajectory

As the cases have demonstrated, the construction of legality in the common law of Botswana is built on a spatial dimension that is highly circumscribed in terms of its hierarchical, organizational framework. This framework provides for a narrowly delimited discussion of legal issues where what counts as law is restricted to a set of technical legal questions. As a result, social actors' contested claims to land have to be constructed and presented within a specific legal form in order to go before the High Court and the Court of Appeal, regardless of whether they fit better into the customary model of law characterized by a different approach to adjudication. Narratives about law that do not comply with the specific legal form upheld by the common law are set aside and excluded from consideration.

The case law also reveals a temporal dimension founded on a linear understanding of time. This dimension embraces a model of time that is evolutionary in nature, in that it is seen to be constantly moving forward. In this process, what becomes important is the affirmative power of selection that such a model embodies. This model is one that upholds a singular perception of development that denies any legitimacy to any other form of temporality. It involves a particular reconstruction of history that, for law, presents a picture of continuity over time that is timeless in nature. Thus, the Court of Appeal in *Mpofu* did not disrupt the notion of precedent but merely found that the ruling in *Matlho* could be departed from because it did not accurately represent what the law really was. Such an approach makes it possible to reformulate the logic of the past in order to meet the interests of the present and the future. This reformulation allows for the possibility of change without displacing law's ideological claim to timelessness. Yet, despite law's perceived sense of continuity, it is nonetheless located in time and formulates its logic from linear events created by finite human beings who make legal decisions based on these events. Reconciling these divergent aspects of temporality in law is an onerous task that, as the case law discloses, is constantly in the making.

Notes

1. See *S. v. Mbaiwa*, 1988 BLE 314, where the court observed that a right of appeal is confined to a point of law, which "means that the Attorney General must *accept the facts as found by the subordinate court* [own italics] in formulating his ground of appeal" (at p. 318). Under Section 12(2) of the Court of Appeal Act, "Any question as to whether there was any evidence upon which the court could have come to the conclusion which it did come . . . shall be deemed to be a question of fact and not law."

2. But the courts may provide some degree of latitude; see *Charlotte Marokane and Others v. Joel Sello Kereng*, Court of Appeal, Civil Appeal No. CACGN-12 (transcript), judgment given February 4, 2016, where the appellants were permitted to pursue their appeal despite the failure to timely file their Notice and Grounds of Appeal.

3. My understanding of these texts has been enhanced over the years by discussions with colleagues in the Law Department at the University of Botswana and with legal practitioners, such as Doreen Khama and Kagalelo Monthe, who have so generously given of their time and provided me with copies of unreported cases.

4. Botswana (2015, No. 4).

5. Section 10(1) TLA in its original form. An amendment to the Act under the Tribal Land Amendment Act of 1993 substituted the term *tribesman* with the term *all citizens of Botswana*, thus removing tribal affiliation as a basis for allocating customary land.

6. In Botswana, common law includes statutory law as it covers all law in force other than customary law. Section 2 of the Customary Law [Application and Ascertainment] Act 1969.

7. The 1992 *Report of the Presidential Commission of Enquiry into Land Problems in Mogoditshane and Other Peri-Urban Villages* noted that serious allegations were leveled at KLB's staff involving criminal activities in relation to land, and even went so far as to recommend the disbanding of KLB to "make a fresh start" (Botswana 1992a, p. 102, para. 3.39). At a higher level, two government ministers were also alleged to have engaged in illegal activities relating to land transactions in this area; for discussion of the context in which this took place, see Lekorwe (2005).

8. This bias gave rise to questions at KLB's annual public meeting held in Mogoditshane in October 2009, where residents were very vocal in their complaints about the board and the way it was operating.

9. Misca. No. 137 of 1990 (HC).

10. *Tribesmen* was the term that the Attorney General used to denote tribal affiliation that was a prerequisite for the application of the TLA before the 1993 amendment to it.

11. While Morolong and Ng'ong'ola (2007, 143) point out that it was Roman-Dutch law and not English law that was adopted under British colonial rule in the Protectorate, the concepts of ownership and dominium under Roman-Dutch common law are not dissimilar to those embedded in European systems of law.

12. *Kweneng Land Board v. Matlho and Another*, 1992 BLR 292.

13. Ibid., p. 297 F.

14. Ibid., p. 297 F-G.

15. Ibid., p. 304 B-C.

16. Ibid., p. 304 C-D.

17. Ibid., p. 305 A.

18. See chapter 2 where the politico-administrative structure of a morafe and its interconnected social structure is discussed. Under the customary system, oral testimony, which is often the only kind of evidence available in these cases and which may be given by senior members of the Kwena polity who may be related to disputants, is not automatically treated as being inadmissible.

19. 1992 BLR, p. 316 B.

20. Ibid., p. 314 A-B.

21. Ibid., p. 316 C-D.

22. Ibid., p. 306 A.

23. Given the 1993 amendment to the TLA and the changes it has brought about with regard to citizens being able to apply for customary land anywhere in the country, this knowledge may well fall into abeyance in the future.

24. 1992 BLR, p. 306 G-H.

25. This change in policy has been challenged by some dikgosi, most notably those representing Batlokwa who wanted to reject this approach with regard to Tlokweng Land Board because of the scarcity of land available in TLB's jurisdiction. TLB is located between the capital city and the South African border. Dikgosi argued that priority ought to be given to Batlokwa over incoming residents from elsewhere in the country. This contestation echoes arguments that Berry (2009) documents as being introduced elsewhere in Africa where distinctions are made between "strangers" and "locals" in order to treat the former unfavorably in relation to the latter, or even to dispossess them of their access to and control over land.

26. For details, see Morolong and Ng'ong'ola (2007, 157–161).

27. *Hypothecation* is a legal term that in practice involves a borrower pledging an asset as collateral for a loan, while retaining ownership of the assets and enjoying the benefits therefrom.

28. See *Tlokweng Land Board v. Segakise* (1999) 1 BLR 526 and *Murima and Another v. Kweneng Land Board*, (2002) 1 BLR 18 (HC).

29. 2005 (1) BLR 3 (CA).

30. *Mpofu and Another v. Kweneng Land Board*, 2004 (1) BLR 213 (HC).

31. Ibid., p. 216 B-C.

32. The second applicant's evidence was hearsay because it was based on an oral understanding of events that took place before she was born that had been passed down to her by the testimony of family members.

33. *Mpofu*, p. 220 F-G.

34. Ibid., p. 224 B.

35. Ibid., p. 224 C-D.

36. Ibid., p. 223 B.

37. Stare decisis, that is, being bound by precedent.

38. This refers to the core legal rationale of a case.

39. *Kweneng Land Board v. Mpofu and Another*, 2005 (1) BLR 3 (CA), at p. 12 B.

40. In the 1992 report (Botswana 1992a, 14–15), the government acknowledged that, given the scale of informal sales in land, it was not feasible to deal with illegal occupation of land through wholesale evictions (which would be politically unpopular). Nor was it feasible for the land board to administer these developed plots of land given their lack of resources. Instead, in this report it elected to evict those who did not have proper title to undeveloped land but to permit those whose land was developed to pay a penalty based on size, that would be levied by the land board which would then regularize their occupation. This approach was later abandoned, but it still gives rise to problems today; see Pini Bothoko, "Mogoditshane Still a Squatters Haven," *Mmegi Online*, August 11, 2017, accessed February 12, 2018, www .mmegi.bw/index.php?aid=7091&dir=2017/august/11.

41. *Land Problems in Mogoditshane and Other Peri-Urban Village.*, Government White Paper No. 1 of 1992 (Botswana 1992b).

42. About USD 500 at that time.

43. *Murima and Another v. Kweneng Land Board,* (2002)1 BLR 18 (HC).

44. Ibid., p. 24 G-H.

45. Ibid., p. 25 G. In this case, the judge held that a cabinet directive did not have the force of law where there was no state of emergency and that the way KLB operated in demolishing Mr. Murima's property was unlawful.

46. See *Abraham Malan v. Kgatleng Land Board and the Estate of the Late Phadi Maribe*, Land Tribunal Case No. 223/2004 (Gaborone), judgment given October 12, 2010.

47. *Malan*, CAHLB-000074-10.

48. *Malan*, Court of Appeal Civil Appeal No. CACGB-040-12.

49. *Malan*, CACGB-040 at 26–27.

50. *Charlotte Marokane and Others v. Joel Sello Kereng,* Court of Appeal, Civil Appeal No. CACGB-12-12 (transcript), judgment given February 4, 2016.

51. *Joel Sello Kereng v. Charlotte Marokane and Others,* High Court, Civil Case No. 2841-05 (transcript), judgment given August 30, 2012.

52. Ibid., p. 9, paras. 9.2 and 9.3.

53. Ibid., p. 9, para. 9.1.

54. Ibid., p. 16, para. 35.

55. Ibid., p. 17, paras. 17 and 20.

56. Ibid., p. 21, para. 48.

57. Ibid., p. 21, paras. 50 and 51.

58. *Rutang v. Rutang*, MC 160 of 1987 (unreported), referred to in *Marokane* High Court at p. 22 para. 53.

59. See Court of Appeal case *Shane Junius Seaman and Tynos Enterprises (Pty) Ltd and Others*, CACLB-024-08, referred to in *Marokane* High Court at p. 22, para. 54.

60. See the unreported case of *Kgatleng Land Board v. Bontsi Chelne* and 13 others, cited in Morolong and Ng'ong'ola (2007, 173–174), which highlights the unsatisfactory wording of Section 38 and the legal problems that it raises.

61. The defendants argued that the sale constituted a fraud on the property that was held in community of property with the deceased's wife. However, since the sale was finalized before the Abolition of Marital Power Act 2004 came into effect, the court held that he was legally entitled to sell the property without her consent and that there was no evidence of any form of fraud as the transactions were drafted by attorneys at arm's length and records of payments made and received were documented.

62. *Marokane* Court of Appeal, p. 8, para 10.

63. Ibid.

64. *Marokane* Court of Appeal, p. 11, para, 12.

65. Ibid.

FINAL REFLECTIONS
The Myth of a Single Global Vision

W HAT HAS EMERGED FROM MY STUDY OF INTERNATIONAL, national, regional, and local domains is a form of governance that differs from classic, traditional models of government. My study has documented the ways in which these domains intersect and overlap and how they come into conflict with one another in processes that are constantly evolving. These processes entail both negative and positive aspects. On the one hand, they may reflect the imposition of a dominant ideological paradigm with all its adverse consequences. Yet, on the other, they may create the potential for transformations that enable people and the systems they engage with to remake themselves in new ways. What emerges in these contexts is the contradictory quality of state power that, as Pauline E. Peters (1984, 29) observes, does not operate in a single direction but allows for contestation and competition "between the dominating and dominated" that are constituted by "different social groups and categories."

In exploring these dimensions, my study highlights how a whole range of social actors negotiate and contextualize relationships to land according to how they are situated within interconnecting transnational, national, regional, and local spaces that shape their capacity to regulate, construct discourses about, and make claims on land. Notions of the global and the local involve a dialectical relationship that is dependent on the perspective and analytical orientation from which it is addressed. This relationship between local and global is one that involves questions of scale and projection operating on many levels and which, as this book demonstrates, vary according to the lenses through which they are articulated and the viewpoints from which they are perceived. These may range from a more narrowly focused form of analysis, concerning, for example, families and households, to a more extended domain evident, for example, in the state's engagement with national and international relations that embrace a broader range of interests and goals.

The multiple and cross-cutting dimensions at work in these relations at a number of levels are made visible through a social-scientific, methodological perspective involving fieldwork. This perspective brings to light factors that would otherwise remain hidden from view (Griffiths 2007); for example, the ways in which differential status and gender operate in a variegated manner, according to whether women and men are married, unmarried, widowed, or childless. How these factors come together, with their position in the lifecycle and location within social networks, is key to comprehending how access to resources, including land, is determined. Such knowledge provides for a more informed understanding of the uneven and unequal outcomes that combinations of differing scales of global and local interactions give rise to in a number of contexts. A recognition of what these contexts involve is valuable because it undermines any simplistic dichotomy that might be drawn between the local and the global, for "it dissolves opposites and entertains internal contradictions" (Mensah 2008, 50) by documenting the ways in which these concepts inhabit spaces that make and remake themselves across a whole range of domains.

It also highlights how these spaces, which include transnational values embodying access to justice, good governance, and accountability, are at work in institutions in Botswana and are measured through indicators, targets, and audits. This quantitative approach to management based on results is, as we have seen in the case of Kweneng Land Board, centered around a set of techniques applied on an international scale in order to rank the performance of nation-states according to a neoliberal, capitalist view of what it means to be *global*. In reality, however, this assessment is judged on the basis of a particular ideological approach to development, one that is nonetheless treated as the foundational base for policy making and regulation worldwide when it comes to dealing with poverty, access to justice, and land reform. At the same time, these concerns associated with sustainable development that promotes an international mandate to improve the lives of women and the poor, including land reform, are framed on the basis of a particular viewpoint that endorses a singular trajectory for current and future progress. This trajectory lays claim to a universal and global outreach, yet it has been formulated on the basis of a more parochial and ethnocentric vision of what development entails.

The techniques through which these global standards are to be implemented in countries across the world have created a situation that requires rethinking what government entails, beyond a traditional interpretation of the nation-state, in order to accommodate a broader concept of governance and governmentality that stretches across boundaries and coordinates via "common knowledge and technology" (Sand 2004, 46). What is at work here are multiple networks of relations that cross territorial boundaries, involving multilevel arrangements that reflect a "great diversity of circumstance," creating "complex coordination issues" that display a more "fluid and complex regulatory environment" (Cottrell and Trubek 2012, 361) than has hitherto been the case. As this work highlights, state institutions dealing with land in Botswana today display a mix of both local and global features that represent "a product of layer upon layer of different sets of linkages, both local and to the wider world" (Massey 1994, 156). Thus they create varying spaces with regard to the administration of land that may overlap or conflict with one another in ways that create differential access for Botswana's citizens, underpinning structural forms of social inequality referred to earlier.

The Power of the Global to Create Structures of Inequality

The local/global linkages that affect institutions are also at work in ordinary people's relations to land. While the spaces within which they operate are more narrowly constituted than those of government and state institutions embodying a more far-reaching and wide-ranging set of relations, nonetheless, as the life histories of Makokwe's and Radipati's descendants demonstrate, they are also "the product of interrelations' (Massey 2005, 9) that reflect "the focus of a distinct mixture of wider and more local social relations" (Massey 1994, 156). Importantly, these life histories highlight how global influences create uneven effects on these relations that give rise to social stratification and inequality lurking behind Botswana's image as a prosperous, middle-income country. The life histories reveal the spatialization of social relations to land through a range of factors that have led these families and households to experience very different life trajectories.

In the case of Makokwe's descendants, their relationship to land has crystallized around the traditional spatial organization of Kwena livelihoods centered on rotation between the village, the lands, and the cattlepost. Traditional social relations were closely associated with agro-pastoral activities based on extended family networks. This spatial form of organization, however, became integrated with a wider economy of social relations, involving massive transient migration to South Africa, with the resulting consequences in the formation and substance of family relationships. These relationships continue to be affected by the global markets for Botswana's products today, such as cattle and diamonds, as well as by changes in the labor market, which are subject to the vicissitudes of fluctuating world demand.

Over time, transformations have occurred, such as the closing of access to the South African mines, but Makokwe's and his family members' livelihoods continue to revolve around subsistence agriculture, raising of livestock (where possible), and on intermittent and insecure employment. These forms of work are not highly remunerated, and their low-income return is such that they do little to contribute to the enhancement of family members' access to resources. The younger generations' attempts to move beyond rural activities and farming have not met with much success. They find themselves among that section of the population who find it difficult to transform their agricultural activities into a commercial enterprise or to make the transition to an urban way of life that would provide them with sufficient resources to invest in land.

As a consequence, their experience of local and global trajectories has placed Makokwe's family members in a precarious position, among those who have not benefited from Botswana's success and who fall among the third of her population that the African Development Bank associates with poverty and unemployment (AfDB 2009–2013, 5). They remain among those for whom, as the Bank of Botswana report (2015, 87) observes, "Poverty and inequality remain widespread at levels unacceptable for a country in Botswana's position." They can be seen to reflect an African working class in the making (Werbner 2014).

The same does not hold true for their relatives in Radipati's family, who have been able to profit from the government's policies toward land. For Radipati's family members, educational attainment and acquisition of professional skills have enabled them to engage in a more productive relationship with land. As members of an emergent middle class, they have been able to diversify their livelihoods. This upward mobility has provided them with the opportunity to take advantage of the government's land policy by investing in land in a number of areas that can be rented out and put to commercial use. They are in a position to participate in the entrepreneurial vision of development that the government envisages for Botswana, one that is in tune with international and transnational agencies' agendas for land administration and sustainable development goals. So, once again, through a different set of connective threads, the local and the global come together to situate the two brothers' descendants in very different positions with regard to social class and land.

What emerges from these extended families' histories are the factors that give rise to differing resource bases on which their networks can draw. They underline the extent to which the current position of family members cannot simply be attributed to arbitrary, or ad hoc, features, but derives from factors, such as education, gender, and employment, that have shaped their status and created divergent patterns of accumulation concerning human, social, and economic capital over generations. It lays bare the conditions under which class formations, influenced by global dimensions, come into being. The importance of this type of "micro historical analysis" is that it not only highlights the role that kinship networks play in "their contribution to the formulation of class alliances," but also marks their involvement in "the creation and persistence of socially differentiated class structure" (Sabean 1999; Tranter 1999, 749–750).

The Power of Time in Ordering Space

At another level, the power of the global invested in bodies such as the UN and the World Bank carries enormous normative authority in dealing with inequality, despite being predicated on a singular world vision. Their assessments of progress and the way in which policies on land are formulated and implemented treats land as space in a very particular manner; for example, in their rankings of countries as being *developed* or *undeveloped* on the basis of techniques that measure GDP and other factors such as the Human Development Index. Yet, as Massey (2013) observes, where space "represents that dimension of the world in which we live," it is one "within which distinct trajectories coexist." This perspective, however, is negated by ranking countries, as these international agencies do. By classifying a country as *developing*, the country is no longer viewed as being on par with *developed* countries, and thus, even though it exists simultaneously in space, in terms of time it is "a country which is following our path to becoming a developed country like us." In employing this form of categorization, "we are denying the simultaneity, the multiplicity of space . . . and turning all these differences into a single historical trajectory."

This negative aspect of governance is based on a trajectory that derives from a linear notion of time. It is built on the concept of progressively ongoing intervals underpinning a single, evolutionary narrative operating as *the* only authentic, authoritative, and legitimate perspective to the exclusion of all others. It also represents that aspect of the global and globalization that is premised on moral superiority or hegemonic discourse that relies "on exclusion as much as inclusion" (Fassin 2012, 99). This perspective results in "turning space into time, turning geography into history . . . [and] is a way of denying the possibility of something different" and of opening up "politics to the possibility of alternatives" (Massey 2013). Where, however, the power of time that operates in this way is challenged, by confronting claims to a historical authenticity that is based on an assumed natural order of things and where one reconstruction of the past (or construction of the present) may be displaced, then there is the possibility of creating a disjunction, so that what Christian Lund (2013, 30) has called "the inevitability of history" may become "unsettled." This disruptive juncture is necessary because, as Boaventura de Sousa Santos (2005, 31) observes, "The linear time presiding over the Western logic of development—based on a linear conception of development, according to which different pasts converge in a single future" must be contested by acknowledging "a pluralistic conception of time based on the idea that there are alternative development paths and that therefore different pasts underlie different presents and may lead to different futures." Thus, globalization must be thought of "as a heterogeneous and historical phenomenon . . . that can always be challenged" (Fassin 2012, 99).

Nonetheless, as the legal narratives demonstrate, where this linear notion of time controls the space in which it operates, it exerts a powerful influence on how matters are handled. This influence is evident not only in the way the Kweneng Land Board handles land administration and disputes but also in the handling of cases by the High Court and the Court of Appeal where, as the case law reveals, linear notions of time promote an affirmative power of selection. This particular reading of history or the past in effect denies any other legal form of construction that might provide for an alternative legal approach to land.

The Power of the Global through Legal Plurality and Soft Law

The power of law in regulating land is universally acknowledged. However, Peters (2004, 270) has argued for the need to study land "in broader political, economic and social changes taking place over the last century." With respect to customary law, this study requires understanding how actors are positioned with regard to their access and use of customary law in ways that acknowledge and highlight the circumstances that give rise to their inequality. An understanding of what lies behind the widespread appropriation of land by elites requires situating them "within broader processes of social inequality and class formation as well as within . . . new forms of governing" (271). Law has an important role to play in these processes. From the perspective of the World Bank and other international agencies, the image of customary law is that of a static, backward, and unprogressive system as compared with Western or European law, although it has acquired some recognition as a form of *informal* justice acknowledged to be an important phenomenon worldwide—that in sub-Saharan Africa is estimated to process 80 percent of disputes (Piron 2005). Its *global* presence is such that international agencies recognize it has deficits that require attention in order to bring it up to what they perceive as the standards of Western justice. Thus, what is viewed as *local* law is promoted to the worldwide stage as a lesser form of law which people, especially the poor and vulnerable, must use only because they do not have access to the perceived superior Western model of law.

Yet as discussions of and research on customary law in Botswana show, this law is not necessarily inferior to Western style law. An example is found in the data on women's access to and control over land in terms of family arrangements and certificates that demonstrate how customary law has adapted to allow for transformation. Its malleability is evident. However, Peters (2004, 270) warns about "privileging contingency, flexibility, and negotiability" that results in "suggesting an open field." And she observes that "an overemphasis on ambiguity and open-endedness is in danger of deflecting research from the patterns of inequity in landholding and the relations between the latter and broader processes of differentiation and class formation" (61).

Ethnography provides a means of redressing the balance, and the life histories of the Makokwe family remind us of what is at stake, by providing concrete evidence of the limits of "negotiation and flexibility for certain social groups and categories" (Peters 2004, 270).

What is clear from empirical research is the extent to which customary and common law are articulated within a wider social, political, and economical structure that engages with national, international, and transnational domains. My presentation of the ways in which this takes place derives from an anthropological perspective, which conforms to Sally Falk Moore's (1969, 253) observation that "whatever is special about the anthropologist's view lies in his tendency to see the legal system as part of a wider social milieu." In adopting this approach, my study moves beyond those that confine their examination of globalization and law to the remit of the nation-state. This wider view is important because neither the fate of transnational law nor its impact on local legal constellations can be understood without attending to the interactions connecting actors at all levels in multisited arenas of negotiation, as well as to the power relations that underpin these interactions.

Power in this sense represents a "subcategory of transformative capacity where transformative capacity is harnessed to actors' attempts to get others to comply with their wants" (Giddens 1979, 93). Characterized in this way, power is relational, relative, and embedded in social relationships such as those addressed in chapters 4 and 5, as well as being engaged in contestations over whose interpretation of law is to be applied in the adjudication of land disputes as discussed in chapters 6 and 7. For in these encounters, which invoke plural legal orders, more than one set of interpretative legal constructions define law and its relationship to land, often in contradictory ways.

In these disputes then, giving priority to some legal orders over others creates dilemmas and opportunities for contestation. Which legal space prevails—whether it be common law based on a linear evolution that is timeless in nature or customary law based on a timeless past—largely depends on the historical moment in time and on which social actors hold the power to interpret it (F. Benda-Beckmann, K. Benda-Beckmann, and Griffiths 2009a, 7). Such a depiction of law highlights the ways in which actors seek to reinvent or revitalize the legal landscape by restructuring the legal spaces to which they have access. Thus law embodies a complex constellation of relations that create fluid and shifting domains for action. Its multifaceted nature underlines the extent to which legal spaces are embedded in broader social and political claims involving intricate negotiations which cannot be ignored (F. Benda-Beckmann, K. Benda-Beckmann, and Griffiths 2009b). It represents an arena in which the politics of space in relation to land is enacted and negotiated because when engaging with the complexity and uncertainty of social life "legal agents—whether judges, legal theorists, administrative officers or ordinary people—represent and evaluate space in various ways" (Blomley 1994, xi). Taking account of these complex and uncertain social factors requires the legal representation of space and temporality to be seen "as constituted by—and in turn constitutive of—complex, normatively charged, and often competing visions of social and political life under law" (xi). It is these connections, involving legal plurality, that have been explored throughout this book in order to present a picture of continuity and transformation of the use, access to, and control over land that has taken place over time and their accompanying dilemmas.

Closing Thoughts

Framing the global is not a concept easily captured, for the term *global* represents different things to different people. To understand the global is to understand representations of power. In the case of Botswana, power is not simply exerted in terms of a top-down model found in traditional government associated with a nation-state, but rather by means of horizontal as well as vertical dimensions of control through its bureaucratic bodies. It is crucial that we recognize this horizontal form of power, for it operates in ways that render it less visible than vertical power, which is displayed and commanded by Western- or European-style models of law and policy. Yet, as my book demonstrates, it has important consequences (both negative and positive) that form part of its extensive reach in keeping with the multidimensional aspects of a postnational landscape. In Botswana, laws and policies relating to land are inextricably linked to transnational and international institutions and agencies' global agendas, whatever their nature. For this reason, Botswana is caught up in a broader world of values, principles, and legal approaches to land administration circulating beyond and within its borders and framing a version of the global that serves both as a potential model for change and transformation as well as a wake-up call for the recognition of social inequality and exclusion that must be factored into our understanding of what it means to be global.

APPENDIX

DRAWING TOGETHER THE DOCUMENTARY MATERIAL FROM DIFFERENT SOURCES required the collation of data on the number and types of appeals that the Land Tribunal has processed over the years, not an easy task. Between 2009 and 2010, my research assistant Phidelia Dintwe and I carried out a comprehensive search of tribunal records, attended cases at the Gaborone and Palapye Tribunal, and conducted interviews with tribunal members.[1] As far as we are aware, this study was the first time such a search of the records has been completed. Our search involved working with old registers as well as with the online court rolls, as up until 2005 appeals were recorded in individual land board registers before being lodged within the Consolidated Land Tribunal Register.

The data can only provide a rough estimate of the number of cases heard, as it was difficult to establish from the records which cases had been completed, as opposed to those that were recorded twice because of postponement. As Mr. Manase, the Principal Clerk (now Registrar) at the Gaborone Tribunal explained, the online database was not accurate because tribunal staff were updating it all the time, and there was no record of the complete number of cases dealt with in a year. There was also the problem of the online database being susceptible to viruses. Nonetheless, our findings provide a guide to the number and types of cases that the Land Tribunal deals with throughout the country and demonstrate how the caseload has increased over time. These records and current Land Tribunal registers indicate that the number of appeals have dramatically increased since the tribunal came into operation.

Table A.1 shows the total number of cases in the Land Tribunal in Gaborone and Palapye broken down according to the land boards whose decisions were appealed. Notice how the caseload has increased from 394 appeals, during the twenty-five-year period from 1971 to 1996, to 3,725 appeals occurring within a thirteen-year period from 1997 to 2010. There were also 124 appeals where the date was unclear, bringing the total number of appeals between 1971 and 2010 to 4,241.

Table A.1. Caseload of appeals up to introduction of Land Tribunal and to 2010

Land Board	1971–1996	n.d.	1997–2010	Total
Gaborone Tribunal				
Kweneng	48	25	797	870
Kgatleng	24	10	268	302
Malete	27	7	144	178
Rolong	14	8	68	90
Kgalagadi	8	12	139	159
Ngwaketse	58	9	265	332
Tlokweng	62	16	300	378
Palapye Tribunal				
Ngwato	100	18	1,173	1,291
Tawana	29	9	356	394
Tati	9	4	52	65
Chobe	12	1	58	71
Gahnzi	3	5	103	111
Total	394	124	3,723	4,241

Tables A.2 and A.3 show a breakdown of appeals according to designated land use within each land board. As is evident from the tables, Ngwato Land Board has the largest number of appeals, amounting to 30 percent of cases overall, with 67 percent of those cases heard at its Palapye branch. Kweneng Land Board follows with 21 percent of overall appeals and

Table A.2. Appeals by tribunal, from 1971 to February 2010

Type of Appeal	Gaborone Tribunal	Palapye Tribunal	Total
Residential (Res)	500	225	725
Commercial (Com)	709	674	1,383
Water Point/Borehole (WP/B)	252	603	855
Agricultural (Agr)	340	177	517
Tribunal Order (T.O.)	180	0	180
Civic and Community (C&C)	60	55	115
Miscellaneous (Misc)	125	76	201
Unclear (Unc)	137	55	192
Canceled (Can)	40	33	73
Total	2,343	1,898	4,241

Table A.3. Appeals by land board, from 1971 to February 2010

Land Board	Res	Com	WP/B	Agr	T.O.	C&C	Misc	Unc	Can	Total
Kweneng	143	306	95	86	71	35	70	48	16	870
Kgatleng	41	96	36	48	27	9	12	22	11	302
Malete	83	52	2	18	9	4	3	7	0	178
Rolong	14	16	3	43	6	0	0	8	0	90
Nkgwaketse	35	138	45	66	22	3	11	12	0	332
Tlokweng	181	50	6	60	18	7	21	31	4	378
Kgalagadi	1	39	56	16	20	1	8	9	9	159
Ngwato	99	471	489	106	9	39	31	28	19	1,291
Tawana	89	157	45	39	0	15	24	17	8	394
Tati	19	18	3	12	0	0	4	6	3	65
Chobe	15	25	1	14	0	0	11	4	1	71
Ghanzi	5	13	74	9	0	2	6	0	2	111
Total	725	1381	855	517	182	115	201	192	73	4,241

37 percent of those appeals lodged with its Gaborone branch. The largest number of appeals involved commercial appeals, followed by water point/ borehole, and then by residential cases.

Note

1. Interviews were held October 12, 2009; January 13, 2010; June 14, 2010; and July 14, 2015 with the following personnel: Mr. Baruti, President, Main Tribunal, Gaborone (who left to go to the High Court and who has been replaced by Mrs. S. Kaisara [formerly Ms. S. Chuma]); Ms. S. Chuma, President, Ad Hoc Tribunal, Gaborone; Ms. Moremong, Registrar; Mr. Motlogelwa Administrator Land Tribunal and Mr. Manase, Principal Clerk of court; Mr. K. Rutherford, Mr. S. Rapinyana, and Mr. G. Tobedza, all Members of the LT in Gaborone; as well as with Mr. Nare, President, Main Tribunal, Palapye; and Mr. Mareng, Acting Registrar, Palapye.

REFERENCES

Aalders, Marius. 1993 "Regulation and In-Company Environmental Management in the Netherlands" *Law & Policy* 15(2): 75–94.

African Development Bank (AfDB). "Botswana Economic Outlook." *African Economic Outlook.* Accessed on May 1, 2017. https://www.afdb.org/en/countries/southern-africa /botswana/botswana-economic-outlook/.

———. 2004–2005. "Country Studies—Botswana." *African Economic Outlook.* Accessed January 15, 2017. www.oecd.org/dev/emea/africaneconomicoutlook20042005country studies.htm.

———. 2007. "Country Studies—Botswana." *African Economic Outlook.* Accessed January 15, 2017. www.oecd.org/dev/emea/africaneconomicoutlook2007.htm.

———. 2009. *Botswana, 2009–2013.* A Country Strategy Paper. Regional Department—South Region A (May 2009). Accessed August 25, 2014. https://www.afdb.org/fileadmin /uloads/afdb/Documents/Project-and-Operations/BOTSWANA_2009-2012.

———. 2014. *African Economic Outlook.* Accessed January 15, 2017. www.oecd.org/dev/emea /africaneconomicoutlook2014.htm.

———. 2015. "Country Studies-Botswana." *African Economic Outlook.* Accessed January 17, 2019. https://www.norfund.no/getfile.php/134019-1484665185?Bilder/Publictions /AEO2015_EN.pdf.

———. 2016. *AfDB Supports Botswana's Economic Diversification Programme, 2016.* Accessed May 1, 2017. https://www.afdb.org/en/nes-and-events/afdb-supports-botsanas -economic-diversification-programme-156.

Akram-Lodhi, A. Harron, and Cristobal Kay. 2010. "Surveying the Agrarian Question: Current Debates and Beyond." Pt. 2. *Journal of Peasant Studies* 37(2): 255–284.

Alverson, Hoyt. 1978. *Mind in the Heart of Darkness: Value and Self-Identity among the Tswana of Southern Africa.* New Haven, CT: Yale University Press.

Amanor, Kogo Sebastian, and Sam Moyo. 2008. *Land and Sustainable Development in Africa.* London: Zed.

Banda, Fareda. 2004. "The End of Culture? African Women and Human Rights." In *Remaking Law in Africa: Transnationalism, Persons and Rights*, edited by Jude Muirison, Anne Griffiths, and Kenneth Kings, 115–137. Edinburgh: Centre of African Studies, University of Edinburgh.

Bank of Botswana. 2015. *Annual Report.* Gaborone, Botswana.

Benda-Beckmann, Franz von. 2003. "Mysteries of Capital or Mystification of Legal Property?" *European Journal of Anthropology* 41:187–191.

Benda-Beckmann, Franz von, and Keebet von Benda-Beckmann. 2014. "Temporalities of Property Relations under Plural Legal Orders: Minankabau Revisited." *Journal of Legal Pluralism and Unofficial Law* 46(1): 18–36.

Benda-Beckmann, Franz von, Keebet von Benda-Beckmann, and Anne Griffiths, eds. 2005. *Mobile People, Mobile Law: Expanding Legal Relations in a Contracting World.* Aldershot, UK: Ashgate.

——. 2009a. *The Power of Law in a Transnational World: Anthropological Enquiries*. New York: Berghahn.

——. 2009b. *Spatializing Law: An Anthropological Geography of Law in Society*. Surrey, UK: Ashgate.

Benda-Beckmann, Franz von, Kebeet von Benda-Beckmann, and Melanie Wiber, eds. 2006. *Changing Properties of Property*. New York: Berghahn.

Bernstorff, Jochen von. 2004. "The Structural Limitation of Network Governance: ICANN as a Case in Point." In *Transnational Governance and Constitutionalism*, edited by Christian Joerges, Inger-Johanne J. Sand, and Gunther Teubner, 257–281. Oxford: Hart.

Berry, Sara. 2002. "Debating the Land Question in Africa." *Comparative Studies in Society and History* 44(4): 638–668.

——. 2009. "Property, Authority and Citizenship: Land Claims, Politics and the Dynamics of Social Division in West Africa." *Development and Change* 40(1): 23–45.

Bledsoe, C. 1990. "Transformations in Sub-Saharan African Marriage and Fertility." *Annals of the American Academy of Political and Social Science* 510(1): 115–125.

Blomley, Nicholas K. 1994. *Law, Space and the Geographies of Power*. New York: Guilford.

Borras, Saturnino M., Jr., and Jennifer Franco. 2010. "Towards a Broader View of the Politics of Global Land Grab." Initiatives in Critical Agrarian Studies (ICAS) Working Paper Series No. 001 (May). Land Deal Politics Initiative and Transnational Institute.

Botswana, Government of. 1975. *National Policy on Tribal Grazing Land Policy*. Government Paper No. 2 of 1975. Gaborone: Government Printer.

——. 1981. *Report of the Commission of Inquiry into Nkgwaketse Development Area Ranches and Government Decision on the Recommendations of the Commission*. Gaborone: Government Printer.

——. 1983. *Report of the Presidential Commission on Land Tenure*. Gaborone: Government Printer.

——. 1985–1990. National Development Plan (NDP6). Ministry of Finance and Development Planning. Central Statistics Office. Gaborone: Government Printer.

——. 1990. National Conservation Strategy. Government Paper No 1. Gaborone: Government Printer.

——. 1991a. National Policy on Agricultural Development. Government Paper No. 1. Gaborone: Government Printer.

——. 1991b. *Report of the Presidential Commission of Enquiry into Land Problems in Mogoditshane and Other Peri-Urban Villages*. Gaborone: Government Printer.

——. 1991–1997. National Development Plan (NDP7). Ministry of Finance and Development Planning. Central Statistics Office. Gaborone: Government Printer.

——. 1992a. *Report of the Presidential Commission of Inquiry into Land Problems in Mogoditshane and Other Peri-Urban Villages* (otherwise known as the Kgabo Land Commission Report). Gaborone: Government Printer.

——. 1992b. *Land Problems in Mogoditshane and Other Peri-Urban Villages*. Gaborone: Government Printer.

——. 1997. Vision 2016: Prosperity for all last accessed 17th January 2019. https://www.gov .bw/en/Ministries--Authorities/Minnistries/Ministry-of-Local-Government-ML91? News/VISION-2036-Proeperity-for-all

——. 1998. Botswana National Settlement Policy of 1998. Government Paper No. 2. Gaborone: Government Printer.

——. 2000. National Policy on Housing in Botswana. Gaborone: Government Printer.

———. 2002a. *Botswana National Land Policy: Issues Report.* Rev. ed. Vol. 1. Ministry of Lands and Housing. Department of Lands. Gaborone: Government Printer.

———. 2002b. National Master Plan for Arable Agriculture and Dairy Development. Government Paper No. 1. Gaborone: Government Printer.

———. 2002c. Revised National Policy on Rural Development. Government Paper No. 1. Gaborone: Government Printer.

———. 2003a. "Botswana Land Policy." By B. M. Mathuba. Ministry of Lands and Housing. Unpublished paper presented at an International Workshop on Land Policies in Southern Africa, Berlin, Germany (May 26–27).

———. 2003b. *Review of Botswana National Land Policy: Final Report.* Vol. 1. (January 31). National Resources Services (Pty) in association with LANDflow Solutions (Pty), Ministry of Lands and Housing, Department of Land. Gaborone: Government Printer.

———. 2003–2009. Kweneng District Development Plan (NDP6). Ministry of Local Government. Kweneng District Council. Kweneng District Development Committee. Gaborone: Government Printer.

———. 2003/04–2008/09. National Development Plan (NDP9). Ministry of Finance and Development Planning. Central Statistics Office. Gaborone: Government Printer.

———. 2004. *Household Income and Expenditure Survey 2002/03: Main Report.* Vol. 1. Central Statistics Office. Gaborone: Government Printer.

———. 2006. *Botswana Demographic Survey.* Central Statistics Office. Gaborone: Government Printer.

———. 2007a. *Informal Sector Survey Report (ISS).* Central Statistics Office. Gaborone: Government Printer.

———. 2007b. *Report of the Auditor General.* Office of the Auditor General. Gaborone: Government Printer.

———. 2009a. *Education Statistics 2000: Stats Brief.* Central Statistics Office. Gaborone: Government Printer.

———. 2009b. *Long Term Vision for Botswana: Vision 2016, Botswana Performance Report; A Report on the Progress Being Achieved against the Vision 2016 Goals.* Vision Council. Gaborone: Government Printer.

———. 2009c. Presentation to the 64th Session of the UN General Assembly (October 6) by Botswana Youth Delegates, Bogolo Kenewendo and Yolise Modise.

———. 2010–2016. National Development Plan (NDP10). Ministry of Finance and Development Planning. Central Statistics Office. Gaborone: Government Printer.

———. 2011a, 2012a, 2013, 2014. Draft Botswana Land Policy. Ministry of Lands and Housing. Gaborone: Government Printer.

———. 2011b. *Population and Housing Census: Preliminary Brief.* Accessed May 18, 2013. ecstats.uneca.org/aimcd/Portals/0/Census2011 Preliminary Brief September 29 2011 .pdf.

———. 2012b. *Keynote Policy Paper for Mid-Term Review of NDP 10* (June). Ministry of Finance and Development Planning. Gaborone: Government Printer.

———. 2015. Botswana Land Policy (BLP). Government Paper No. 4. Approved by the National Assembly (July 16). Ministry of Lands and Housing. Gaborone: Government Printer.

Botswana Institute for Development Policy Analysis (BIDPA). 2016. *Botswana* (May 9). Accessed May 1, 2017. https://www.bidpa.bw/research/content.php?id=1.

Bruce, John. 1998. "Learning from the Comparative Experience with Agrarian Reform." In *Proceedings of the International Conference on Land Tenure in the Developing World*, edited by Michael Barry. Cape Town: University of Cape Town Press.

Center for International Governance Innovation (CIGI) and Korea Development Institute (KDI). 2012. "Post-2015 Development Agenda: Goals, Targets and Indicators." Special Report by Nicole Bates-Earner, Barry Carin, Min Ha Lee and Wonhyuk Lim, with Min Kesh Kapila. https://sustainabledevelopment.n.org/contents/documents/775cigi.pdf.

Chanock, Martin. 1985. *Law, Custom and Social Order: The Colonial Experience in Malawi and Zambia*. Cambridge: Cambridge University Press.

———. 2002. "Human Rights and Cultural Branding: Who Speaks and How." In *Cultural Transformation and Human Rights in Africa*, edited by A. A. An-Na'im, 38–67. London: Zed.

Chiagra, Ben, ed. 2012. *African Development Community Land Issues: Towards a New Sustainable Land Relations Policy*. Oxford: Routledge.

Claassens, Aninka, and Ben Cousins. 2008. *Land, Power and Custom: Controversies Generated by South Africa's Communal Land Rights Act*. Cape Town: University of Cape Town Press.

Colclough, Christopher, and Stephen McCarthy. 1980. *The Political Economy of Botswana: A Study of Growth and Distribution*. Oxford: Oxford University Press.

Comaroff, John L., and Simon A. Roberts. 1981. *Rules and Processes: The Cultural Logic of Dispute in an African Context*. Chicago: University of Chicago Press.

Commission on Legal Empowerment of the Poor and the UN Development Program. 2008. *Making the Law Work for Everyone*. Vol. 1. Accessed September 18, 2016. https://www.un.org/ruleoflaw/files/Making_the_Law_Work_for_Everyone.pdf.

Cooper, David M. (1980) 1982. *Botswana Class Structure and Its Articulation with the Rural Mode of Production: Insights from Selebi-Pikwe*. Cape Town: Center for African Studies, University of Cape Town.

Cooper, Frederick. 2001. "What Is the Concept of Globalization Good For? An African Historian's Perspective." *African Affairs* 100:189–193.

Cottrell, M. Patrick, and David M. Trubek. 2012. "Law as Problem Solving: Standards, Networks, Experimentation and Deliberation in a Global Space." *Transnational Law and Contemporary Problems* 21:359–393.

Cotula, Lorenzo. 2015a. "Harnessing the Law to Contest 'Land Grab.'" *Reflect and Act* (October). London: International Institute for Environment and Development (IIED).

———. 2015b. "Land Rights, International Law and a Shrinking Planet." *Briefings* (July). London: IIED.

———. 2016. *Foreign Investment, Law and Sustainable Development: A Handbook on Agriculture and Extractive Industries*. 2nd ed. London: IIED.

Crang, Mike, and Nigel Thrift, eds. 2000. *Thinking Space*. London: Routledge.

Davis, Kevin, Angelina Fisher, Benedict Kingsbury, and Sally Engle Merry. 2012. *Governance by Indicators: Global Power through Quantification and Ranking*. Oxford: Oxford University Press.

De Soto, Hernando. 2000. *The Mystery of Capital: Why Capitalism Triumphs in the West and Fails Everywhere Else*. New York: Basic Books.

Dintwat, Kakanyo Fani. 2010. "Changing Family Structure in Botswana." *Journal of Comparative Family Studies* 41(3): 281–297.

Duffield, Mark R. 2001. *Global Governance and the New Wars*. London: Zed.

Ehrlich, Eugen. (1913) 1936. *Fundamental Principles of the Sociology of Law.* Translated by W. L. Moll. Harvard Studies in Jurisprudence No. 5. Cambridge, MA: Harvard University Press.

Engle, David M. 1995. "Law in the Domain of Everyday Life: The Construction of Community and Difference." In *Law in Everyday Life,* edited by Austin Sarat and Thomas R. Kearns, 123–170. Ann Arbor: University of Michigan Press.

Fabian, Johannes. 1983. *Time and the Other: How Anthropology Makes Its Object.* New York: Columbia University Press.

———. 1996. *Remembering the Present: Painting and Popular History in Zaire.* Berkeley: University of California Press.

Fassin, Didier. 2012. "That Obscure Object of Global Health." In *Medical Anthropology at the Intersections: Histories, Activisims and Futures,* edited by Marcia C. Inhorn and Emily A. Wentzell, 95–115. Durham, NC: Duke University Press.

Fawcus, Peter, and Alan Tilbury. 2000. *The Road to Independence.* Gaborone: Pula Press and the Botswana Society.

Ferguson, James. 2006. *Africa in the Neoliberal World Order.* Durham, NC: Duke University Press.

Ferguson, Marjorie. 1992. "The Mythology about Globalization." *European Journal of Communication* 7(1): 69–93.

Fitzpatrick, Peter. 1992. *The Mythology of Modern Law.* London: Routledge.

Ghai, Yash P., and J. Patrick B. W. McAuslan. 1970. *Public Law and Political Change in Kenya: A Study of the Legal Framework of Government from Colonial Times to the Present.* Nairobi: Oxford University Press.

Giddens, Anthony. 1979. *Central Problems in Social Theory: Action, Structure and Contradiction in Social Analysis.* London: Macmillan.

———. 1990. *The Consequences of Modernity.* Stanford, CA: Stanford University Press.

Gilpin, Robert. 2001. *Global Political Economy.* Princeton, NJ: Princeton University Press.

Gluckman, Max. 1971. *Politics, Law, and Ritual in Tribal Society.* New York: Basil Blackwell.

Good, Kenneth. 1992. "Interpreting the Exceptionality of Botswana." *Journal of Modern African Studies* 30(1): 69–95.

Greenhouse, Carol. 1998. "Just in Time: Temporality and the Cultural Legitimation of Law." *Yale Law Journal* 98(8): 1631–1651.

Greenhouse, Carol, Barbara Yngvesson, and David Engle. 1994. *Law and Community in Three American Towns.* Ithaca, NY: Cornell University Press.

Griffiths, Anne. 1988. "Support among Bakwena." In *Between Kinship and the State,* edited by F. von Benda-Beckmann et al., 289–316. Dordrecht: Foris.

———. 1990–1991. "The 'Women's Question' in Kwena Family Disputes." *Journal of Legal Pluralism and Unofficial Law* 30–31:223–254.

———. 1996. "Between Paradigms: Differing Perspectives on Justice in Molepolole, Botswana." *Journal of Legal Pluralism and Unofficial Law* 36:195–214.

———. 1997. *In the Shadow of Marriage: Gender and Justice in an African Community.* Chicago: University of Chicago Press.

———. 2001. "Gendering Culture: Towards a Plural Perspective on Kwena Women's Rights." In *Culture and Rights: Anthropological Perspectives,* edited by Jane K. Cowan, Marie-Bénédicte Dembour, and Richard Wilson, 102–126. Cambridge: Cambridge University Press.

———. 2002. "Legal Pluralism." In *An Introduction to Law and Social Theory,* edited by Reza Banakar and Max Travers, 289–310. Oxford: Hart.

———. 2007. "Making Gender Visible in Law: Kwena Women's Access to Power and Resources." In *Human Rights, Plural Legalities and Gendered Realities: Paths Are Made by Walking.* Harare: Weaver.

———. 2010. "International Human Rights, Women, Gender and Culture: Perspectives from Africa." In *Cultural Diversity and the Law: State Responses from Around the World,* edited by Marie Claire Foblets, Jean-François Gaudreault-Desbiens, and Alison Dundes Renteln, 737–761. Bruxelles: Bruylant.

———. 2012. "The Changing Dynamics of Customary Land Tenure: Women's Access to and Control over Land in Botswana." *Acta Juridica* 11:65–96.

———. 2013. "Reviewing Legal Pluralism." In *Law and Social Theory,* edited by Rexa Banakar and Max Travers, 269–286. Oxford: Hart.

———. 2014. "Embodied Histories: Exploring Law's Temporality in Relation to Land in Botswana." *Journal of Legal Pluralism and Unofficial Law* 46(1): 37–59.

Griffiths, John. 1986. "What Is Legal Pluralism?" *Journal of Legal Pluralism and Unofficial Law* 18(24): 1–55.

Gulbrandsen, Ornulf. 1980. *Agro Pastoral Production and Communal Land Use.* Gaborone: Government Printer.

———. 2012. *The State and the Social: State Transformation in Botswana and Precolonial and Colonial Genealogies.* New York: Berghahn Books.

Habitat III. 2016. New Urban Agenda. Adoped at the UN Conference on Housing and Sustainable Urban Development, October 17–20, 2016, Quito, Ecuador. Accessed January 14, 2017. https://habitat3.org/the-new-urban-agenda/.

Hardin, Garrett. 1968. "Tragedy of the Commons." *Science* 162 (3859): 1243–1248.

Harvey, David. 1990. "Between Space and Time: Reflections on the Geographical Imagination." *Annals of the Association of American Geographers* 80(3): 418–434.

Held, David, Anthony McGrew, David Goldblatt, and Jonathan Perraton. 1999. *Global Transformations: Politics, Economics and Culture.* Stanford, CA: Stanford University Press.

Hellum, Anne. 1998. "Women's Human Rights and the Dynamics of African Customary Laws in a Changing World: Three Studies of Procreative Problems, Patrilineal Continuity and Gender Equality in Zimbabwean Family Law and Practice." PhD diss., Faculty of Law, University of Oslo.

Hellum, Anne, Sardar Ali, and Anne Griffiths, eds. 2011. *From Transnational Relations to Transnational Laws: Northern European Laws at the Crossroads.* Surrey, UK: Ashgate.

Hellum, Anne, Patricia Kaberi-Mbote, Barbara von Koppen, et al. 2015. *Water Is Life: Women's Human Rights in National and Local Water Governance in Southern and Eastern Africa.* Harare: Weaver.

Hirsch, Eric, and Charles Stewart. 2005. "Introduction: Ethnographies of Historicity." *History and Anthropology* 16(3): 261–274.

Holleman, Johan Frederik. 1973. "Trouble-Cases and Trouble-less Cases in the Study of Customary Law and Legal Reform." *Law and Society Review* 7:585–609.

Hooker, Michael Barry. 1975. *Legal Pluralism. An Introduction to Colonial and Neo-Colonial Laws.* Oxford: Clarendon Press.

Home, Robert. 2012. "The Colonial Legacy in Land Rights in Southern Africa." In *African Development Community Land Issues: Towards a New Sustainable Land Relations Policy,* edited by B. Chiagra, 8–26. Oxford: Routledge.

Hove, Mediwl, Emmaculate Tsitsi Ngwerume, and Cyprian Muchemwa. 2013. "The Urban Crisis in Sub-Saharan Africa: A Threat to Human Security and Sustainable

Development." *Stability: International Journal of Security and Development* 2(1): Art. 7:1–14.

Hubbard, Phil, Rob Kitchin, Bartley Brendan, and Duncan Fuller. 2002. *Thinking Geographically: Space, Theory and Contemporary Human Geography.* London: Continuum.

Hunt, Alan, and Wickham, Gary. 1994. *Foucault and Law: Towards a Sociology of Law as Governance.* London: Pluto Press.

Ijagbemi, Bayo. 2006. "Land Tenure Reform and Social Transformation in Botswana: Implications for Urbanization." PhD diss., University of Arizona, Tucson. http://hdl .handle.net/10150/196133.

Isaacs, Senwelo M., and Boga Thura Manatasha. 2016. "Will the Dreaded 'Yellow Monster' Stop Roaring Again? An Appraisal of Botswana's 2015 Land Policy." *Botswana Notes and Records* 48:383–395.

James, Deborah. 2007. *Gaining Ground? Rights and Property in South African Land Reform.* Abingdon, UK: Routledge-Cavendish.

James, Rodin William. 1971. *Land Tenure and Policy in Tanzania.* Toronto: University of Toronto Press.

Kalabamu, Faustin, and Siamsang Morolong. 2004. *Informal Land Delivery Processes and Access to Land for the Poor in Greater Gaborone, Botswana.* Working Paper No. 3. Project on Informal Land Delivery Processes in African Cities. International Development Department, University of Birmingham / Department of Architecture and Town Planning and Department of Law, University of Botswana.

Kalabamu, Faustin Tirwirukwa. 2003. *Changing Gender and Institutional Roles in Self-Help Housing in Botswana: The Case of Lobatse.* Institute of Southern African Studies. Lesotho.

———. 2005. "Perceptions on Renegotiated Customary Inheritance in Tlokweng, Botswana." In *Gender, Generation and Urban Living Conditions in Southern Africa*, edited by Faustin. T. Kalabamu, Matlelise M. Mapetla, and Ana Schlyter, 67–80. Lesotho: Institute of Southern African Studies.

———. 2006. "Patriarchy and Women's Land Rights in Botswana." *Land Use Policy* 23(3): 237–246.

———. 2009. "Towards Egalitarian Inheritance Rights in Botswana: The Case of Tlokweng." *Development Southern Africa* 26(2): 209–223.

Kerven, Carol. 1982. "The Effects of Migration on Agricultural Production." In *Migration in Botswana: Patterns, Causes and Consequences*, 526–622. Final Report of the National Migration Study 3. Gaborone: Government Printer.

Khan, Liaquat A. 2009. "Temporality of Law." *McGeorge Law Review* 40:55–106.

Kinsman, Margaret. 1983. "'Beasts of Burden': The Subordination of Southern Tswana Women, ca. 1800–1840." *Journal of Southern African Studies* 10(1): 39–54.

Kocken, Elizabeth Maria, and George Christiaan Uhlenbeck. 1980. *Tlokweng, A Village Near Town.* ICA Publication No. 39. Institute of Cultural and Social Studies, Leiden University.

Lawson, Stephanie. 2011. "Is the Future a Foreign Country?" *Australian Journal of Politics and History* 57(3): 420–433.

Lefebvre, Henri. 1991. *The Production of Space.* Oxford: Blackwell. First published in French as *La Production de l'espace.* Paris: Anthropos.

Lekorwe, Mogopodi. 2005. "The Organisation of Political Parties." In *40 Years of Democracy in Botswana, 1965–2005.* Gaborone: Mmegi.

Letsididi, Bashi. 2014. "Botswana's Income Inequality Still among Highest in the World." *Sunday Standard* (April 27). Accessed April 19, 2017. www.sundaystandard.into /botswana's-income-inequality-still-among-highest-world.

Llewellyn, Karl Nickerson, and Edward Adamson Hoebel. (1941) 1953. *The Cheyenne Way: Conflict and Case Law in Primitive Jurisprudence.* Reprint, Norman: University of Oklahoma Press.

Low, Setha M., and Denise Lawrence-Zuniga, eds. 2003. *The Anthropology of Space and Place: Locating Culture.* Oxford: Blackwell and Carlton.

Lund, Christian. 2013. "The Past and Space: On Arguments in African Land Control." *Africa* 83(10): 14–35.

Lynd, Alice, and Staughton Lynd. 1996. "'We Are All We've Got': Building a Retiree Movement in Youngstown, Ohio." In *Law Stories*, edited by G. Bellow and M. Minow, 77–99. Ann Arbor: University of Michigan Press.

Makgala, John, and Mokganedi, Sara Botlhomilwe. 2017. "Elite Interests and Political Participation in Botswana, 1966–2011." *Journal of Contemporary African Studies* 35(1): 54–72.

Manji, Ambreena. 2001. "Land Reform in the Shadow of the State: The Implementation of New Land Laws in Sub-Saharan Africa." *Third World Quarterly* 22(3): 327–342.

———. 2003a. "Capital, Labor and Land Relations in Africa: A Gender Analysis of the World Bank's Policy Research Report on Land Institutions and Land Policy." *Third World Quarterly* 24(1): 97–114.

———. 2003b. "Remortgaging Women's Lives: The World Bank's Land Agenda in Africa." *Feminist Legal Studies* 11:139–162.

———. 2005. Review of "Cause and Consequence in Law and Development." *Journal of Modern Africa Studies* 43(1): 119–138.

———. 2010. "Eliminating Poverty? 'Financial Inclusion,' Access to Land, and Gender Equality in International Development." *Modern Law Review* 73(6): 985–1025.

———. 2014. Review of *Land Law Reform in Eastern Africa: Traditional or Transformative? A Critical Review of 50 years of Land Law Reform in Eastern Africa, 1961–2011.* By Patrick McAuslan. *Journal of Law and Society* 41(2): 327–332.

Massey, Doreen. 1994. "A Global Sense of Place." In *Space, Place and Gender*, 146–156. Minneapolis: University of Minnesota Press.

———. 2013. "A Dialogue between Doreen Massey and Nigel Warburton." *Social Science Bites* (February 1). Accessed November 11, 2016. http://www.socialsciencespace.com/2012 /02/podcastdoreen.-massey-on-space.

Mathuba, Botselo M. 1982. *Customary and Modern Land Tenure Systems in Botswana.* Madison: University of Wisconsin Press.

May, John, and Nigel Thrift. 2001. *Timespace: Geographies of Temporality.* London: Routledge.

McAuslan, Patrick. 1997. "Law, Governance and the Development of the Market: Practical Problems and Practical Solutions." In *Good Government and Law: Legal and Institutional Reform in Developing Countries*, edited by J. Faundez, 25–44. London: Macmillan/St. Martin's Press.

———. 2003. *Bringing the Law Back In: Essays in Land, Law and Development.* Aldershot, UK: Ashgate.

———. 2014. *Land Law Reform in Eastern Africa: Traditional or Transformative? A Critical Review of 50 Years of Land Law Reform in Eastern Africa, 1961–2011.* London: Routledge.

McGrew, Anthony G. 2010. "Globalization and global Politics." In *The Globalization of World Politics: An Introduction to International Relations,* edited by John Baylis, Steve Smith, and Patrica Owens, 5th ed. Oxford: Oxford University Press.

Mensah, Joseph. 2008. Introduction to *Neoliberalism and Globalization in Africa: Contestations on the Embattled Continent,* edited by Joseph Mensah, 1–32. New York: Palgrave Macmillan.

———. 2008. "Cultural Dimensions of Globalization in Africa: A Dialectical Interpretation of the Local and the Global." In *Neoliberalism and Globalization in Africa: Contestations on the Embattled Continent,* edited by J. Mensah, 33–54. New York: Palgrave Macmillan.

Merry, Sally Engle. 1988. "Legal Pluralism." *Law and Society Review* 22(5): 869–896.

———. 2000. "Crossing Boundaries: Ethnography in the Twenty-First Century." *PoLar* 23(2): 127–133.

———. 2011. "Measuring the World: Indicators, Human Rights and Global Governance." *Current Anthropology* 52(S3): S85–S95.

Mmegi Online. 2012. "Squatter Settlement Ordered to Make Way for BDC [Botswana Development Corporation] Project." (March 16). Accessed May 20, 2012. www.mmegi .bw/index.php?sid=4&aid=17&dir=2012.

———. 2015. "Botswana Third Most Unequal Country in the World." (December 10). By Brian Benza. Accessed April 19, 2017. www.mmegi.bw/index.ph?paid=564068dir=2015 /december10.

———. 2017. "Mogoditshane Still a Squatters' Haven." (August 11). By Pini Bothoko. Accessed February 12, 2018. www.mmegi.bw/index.php?aid=7091&dir=2017/august/11.

Mogalakwe, Monagang, and Francis Nyamnjoh. 2017. "Botswana at 50: Democratic Deficit, Elite Corruption and Poverty in the Middle of Plenty." *Journal of Contemporary African Studies* 35(1): 1–14.

Molenaar, Marja. 1980. "Social Change within a Traditional Pattern: A Case Study of a Tswana Ward." MA thesis, University of Leiden.

Molokomme, Athaliah. 1991. *"Children of the Fence": The Maintenance of Extra-marital Children under Law and Practice in Botswana.* Research Report No. 46. Leiden: African Studies Centre.

Moore, Sally Falk. 1969. "Law and Anthropology." *Biennial Review of Anthropology* 6:252–300.

———. 1973. "Law and Social Change: The Semi-Autonomous Social Field as an Object of Study." *Law and Society Review* 7(4): 719–746.

Morison, John. 2003. "Modernising Government and the E-Government Revolution: Technologies of Government and Technologies of Democracy." In *Public Law in a Multi-Layered Constitution,* edited by Nicholas Bamforth and Peter Leyland, 157–188. Oxford, UK: Hart.

Morolong, Siamisung Thoki, and Clement Ng'ong'ola. 2007. "Revisiting the Notion of Tribal Land." In *Essays on the Law of Botswana,* edited by Charles M. Fombad, 142–175. South Africa: Juta Law.

Morten, Jerven. 2013. *Poor Numbers: How We Are Misled by African Development Statistics and What to Do about It*. Ithaca, NY: Cornell University Press.

Motzafi-Haller, Pnina. 1986. "Whither the 'True Bushman': The Dynamics of Perpetual Mariginality." In *Proceedings of the International Symposium on African Hunters and Gatherers*, edited by Franz Rottland and Rainer Vossen, 295–328. Sankt Augustin. *Sprache und Geschichte in Afrika* 7(1).

Munn, Nancy D. 1992. "The Cultural Anthropology of Time: A Critical Essay." *Annual Review of Anthropology* 21:93–123.

Murphy, Sophia. 2013. *Land Grabs and Fragile Food Systems: The Role of Globalization*. Report of the Institute for Agriculture and Trade Policy (February 20). Accessed January 11, 2017. www.latp.org/documents/land-grabs-and-fragile-food-systems.

Murray, Andrew, and Neil Parsons. 1987. "The Modern Economic History of Botswana." In *Studies in the Economic History of Southern Africa: The Front-Line States*, edited by Simon Katzenellenbogen, Zbigniew A. Konczacki, Jane L. Papart, and Timothy M. Shaw, 159–199. London: Frank Cass.

Naganti, Fanual. 1982. "Early Capitalist Penetration: The Impact of Precolonical Trade in Kweneng (1840–1876)." In *Settlement in Botswana*, edited by Renee Hitchcock and Mary R. Smith. Marshalltown, South Africa: Heinemann and the Botswana Society.

Ng'ong'ola, Clement. 1997. "Land Rights for Marginalized Ethnic Groups in Botswana, with Special Reference to Basarwa." *Journal of African Law* 41:1–26.

Nyamu-Musembi, Celestine. 2002. "Are Local Norms and Practices Fences or Pathways? The Example of Women's Property Rights." In *Cultural Transformation and Human Rights in Africa*, edited by Abdullahi A. An-Na'im, 126–150. London: Zed.

———. 2007. "De Soto and Land Relations in Rural Africa: Breathing Life into Dead Theories about Property Rights." *Third World Quarterly* 28(8): 1457–1478.

Okatch, Zelda. "Determinants of Poverty and Inequality in Botswana." PhD diss., University of Western Australia. Accessed April 17, 2017. http://research-repository.uwa.edu.au /files/9839128/THESIS_DOCTOR_OF_PHILOSOPHY_OKATCH_Zelda_Achieng _2015.pdf.

Okihiro, Gary Y. 1976. "Hunters, Herders, Cultivators and Traders: Interaction and Change in the Kgalagadi, Nineteenth Century." PhD diss., University of California, Los Angeles.

———. 1981. "Population Change among the Kwena of Botswana." Paper presented in a seminar at the Centre of African Studies (April 24–25). Edinburgh: Centre of African Studies, Edinburgh University.

O'Meally, Simon. 2014. "The Contradiction of Pro-Poor Participation and Empowerment: The World Bank in East Africa." *Development and Change* 45(6): 1248–1283.

Parson, Jack. 1981. "Cattle, Class, and State in Rural Botswana." *Journal of Southern African Studies* 7:236–255.

Parsons, Neil. 1977. "The Economic History of Khama's Country in Botswana, 1844–1930." In *The Roots of Rural Poverty in Central and Southern Africa*, edited by Neil Parsons and Robin Palmer, 113–143. Berkeley: University of California Press.

Patomaki, Heikki. 2011. "On the Complexities of Time and Temporality: Implications for World History and Global Futures." *Australian Journal of Politics and History* 57(3): 339–352.

Peluso, Nancy Lee. 2009. "Rubber Erasures, Rubber Producing Rights: Making Racialized Territories in West Kalimantan, Indonesia." *Development and Change* 40(1): 47–80.

Perche, Diana. 2011. "Dialogue between Past and Present: Policy Evaluation and History." *Australian Journal of Politics and History* 57(3): 403–419.

Perry, Richard Warren, and Bill Maurer. 2003. "Globalization and Governmentality: An Introduction." In *Globalization under Construction: Governmentality, Law and Identity*, edited by Richard W. Perry and Bill Maurer. Minneapolis: University of Minnesota Press.

Peters, Pauline E. 1984. "Struggles over Water, Struggles over Meaning: Cattle, Water and the State in Botswana." *Africa: Journal of the International African Institute* 54(3): 29–49.

———. 1994. *Dividing the Commons: Politics, Policy and Culture in Botswana*. Charlottesville: University Press of Virginia.

———. 2002. "The Limits of Negotiability, Security, Equity and Class Formation in Africa's Land Systems." In *Negotiating Property in Africa*, edited by Kristine Juul and Christian Lund, 45–66. Portsmouth, NH: Heinemann.

———. 2004. "Inequality and Social Conflict Over Land in Africa." *Journal of Agrarian Change* 4(3): 269–314.

———. 2013. "Land Appropriation, Surplus People and a Battle over Visions of Agrarian Futures in Africa." *Journal of Peasant Studies* 40(3): 537–562.

———. 2014. "Analysing Land Law Reform." *Development and Change* 46(1): 167–193.

Picard, Louis A. 1987. *The Politics of Development in Botswana: A Model for Success?* Boulder, CO: Lynne Reiner.

Power, Michael. 1997. *The Audit Society: Rituals of Verification*. Oxford: Oxford University Press.

Piron, Laure-Hélène. 2005. "Donor Assistance to Justice Sector Reform in Africa: Living Up to the New Agenda?" Open Society Justice Initiative, New York. http://gsdrc.org/document-library/donor-assistance-to-justice-sector-reform-in-africa-living-up-to-the-new-agenda/.

Ramsay, Jeff. 1991. "The Rise and Fall of the Bakwena Dynasty of South Central Botswana." PhD diss., Boston University.

Roberts, Simon A. 1979. *Order and Dispute: An Introduction to Legal Anthropology*. London: Penguin.

Robertson, Roland. 1995. "Glocalization: Time-Space and Homogeneity-Heterogenity." In *Global Modernity*, edited by Mike Featherston, Scott Lash, and Roland Roberston, 25–45. London: Sage.

Rose, Nikolas, and Miller, Peter. 1992. "Political Power Beyond the State: The Problematics of Government." *British Journal of Sociology* 43(2): 173–205.

Rottenburg, Richard. 2009. *Far Fetched Facts: A Parable of Development Aid*. Translated by Alison Brown and Tom Lampart. Cambridge: Massachusetts Institute of Technology Press.

Sabean, David. 1999. *Kinship in Neckarhausen, 1700–1870*. Cambridge: Cambridge University Press.

Saghir, Jamil, and Santoro, Jena. 2018 "Urbanization in Sub-Saharan Africa: Meeting Challenges by Bridging Stakeholders" for *Centre for Strategic Development* Project on Property and Development. Accessed January 4, 2019. Downloaded from csis-prod.s2.amazonas.com/s3fs-public/publication/180411_saghir_UrbaizationAfrica.web-1.pdf.

Sand, Inger-Johanne. 2004. "Polycontextuality as an Alternative to Constitutionalism." In *Transnational Governance and Consitutionalism*, edited by Christian Joerges, Inger-Johanne Sand, and Gunter Teubner, 41–66. Oxford, UK: Hart.

Santos, Boaventura de Sousa. 1987. "Law: A Map of Misreading: Toward a Postmodern Conception of Law." *Journal of Law and Society* 14(3): 279–302.

———. 2005. "Beyond Neoliberal Governance: The World Social Forum as Subaltern Cosmopolitan Politics and Legality." In *Law and Globalization from Below: Towards a Cosmopoltan Legality*, edited by Boaventura de Sousa Santos and Cesar A. Rodriguez-Garavito, 29–63. Cambridge: Cambridge University Press.

———. 2006. "Globalizations and Theory." *Theory, Culture and Society* 23:393–399.

Sassen, Saskia. 2014. Forward to *Framing the Global: Entry Points for Research*, edited by Hilary H. Kahn, ix–xiii. Bloomington: Indiana University Press.

Schapera, Isaac. 1947. *Migrant Labor and Tribal Life: A Study of the Conditions of the Bechuanaland Protectorate*. London: Oxford University Press.

Scholte, Jan Aarte. 2000. *Globalization: A Critical Introduction*. New York: St. Martin's Press.

Shore, Chris, and Susan Wright. 2000. "Coercive Accountability: The Rise of Audit Culture in Higher Education." In *Audit Cultures: Anthropological Studies in Accountability Ethics and the Academy*, edited by Marilyn Strathern, 57–90. London: Routledge.

Silitshena, Robson Modilaliso Kudiakwempi. 1978. "Notes on Some Characteristics of Population That Has Migrated Permanently to the Lands in the Kweneng District." *Botswana Notes and Records* 10:149–157.

———. 1982. "Population Movements and Settlement Patterns in Contemporary Botswana." In *Settlement in Botswana*, edited by Renée Hitchcock and Mary Smith, 31–43. Marshalltown: Heinemann.

Stephens, Phoebe. 2011. "The Global Land Grab: An Analysis of Extant Governance Institutions." *International Affairs Review* 20(1). Accessed January 16, 2017. http://www.iar-gwu.org/node/336.

Stewart, Ann. 2011. *Gender, Law and Justice in a Global Market*. Cambridge: Cambridge University Press.

Strathern, Marilyn, ed. 2000. *Audit Cultures: Anthropological Studies in Accountability, Ethics and the Academy*. London: Routledge.

Thompson, Edward Palmer. 1993. *Customs in Common*. New York: New Press.

Timaeus, Ian, and Wendy Graham. 1989. "Labor Circulation, Marriage and Fertility in Southern Africa." In *Reproduction and Social Organization in Sub-saharan Africa*, edited by Ron Lesthaeghe, 365–400. Berkeley: University of California Press.

Tlou, Thomas. 1985. *A History of Ngamiland, 1750–1906*. Madison: University of Wisconsin Press.

Tranter, Neil. 1999. Review of *Kinship in Neckarhausen 1770–1870*. By David Sabean. *English Historical Review* 114(457): 749–750.

Tsing, Anna. 2000. "The Global Situation." *Cultural Anthropology* 15(3): 327–360.

Turek, Ivan. 2016. "Getting Urbanization to Work in Africa: The Role of the Urban-Land-Infrastructures-Finance Nexus." *Area Development Policy* 1(1): 30–47.

Twining, William. 2000. *Globalisation and Legal Theory*. Cambridge: Cambridge University Press.

———. 2009. *General Jurisprudence: Understanding Law from a Global Perspective*. Cambridge: Cambridge University Press.

Ubink, Janine. 2011. "Land, Chiefs and Custom in Peri-Urban Ghana: Traditional Government in an Environment of Legal and Institutional Pluralism." In *The Governance of Legal Pluralism: Empirical Studies from Africa and Beyond*, edited by Werner Zips and Marcus Weilenmann, 81–108. Berlin, Münster, Wien, Zurich, and London: LIT Verlag.

Ulriksen, Marianne S. 2017. "Mineral Wealth and Limited Redistribution, Social Transfers and Taxation in Botswana." *Journal of Contemporary African Studies* 35(1): 73–92.

UNICEF (United Nations Children's Fund). 1993. *Children, Women and Development in Botswana: A Situational Analysis*. Report prepared by Maendeleo (Botswana) for the Government of Botswana and UNICEF.

United Kingdom. Department for International Development (DfID). 2009. "Eliminating World Poverty: Building Our Common Future." White paper (July). Cm. 7656.

United Nations. 2007. *Second Common Country Assessment for Botswana: Final Report*. United Nations System in Botswana.

———. 2000. Millenium Development Goals (MDGs). Accessed January 14, 2017. http://www.un.org/milleniumgoals/.

———. 2015a. Sustainable Development Goals (SDGs). Accessed January 14, 2017. http://www.un.org/sustainabledevelopment/news/communications-material/.

———. 2015b. The 2030 Agenda for Sustainable Development. Accessed January 14, 2017. http://www.un.org/sustainabledevelopment/development-agenda/.

United States. Department of State. 2015. *Botswana Investment Climate Statement* (June). Accessed May 3, 2017. https://ww.state.gov/documents/organization/241703.pdf.

Van der Molen, Paul. 2012. "After 10 Years of Criticism: What Is left of De Soto's Ideas? https://www.fig.net/resourcs/proceedings/fig_proceedings/fig2012/papers/TS)7B_vandermolen_5503.pdf.

Van Klaveren, Maarten, and Kea Tijdens, Melanie Hughie-Williams, and Naria Ramos Martin. 2009. *An Overview of Women's Work and Employment in Botswana*. AIAS Working Paper No. 09–81 (November). Amsterdam Institute for Advanced Labor Studies, University of Amsterdam.

Walker, Neil. 2014. *Intimations of Global Law*. Cambridge: Cambridge University Press.

Weilenmann, Markus. 2009a. "Project Law—A Legal Intermediary between Local and Global Communities: A Case Study from Senegal." *Anthropologica* 51(1): 39–51.

———. 2009b. "Project Law—A Power Instrument of Development Agencies: A Case Study from Burundi." In *The Power of Law in a Transnational World: Anthropological Enquiries*, edited by Franz von Benda-Beckmann, Keebet von Benda-Beckmann, and Anne Griffiths, 156–175. Oxford: Berghahn.

Werbner, Pnina. 2014. *The Making of an African Working Class: Politics, Law, and Cultural Protest in the Manual Workers' Union of Botswana*. London: Pluto Press.

Werbner, Richard. 2004. *Reasonable Radicals and Citizenship in Botswana: The Public Anthology of Kalanga Elites*. Bloomington: Indiana University Press.

Wilmsen, Edwin N. 1989. *Land Filled with Flies: A Political Economy of the Kalahari*. Chicago: University of Chicago Press.

Wistrich, Andrew J. 2012. "The Evolving Temporality of Lawmaking." *Connecticut Law Review* 44(2): 737–826.

World Bank. 2003. *Land Policies for Growth and Poverty Reduction*. Policy Research Report. Oxford: Oxford University Press.

———. 2008. *Finance For All? Policies and Pitfalls in Expanding Access.* Policy Research on Finance Report. Washington, DC: World Bank.

———. 2015. *Botswana Poverty Assessment.* Report No. 88473-BW. Poverty Global Practice, Africa Region. Washington, DC: World Bank.

———. 2017. *Macro Poverty Outlook for Botswana.* Accessed April 19, 2017. http://documents .worldbank.org/curated/en/166451490988706864/Macro-poverty-outlook-for -Botswana.

World Bank Group. 2011. Botswana's Success: Good Governance, Good Policies, and Good Luck by Michael Lewin. World Bank Creative Commons Attribution License. Accessed January 17, 2019. https://siteresources.worldback.org/AFRICAEXT /Resources/258643-1271798012256/Botswana-success.pdf.

Wylie, Diana. 1991. *A Little God: The Twilight of Patriarchy in a Southern African Chiefdom.* Hanover, NH: Wesleyan University Press.

INDEX

Page numbers in italics indicate a table or figure.

185

Before retirement, ANNE M. O. GRIFFITHS held a Personal Chair in Anthropology of Law at the School of Law, Edinburgh University. Her research focuses on anthropology of law, comparative and family law, African law, gender, culture, and rights. She is author of *In the Shadow of Marriage: Gender and Justice in an African Community.*

www.ingramcontent.com/pod-product-compliance
Lightning Source LLC
Chambersburg PA
CBHW070329270326
41926CB00017B/3818